Rockets, Bombs and Bayonets

A Concise History of the Royal Marines and Other British and Canadian Forces in Defence of Canada 1812-1815

ROCKETS, BOMBS AND BAYONETS
Copyright © 2013, Alexander Craig

All Rights Reserved. No part of this publication may be reproduced, stored in a retrieval system or transmitted in any form or by any means—electronic, mechanical, photocopy, recording or any other—except for brief quotations in printed reviews, without the prior permission of the author.

ISBN: 978-1-4600-0094-6
LSI Edition: 978-1-4600-0095-3
E-book ISBN: 978-1-4600-0096-0
(E-book available from the Kindle Store, KOBO and the iBookstore)

Cataloguing data available from Library and Archives Canada

To order additional copies, visit:
www.essencebookstore.com

For more information, please contact:
Alexander Craig
acraig1814@gmail.com

Cover image: *Attack on Fort Oswego, Lake Ontario, N. America, May 6th, 1814, Noon.* John Hewett (known 1806-1869).

Epic Press is an imprint of *Essence Publishing,* a Christian Book Publisher dedicated to furthering the work of Christ through the written word. For more information, contact: 20 Hanna Court, Belleville, Ontario, Canada K8P 5J2
Phone: 1-800-238-6376 • Fax: (613) 962-3055
Email: info@essence-publishing.com
Web site: www.essence-publishing.com

Printed in Canada
by
Epic Press

For Hannah and William.

Contents

Acknowledgements 6
Introduction: From Sea Soldiers to Flying Squadron 9
The American War—Operations in the Chesapeake. 17
Canada and Winter Warfare 23
The Royal Navy's Offensive, 1814 37
Britons Strike Home! John Bull on Capitol Hill 51
Plattsburgh, The Land Invasion Begins. 65
The Battle of Cumberland Bay 81
Actions in Maine, North Point, and Baltimore 117
A Dangerous Voyage 135
Operations Against the Coast of Georgia and Alabama 139
The New Orleans Campaign 145
The Second Attack on Fort Bower,
    the Last Land Action in the South. 177
Appendix I: The Treaty of Ghent 180
Appendix II: Who Won the War of 1812? 181
Appendix III: Timeline of Reconciliation and Co-operation 183
Endnotes. 187
Select Bibliography 190
Index 194

Acknowledgements

There are a number of individuals and institutions to whom I owe my sincere gratitude for the assistance and encouragement they have given me in the preparation of this volume.

Foremost is the Royal Marines Society, which over the last thirty years has provided me with a constant stream of historical articles from their journal Sheet Anchor and other special publications, many of which have intersected in the timeline of the War of 1812. The work of this all-volunteer society has given me the inspiration to develop a more detailed account of the Corps activities during this all-important war for Canada's survival. My special appreciation goes to Miss Bridget E.J. Spiers, Maj. Alistair J. Donald RM, and Col. Brian L. Carter OBE RM.

Next, I am especially grateful to the Royal Marines Association (Ontario). Within the ranks of this organization I have found a constant source of comradeship and appreciation for the history of the Corps. I am deeply indebted to the various members of the RMA Colour party, who have paraded each September at the Battle of Plattsburgh celebrations along with the band of H.M. Royal Marines Association. Also I extend a special thanks to Neil Pennington and Michael J. Smith for their constant support.

A further source of support and kind encouragement has been my friends in the Canadian Forces Museums, the late Maj. E.F. (Tex) Joyner CD of the Princess of Wales Own Regiment Military Museum, Curator Cpt. Neil W.

Acknowledgements

Smith CD, Colonels J.F. Sherry CD, J.D. Inrig CD, and D.J. Kernahan CD all of the Hastings and Prince Edward Regiment Military Museum. They have all contributed much to my knowledge and appreciation of the history of Canada's militia and permanent forces.

The Battle of Plattsburgh Association and the B.O.P. Interpretive Centre have been at the heart of much of my research and inspiration to write this book. Through these twin organizations I have encountered many historians with similar interests, and through them I have found an entire community dedicated to the preservation of the memory of not only a battle, but also the memory of those who fought and died on both sides, giving them the dignity and honour deserved by our glorious dead.

My American associates and friends who have shown me much kindness and support over the last dozen years are, Mr. Kit Booth, Captain Rich Calma, Mr. & Mrs. Roy Carter, Colonel David G. Fitz-Enz, Mr. Keith A. Herkalo, Mrs. Patricia Schwartz, Dr. and Mrs. John Tanner, and especially Mrs. Kit Parlin.

Lastly I would like to recognize the support of Mary, my dear wife of thirty years, our daughter Heather and her husband Don, and my late sister Mrs. Catherine Neely.

GREAT ENCOURAGEMENT.
AMERICAN WAR.

What a Brilliant Prospect does this Event hold out to every Lad of Spirit, who is inclined to try his Fortune in that highly renowned Corps,

The Royal Marines,
When every Thing that swims the Seas must be a
PRIZE!

Thousands are at this moment endeavouring to get on Board Privateers, where they serve without Pay or Reward of any kind whatsoever; so certain does their Chance appear of enriching themselves by PRIZE MONEY! What an enviable Station then must the ROYAL MARINE hold,—who with far superior Advantages to thefe, has the additional benefit of liberal Pay, and plenty of the best provisions, with a good and well appointed Ship under him, the pride and Glory of Old England; furely every Man of Spirit muft blufh to remain at Home in Inactivity and Indolence, when his Country and the beft of Kings needs his Assistance.

Where then can he have fuch a fair opportunity of Reaping Glory and Riches, as in the Royal Marines, a Corps daily acquiring new Honours, and there, when once embarked in the BRITISH FLEET, he finds himself in the midft of Honour and Glory, furrounded by a fet of fine Fellows, Strangers to Fear, and who ftrike Terror through the Hearts of their Enemies wherever they go!

He has likewise the infpiring Idea to know, that while he fcours the Ocean to protect the Liberty of OLD ENGLAND, that the Hearts and good Wifhes of the whole BRITISH NATION, attend him; pray for his Succefs, and participate in his Glory!! Lofe no Time then, my Fine Fellows, in embracing the glorious Opportunity that awaits you; YOU WILL RECEIVE

Sixteen Guineas Bounty,

And on your Arrival at *Head Quarters*, be comfortably and genteely CLOTHED.—And fpirited Young BOYS of a promifing Appearance, who are Five Feet high, WILL RECEIVE TWELVE POUNDS ONE SHILLING AND SIXPENCE BOUNTY and equal Advantages of *PROVISIONS* and *CLOATHING* with the Men. And thofe who wish only to enlist for a limited Service, fhall receive a Bounty of ELEVEN GUINEAS, and Boys EIGHT. In Fact, the Advantages which the *ROYAL MARINE* poffefses, are too numerous to mention here, but among the many, it may not be amifs to state,—That if he has a WIFE, or aged PARENT, he can make them an Allotment of half his PAY; which will be regularly paid without any Trouble to them, or to whomsoever he may direct: that being well Clothed and Fed on Board Ship, the Remainder of his PAY and PRIZE MONEY will be clear in Reserve for the Relief of his Family or his own private Purposes. The Single Young Man on his return to Port, finds himfelf enabled to cut a Oafh on Shore with his GIRL and his GLASS, that might be envied by a Nobleman.—Take Courage then, seize the Fortune that awaits you, repair to the ROYAL MARINE RENDEZVOUS, where in a *FLOWING BOWL of PUNCH*, in Three Times Three, you shall drink

Long live the King, and Success to his Royal Marines

The Daily Allowance of a Marine when embarked, is—One Pound of BEEF or PORK.—One Pound of BREAD —Flour, Raisins, Butter, Cheese, Oatmeal, Molasses, Tea, Sugar, &c. &c. And a Pint of the beft WINE, or Half a Pint of the best RUM or BRANDY; together with a Pint of LEMONADE. They have likewise in warm Countries, a plentiful Allowance of the choiceft FRUIT. And what can be more handsome than the Royal Marine's Proportion of PRIZE MONEY, when a Sergeant shares equal with the First Class of Petty Officers, such as Midshipmen, Assistant Surgeons, &c. which is Five Shares each; a Corporal with the Second Class, which is Three Shares each; and the Private, with the Able Seamen, One Share and a Half each.

☞ *For further Particulars, and a more full Account of the many advantages of this invaluable Corps, apply to Sergeant Fulcher, at the Eight Bells, where the Bringer of a Recruit will receive* THREE GUINEAS.

S. AND J. RIDGE, PRINTERS, MARKET PLACE, NEWARK.

Introduction: From Sea Soldiers to Flying Squadron

The British Corps of Marines and the Royal Marines

The Royal Marines were first raised as The Admiral's Regiment, or the Duke of York and Albany's Maritime Regiment of Foot. The date of their foundation was October 28, 1664, during the Second Dutch War.

It was during this war in the same year that the British annexed New Amsterdam and renamed it New York, after the same Duke of York who had raised the ancestral regiment of the Royal Marines. His title as Duke of Albany was also used to change the name of the former Dutch town of Beverwyck to Albany. So the province and now state of New York have a direct link to the first "Royal" marine, who would succeed his brother and come to the throne as James VII of Scotland and James II of England.

The Royal Navy with its corps of marines served the interests of Great Britain and its overseas colonies throughout numerous wars and conflicts. After the beginning of the Seven Years War (the French and Indian War), the Admiralty Office issued an order on April 26th, 1755, authorizing the raising of twenty permanent companies of marines at Portsmouth, eighteen at Plymouth and twelve at Chatham; each company numbered 100 soldiers some 5,000 marines in all.

This reconstituted force of marines provided a seasoned nucleus for rapid mobilization in times of war. Serving in small detachments on board every warship of ten guns and above ensured that the marines saw action in every naval engagement of the Seven Years War and the American War of Independence.

In 1793 the Corps was expanded to 12,000 and in 1794 to 15,000. By 1805 the demands of the Napoleonic Wars prompted a further expansion to 30,000, and by 1812 the Royal Marines numbered about 32,000.

Deployment in action varied according to a ship's size. Typically a captain or lieutenant would be stationed on the poop deck, with a number of marines used as marksmen. The rest of the detachment was distributed in ones, twos, and occasionally threes amongst the gun crews, depending on size; it took six or as many as thirteen men to efficiently handle a single gun.

Marines working the great guns alongside the seamen had no special training in this role. Naval officers often saw the marines as just another source of manpower, who would learn the necessary skills from within the ranks. The marines were often encouraged to go aloft but were never "to be obliged to go aloft or to be beat or punished for not showing an inclination for doing so."[1] By 1808 naval regulations provided that no serving marine could be discharged and entered as a seaman without a specific order from the Admiralty.

The chief role of the marines was to fight as a seaborne infantry. In a typical 74-gun ship's complement of 120 marines, about 20 would be small-arms men. Admiral Nelson had developed aggressive tactics that increased the importance of boarding enemy ships. In boarding enemy vessels, sailors armed with cutlasses, pistols, axes or pikes would combine with marines armed with muskets and bayonets and provide a deadly combination in most sea battles.

At the close of the eighteenth century, in the Napoleonic Wars, the marines' role had increased dramatically. Next to enforcement and guard duties aboard ship, their most important task was the suppression of mutiny. Apart from sea duties and working with the guns, it was normal practice to segregate marines and seamen, each with their own messes and berths. Under Admiral Lord St. Vincent in 1797—the year of the great naval mutiny at Spithead and Nore—the segregation was greatly reinforced. This was intended to provide the ship's officers with a force of loyal, fully armed soldiers under their command. Marines stood guard whenever punishment was carried out and were kept at drill and parade when the ship was in harbour, the most likely place for open revolt. As a result of this, there were no major mutinies on any ship under the admiral's command.

Introduction: From Sea Soldiers to Flying Squadron

Lord St. Vincent's high regard for the marines led him to recommend to King George III that they be awarded the title of "Royal." This was granted on April 29, 1802. St. Vincent later said, "In obtaining for them the distinction of Royal, I but inefficiently did my duty. I never knew an appeal to them for honour, courage or loyalty that did not more than realize my highest expectations. If ever the hour of real danger should come to England, they will be found the country's sheet anchor."[2]

Amphibious operations created many problems, particularly when army troops were serving on Royal Navy ships. Soldiers at sea would still be under military discipline, not naval, and the blurring of lines of command often produced tactical errors and incompetence. Royal Marines, however, were clearly under naval discipline. They were familiar with boats and used to life aboard ship and were more effective in landing operations. The role of amphibious warfare was evolving continuously and was extremely effective during the Peninsular War in Spain.

When Royal Navy ships visited friendly ports, for resupply of food and water, there was always a danger of seamen deserting. The well-drilled and disciplined Royal Marines were always present to remind sailors of where their duty lay and to prevent seamen from deserting.

The age-old problem of obtaining sailors to man the British fleet was somewhat resolved by the use of press-gangs. The marines were sometimes used to reinforce this rather crude method of conscription. The recruiting system of the marines was similar to that of the army. Recruits were raised in market towns all over the country, tempting suitable young men and boys with the promise of action, adventure, and prize money. In wartime a bounty was offered, in 1794 eight guineas per recruit; this was raised again to fifteen guineas. By 1801 this had risen to twenty-six pounds sterling per man. Marines were never "pressed" into service; they were all volunteers.

The Royal Navy expanded greatly, but the marines could not keep up. Soldiers from the army were used to try to make up the shortfall. Soldiers' wives were allowed to accompany them aboard ship, and many of these women were present during naval battles. Anecdotally, during the Battle of the Glorious First of June, a son was born to Mrs. McKenzie, who was on board HMS *Tremendous*. Fifty-four years later he applied for the Naval General Service Medal and Clasp for June 1, 1794, the battle fought on the day he was born! His name Daniel Tremendous McKenzie; his rank on the medal is given as "Boy."[3]

The Royal Marines, desperate for recruits, also saw foreigners as a potential source. Volunteers were sought from prison hulks containing prisoners who had been forced to serve under the French flag. Dutch, Swiss, and Polish volunteers came from this source. When a recruiting station was opened in the Caribbean, free blacks were also taken to the colours. Malta also had a recruiting station where further foreigners were taken into the ranks.

When ships were commissioned, the captain would send to the nearest marine barracks for a marine detachment. These would be selected by the local commandant and sent to the ship. If the captain wished, he could return any marines he considered below standard as unfit, giving his reasons in writing.

The size of a shipboard detachment varied according to the size of the warship. In 1801, one in six of a ship's company was a marine. By 1808, roughly one in five was a Royal Marine, perhaps as a precaution against mutiny. A marine guard was placed at the captain's door, while others were placed at the storerooms and the "spirit room" and a twenty-four-hour guard at the hatch of the ship's magazine. The relationship between seamen and marines was not always one of guard and prisoner. They were two distinct parts of a very effective war machine.

Officers

In the 18th and 19th centuries, positions in the British government and civil service were entirely dependent on a patronage system. This system operated in the Royal Navy and included marine officers. Boys were taken into the service on the recommendation of uncles, godparents, family, friends, and brother officers, who could also be their father, brother, etc. The system was considered a gift from the Lords of the Admiralty.

This system of interlocking patronage and favouritism could be used to write off debts, gain the favour of a senior officer or advance the prospective officer or the patron himself. Some of these new officers were so young they would be commissioned as a coronet, rather than a second lieutenant.

Not all potential officers were given commissions; some had to first serve as "gentlemen volunteers." This gave the navy a chance to evaluate and educate these young men and boys before offering a commission. When serving at sea these "gentlemen volunteers" were carried as a supernumerary in the ships log and would mess with the midshipmen.

Introduction: From Sea Soldiers to Flying Squadron

One stark difference between army and navy officers was the promotion by purchase system. The army maintained this system till about 1875, while the navy discontinued it in 1755, for the good of the service. This intended that all naval and marine officers were to be promoted by the Admiralty for their ability and zeal or by seniority, whereas the army system could allow a very inexperienced man to lead a regiment or even an army into battle and make life and death decisions that could determine the outcome of an entire war. A good example of this would be Sir George Prevost.

The honour and privilege of being granted the title Royal Marines in 1802 required a change of uniform for both officers and men. The new uniforms were to have facing colours of blue, replacing white. Officers had gilt buttons and gold epaulettes; captains and subalterns were to be distinguished by one epaulette only, on the right shoulder. New Colours were also presented to all divisions. The commandant of the Portsmouth Division made a plea for the inclusion of the sphinx, as allowed to the army regiments for the campaign in Egypt in 1801, but this was not approved.

On August 18, 1804, an order-in council was issued, authorizing the establishment of a company of artillery at each division. The order specifically stated, "The Officers and men to be selected from the most intelligent, and experienced Royal Marines belonging to the respective Divisions." From the very first the Royal Marine Artillery was to be a *corps d'elite*.[4]

It is perhaps worth noting that the Portsmouth Division produced three officers who were to see extensive action during the Napoleonic War and the future War of 1812. These were Captain R. Williams, Lieutenant T. A. Parke, and 2nd Lieutenant G. E. Balchild.

At first the training was directed towards vessels known as bomb ketches; these were heavy barge-like vessels armed with 10" and 13" calibre mortars. Later the RMA would land and service light field guns, howitzers, and land service mortars to support infantry on land.

In 1759 King George III formed a new establishment of marine officers of superior rank, chosen from the officers of the Royal Navy. These high ranking officers were often referred to as "blue colonels." Captain Horatio Nelson RN, was appointed Colonel of Marines in 1795, and Admiral Sir George Cockburn RN, was made Major General of Royal Marines in 1821. This system of appointments was abolished in February of 1837.

The Royal Marines Battalion

Orders were issued on September 25, 1810, to the four Royal Marines divisions to provide companies of eighty rank and file, including ten foreigners "who must be Germans," with a proper proportion of sergeants and drummers, to be selected from the steadiest and best disciplined men. Chatham and Portsmouth were to provide one company each, Plymouth two companies, and a small contingent of RMA from Woolwich. Major R. Williams, the senior RMA captain, was appointed to command with Major T. Abernathie, RMA, as his second in command. The embarkation state, signed by Major Williams, shows two majors, five captains, nine first lieutenants, three second lieutenants, twenty-eight sergeants, eleven drummers, 462 rank and file, one adjutant and two staff sergeants. They embarked for Lisbon on board HMS *Abercrombie* and one other frigate, leaving Devil's Point, Plymouth, at 7:30 a.m. on November 28. One captain of note was Alexander Anderson RM, from the Chatham division.

The battalion arrived in Lisbon on the 4th of December. Duties were to garrison and protect the town and port, as this was an essential part of the lifeline to Wellington's forces inland, who were building the lines of the Torres Vedras. During their stay in Lisbon, they were presented with their own stand of colours at the Grand Rossio Square, by the British envoy to Portugal, Charles Stuart, who later became the first Baron Stuart D'Rothsey. The tour ended in February of 1812 when the unit returned to England.

Two Battalions and the Flying Squadron

After a short respite at Portsea, orders were again issued to reform the battalion. This time it was to be a larger unit, 646 officers and men. It would have its own RMA company, armed with two six-pounder light field guns and one five-and-a-half-inch howitzer, all manned by fifty-four officers and men. A 2nd battalion was also formed, under the command of Major James Malcolm RM, of the Chatham division. This 2nd battalion had fully the exact same numbers of officers and men and a similarly armed company of RMA, under Captain T. A. Parke. This battalion carried the colours of the Portsmouth Division.

The Admiralty had devised a "Flying Squadron." This was a force of Royal Navy ships, consisting of two seventy-four-gun line-of-battle ships, five frigates, troop transports, and a number of smaller vessels. The concept

Introduction: From Sea Soldiers to Flying Squadron

was to land Royal Marines with supplies of arms and ammunition to be distributed amongst the Spanish insurgents along the northern coast of Spain and to combine forces with these local guerrilla bands and attack various French costal garrisons. The enemy mostly occupied old medieval castles, convents, and small forts, with garrisons of 300 to 1,000 men, plus guns mounted on the defences. The British ships would bombard the French from the sea while the marines and the Spanish irregulars attacked by land.

From June 20 to December 14, 1812, the Flying Squadron under Commodore Sir Home Popham RN, with its attached 1st and 2nd battalions of Royal Marines, fought at the battles of Satandar, Santona, Guetaria, Lequito, Plencia, Galeta, Castro Urdiales, Fort St. Ano, and Bermejo. These actions forced the French "Army of the North" to divert 30,000 soldiers away from Wellington's forces during the Salamanca campaign. The Duke of Wellington was so impressed with the Royal Marine battalions that he requested that the Admiralty place them under his command. This request was refused, as the Admiralty had other plans for these battalions.

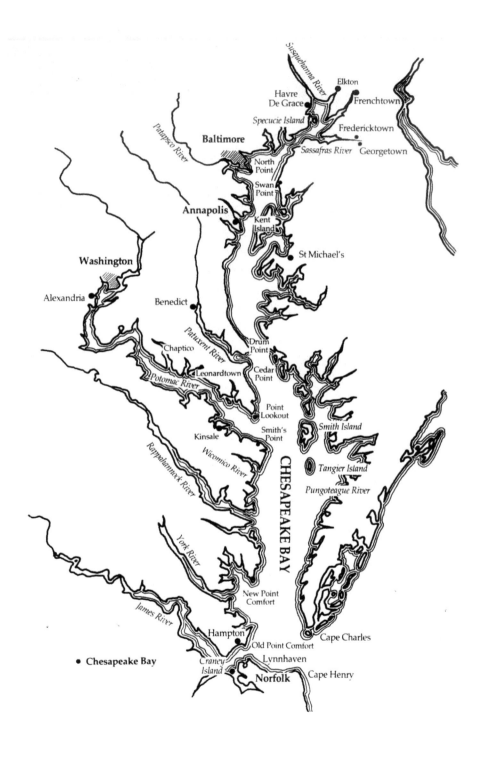

1

The American War—Operations in the Chesapeake

The declaration of war by the United States in June of 1812 found the British army fully committed to the war in Europe against Napoleon. The Royal Navy was blockading the French, protecting British merchantmen against privateers, and maintaining security and communication with her overseas colonies. The comparison of the United States Navy and the Royal Navy in 1812 is as follows:

	Warships	Tonnage	Guns	Manpower.
United States	16	15,300	442	5,025 (including 493 Marines)
Great Britain	1,048	860,990	27,800	151,572 (including 31,400 Marines)

The North American and West Indies stations were under the command of Vice Admiral Sir Herbert Sawyer RN. Little was done to curb the activity of American privateers or the US Navy.

Sawyer was replaced in September 1812 by Vice Admiral Sir John Borlese Warren RN. This officer was authorized to negotiate a truce or an end to the war. However, his communications with Secretary of State James Monroe failed. British naval activity had confined itself to a loosely maintained commercial blockade of the New England ports. Fighting had mostly been taking place along the Canadian frontiers and on the lakes in beating back the American efforts at invasion.

Warren increased efforts to maintain a more aggressive blockade; however, with only twenty-seven vessels, his squadron was inadequate. In December 1812, the British cabinet decided to take aggressive measures on the American coast. A squadron of four ships of the line and frigates were detached from the Cadiz station, under Rear Admiral George Cockburn RN, to reinforce the North Atlantic and West Indies fleet.

Warren and Cockburn met at Hampton Roads in March of 1813. The officers discussed their objectives. These included the expansion of the blockade, the obtaining of intelligence on enemy vessels, the procuring of pilots, the charting and surveying as much of the Chesapeake as possible, the harbouring of refugee slaves, and the capture and collection of prizes and sending them in convoy to Bermuda. The two men also discussed the landing of troops to raid, capture, or destroy federal property and to keep the region in a state of general alarm. Cockburn formed a composite unit of Royal Navy seamen and Royal Marines, all taken from ships then in the Chesapeake region. Warren departed for Bermuda, leaving Cockburn and his forces to carry out a campaign of amphibious attacks. This included raids on Frenchtown, Havre de Grace, Principio Foundry, Georgetown, and Fredericktown.

The British pursued the practice of returning fire when fired upon, then destroying the property of those who opposed their landings. This soon produced much fear and consternation. A price was put on Cockburn's head, while many officials in towns and hamlets wrote letters to the British professing that no US militia were welcome in their town. By June 19th, Admiral Warren returned with a number of transports carrying both Royal Marines battalions, which had been "inspected, disciplined and refreshed." Each battalion now contained six companies of infantry, 801 officers and men, with a Royal Marine Artillery company containing 81, all ranks, and in addition a newly trained rocket company of fifty men, formed from the RMA detachment at Woolwich, commanded by Lieutenants George E. Balchild and John H. Stevens.

The armament of each of the two RMA companies was increased to a "brigade" of four light six-pounders, two light five-and-a-half-inch howitzers, two ten-inch land service mortars on field carriages, and two

The American War—Operations in the Chesapeake

eight-inch howitzers on battery carriages. The rocket company had a variety of Congreve rockets but was mainly armed with the four-inch-diameter thirty-two-pound rockets, which cost the sum of one pound sterling each.

Further additions to the expedition were the British army's New South Wales Corps (The Rum Corps), numbered as the 102nd Regiment, and companies of foreign troops made up from deserters and POWs from Napoleon's armies. These were named "The Canadian Chasseurs" or "Chasseurs Britanniques." The British army was desperately undermanned and was scraping together troops from far and wide to help combat the new American enemy.

It was decided by Admiral Warren and Sir Sydney Beckwith (senior officer in charge of the army contingent) during their voyage, to begin operations with an attack on the arsenal at Norfolk Navy Yard and to attempt to capture or destroy USS *Constellation* (38) on the Elizabeth River.

Craney Island is a low lying strip of land, barring access to the main channel leading to the Norfolk Navy Yard. It was defended by a company of light artillery commanded by Captain Edward Emmerson USA, 580 American troops, mainly Virginia Militia, and a detachment of the US 20th Infantry Regiment, reinforced by 150 seamen and US Marines from USS *Constellation*.

On June 22nd the British attack took place under the command of Captain Samuel J. B. Pechell RN, of HMS *San Domingo* (74). The leading boats grounded on the shallows and were fully exposed to the American battery, a fierce fire of grape and case shot at short range, damaging fifteen boats and sinking three others. The British lost eighty-one dead and numerous others wounded. The casualties were particularly high amongst the Canadian Chasseurs. Admiral Warren's personal barge, known as the *Centipede*, was one of the captured vessels. Its commander, Captain John M. Hanchett, RN, who was wounded, was rumoured to be the illegitimate son of King George III. The loss of this officer may have had far-reaching implications. It is worth noting that the British plan was devised by Admiral Warren, who ignored information and advice by Rear Admiral Cockburn regarding the shoals that grounded the attack boats.

The battle of Craney Island is the first occasion when American troops faced effective rocket fire. Captain Marmaduke Wybourn RM, serving on HMS *Marlborough* (74), described the event as follows:

The Rocket boat under the charge of the gunner (Hepburn) a brave man, was never further off than musket shot, and he proved that the rockets could be fired point blank, and we know that one of those horrid engines proves more destructive than 100-pound shot. It goes further, burns like a comet in appearance,& water will not quench it, and carry such a tremendous appearance altogether and noise like thunder that it terrifies & alarms far out of its vortex.[5]

After the debacle of Craney Island, the British decided to give up on the Norfolk Navy Yard, as batteries, entrenchments, and American reinforcements would have made a further attack too costly. It was also decided to place Admiral Cockburn in charge of all amphibious operations in the Chesapeake. From this moment on, Cockburn, who was also a Lieutenant Colonel in the Royal Marines, would dominate the entire eastern coast of the United States for the remainder of the war.

Cockburn decided to attack Hampton, on the Virginia shore of Chesapeake Bay. This would cut the road to Richmond and cause a shifting of the American army to protect that city. These tactics were exactly the same as those used in Northern Spain.

The attack on Hampton began early on June 25th. Boats carrying the two brigades, under Lt. Colonel Charles Napier of 102nd and Lt. Col. R. Williams RMA, landed three miles west of Hampton. They then moved inland around Hampton to attack from the rear. A second flotilla of armed launches and boats with Lt. Balchild's rocket company on board coasted inshore towards the town. "A noisy demonstration" was made by firing heavily with shells and salvos of rockets and by keeping up a continuous fusillade of musket fire, all to attract the defenders' attention to the river side and away from the main attack by the column on the land side. Napier's 102nd foot, two companies of Canadian Chasseurs, Captain Parke's RMA company with three field pieces, and three companies of ship-marines were nearest to Hampton. Close behind were Lt-Colonel Williams and his two battalions of Royal Marines and a further RMA company with two more six-pounders at the head of this column.

All went as the British had intended. The surprised American garrison of Hampton discovered too late that the British had closed on them and were turning their flank, threatening to cut them off from the high road to

The American War—Operations in the Chesapeake

Richmond, which was their main line of retreat. The fighting resulted in seven American field guns, complete with all their equipment, being captured. 5 Company 1st Battalion Royal Marines, led by Captain Edward N. Louder, captured the colours of the 85th Regiment US Infantry, and 6 Company, led by Captain Alexander Anderson, captured the colours of the 68th Regiment (James City Light Infantry). Both of these colours were later presented to Admiral Warren on board his flagship, *San Domingo*. British losses at

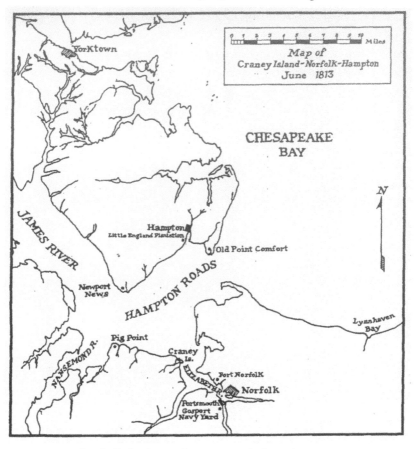

Hampton were five killed, thirty-three wounded, and ten missing. American losses were about thirty killed. A black mark on the British forces was the savage pillaging by the French mercenaries of the Canadian Chasseurs. The worst degradations of the French armies in Spain were now present at Hampton. As a result of the court of inquiry, all the foreign Chasseurs were shipped off to Bermuda and were not again employed anywhere.

The Royal Navy squadron made Lynnhaven Bay its main anchorage, sending out "divisions" of ships to attack specific targets, such as USS *Adams,* a twenty-four-gun frigate in the Potomac River. This vessel was moved out of the reach of the British ships. In consolation landings were made, and a number of small craft were captured.

In July a minor naval battle took place at Ocracoke Bar, where two large American privateers, *Anaconda* and *Atlas,* were taken after rockets were fired at them. The British next occupied Ocracoke Village and the neighbouring town of Beaufort for two days. The "spreading of alarm on all sides" continued, and Admiral Warren came close to attacking Annapolis. He also entered the Patapsco River leading to Baltimore but did not attack at either place. He did capture Kent Island, occupied it with both marine battalions, the 102nd foot and Captain Parke's artillery company, and set up a defensive post at either end of the island.

From Kent Island the British captured Queenston Village, Maryland, on August 13th, in what is known as the battle of Slippery Hill. Later a raid was carried out on an American encampment in Talbot County, but the Americans had retreated before the British arrived. When a sickness broke out in the fleet, Warren decided to leave the Chesapeake and return to Halifax, where his fleet and transports arrived on September 13th. The British assault force camped outside the town to await further orders.

2

Canada and Winter Warfare

Halifax to Montreal

The lieutenant governor of Nova Scotia, Sir John Sherbrooke, carried out an inspection of both Royal Marines battalions on September 23rd. A day previously, the 2nd Battalion had been placed under orders for embarkation to Lower Canada (Quebec) at the request of Lieutenant General Sir George Prevost. Admiral Warren had been sent a dispatch requesting a battalion of marines to be sent at once. Reports had shown that an invasion by two separate United States armies was about to begin.

A week after the 2nd Battalion departed, on *Success, Fox,* and *Nemesis* transport vessels, Admiral Warren received yet another, even more urgent request from Sir George Prevost. This time intelligence had been received of a naval disaster, with the loss of the British Lake Erie squadron, under Captain Robert H. Barclay RN. In addition a British army had been defeated at Moraviantown on the River Thames in Upper Canada (Ontario). A dispatch rider had ridden 700 miles in seven days to bring the request for more Royal Marines.

Warren quickly mobilized the entire 1st Battalion, including the artillery and rocket companies. All were embarked on the transports *Diadem* and *Diomede,* then escorted northward to the mouth of the St. Lawrence. The weather was exceptionally bad, and some of the transports were damaged and leaking severely. Eventually all five transports containing both battalions sheltered off Green Island, on the south shore of the St. Lawrence.

It was decided to move the battalions the last 100 miles by a relay of river schooners. During these transfers, one schooner sank, with no loss of life but a massive loss of camp and personal equipment belonging to the 1st Battalion. Between October 16 and 24 both battalions arrived in Quebec City. The 2nd Battalion marched out towards Montreal just as the 1st was arriving. The road to Montreal was in very poor condition, and the weather was described as "foul."

Eventually the marines reached Trois Rivieres. Here it was decided to again board local vessels, to try to reach Montreal sooner. One vessel was the steamship *Swiftsure,* a recently built side paddle passenger steamboat, owned by John Molson of Montreal. *Swiftsure* carried all three artillery companies, at a breakneck speed of seven mph on its first journey. The other vessels carrying the infantry were again mostly schooners, landing the 2nd Battalion in Montreal by October 30. A return journey to Trois Rivieres was needed to bring down the 1st Battalion. This time *Swiftsure* transported 300 infantry, under the command of Captain Anderson, while Colonel Williams and the rest of the battalion travelled by sailing vessels. This event is possibly the first use of mechanized transport by the Royal Marines in a "rapid reaction" role.

On arrival in Montreal the 2nd Battalion was quickly directed to Coteau du Lac, as part of the defence of the city. However, news of the battle of Chateauguay on October 26 and the defeat of General Hampton's army greatly relieved the populace and allowed the military to direct their attention to the approach of General Wilkinson's army of 8,000 men.

The 1st Battalion of Royal Marines arrived in Montreal on November 6th. They were reunited with Captain Parke's battery and Balchild's rocket company as they encamped at the Champ Des Mars. The following day, in his capacity of commander of the forces, Lieutenant General Prevost and his staff inspected the battalion and welcomed it to the forces under his command. Defensive positions were assigned to the battalion; however, the news of the battle at Chryslers Farm arrived. US General Wilkinson's army had been defeated and retired back to U.S. territory.

Colonel Williams was advised that his battalion would proceed to the Richelieu River and he would take command of the fort on the Island of Ile aux Noix. Here he would assume command of the troops along the frontier with the United States. The 2nd Battalion under Major Malcolm was to be sent to Fort Wellington at Prescott in Upper Canada, to protect the St.

Canada and Winter Warfare

Lawrence River frontier. Both Williams and Malcolm were to report to Prevost and to the Admiralty. The Canadian frontier now had more than 1,700 additional highly trained battle-hardened British regulars, waiting for the next American invasion.

Ile aux Noix and Winter Warfare

The main fortifications at island of Ile aux Noix consisted of a fort and two redoubts. In addition there were chains, floating booms, and several chevaux-de-frise formed to block navigation past the island. Also there were additional fortifications on several of the outer islands.

On arrival, the battalion would have been pleased with their accommodations, as these had been upgraded a year before. The fort and redoubts had six new barrack blocks and four officers' quarters. One barrack block could accommodate 800 soldiers. They would share the accommodation with the three companies of 13th (Somerset Regiment), the 10th Royal Veteran Battalion, a number of Royal Engineers, Royal Artillery, and some local militia regiments.

After relieving Lt-Col. Weller of the 13th, Colonel Williams now found himself commanding a force of over 2,000 troops. The immediate concern was to integrate the newly arrived Royal Marines into the front line duties, such as manning the frontier posts, patrols in the woods, and close observation of the enemy. The winter climate was such that the new arrivals had to learn basic survival techniques. The use of gloves or mittens and scarves to ward off frostbite and the use of snowshoes would all have been taught by the local Canadian militia.

Williams also set up his staff to run the fort efficiently. This included 1st Lieutenant John Mitton as battalion adjutant, 1st Lieutenant Valentine Grifith as quartermaster, 1st Lieutenant John E. Jones as fort major, 1st Lieutenant John Fennell in charge of the sleigh establishment, and Captain Thomas Mould as paymaster. The RMA Company had 1st Lieutenant Richard C. Steele as its adjutant, and transferred from the 2nd Battalion RMA Company was 2nd Lieutenant John Marsh, as the fort's engineering officer. (Marsh was later killed at Fort Erie on September 4, 1814. He was decapitated by an American cannonball whilst supervising a British mortar emplacement.) The other officers concentrated on training for their men and educating themselves as to the enemies' positions and the immediate frontier they would be defending.

Another part of Colonel William's job was to work in close co-operation with the Royal Navy. The naval base and shipyard were adjacent to the fort and protected by its guns. The shipyard had several small gunboats under construction, along with a new brig being built by master shipbuilder William Simons. The larger vessel was expected to be completed and launched by May of 1814.

The senior naval officer was Commander Daniel Pring RN. He had served under Admiral Warren on the flagship HMS *San Domingo*. Warren sent him to the Lake Ontario Squadron, where he served on HMS *Wolfe*. Warren later sent him to Lake Champlain in 1813 as second in command of the Lake Squadron under Captain Thomas Everard RN. Both officers collaborated with Lieutenant Colonel John Murray in a waterborne raid on the city of Plattsburgh in June of 1813. A combined force of 1,400 soldiers, militia, Royal Marines and sailors destroyed the US Army encampment known as Pike's Cantonment. The dockyards and other government buildings were searched for documents and military supplies, which were confiscated. The arsenal, armoury, and blockhouse were set on fire. The raid had been carried out with the aid of a British paid spy, by the name of Mr. Joseph Ackley, who had provided a list of targets and given the disposition of US troops in the area.

When Captain Everard returned to Quebec, he took back with him the fifty seamen from his own ship, HMS *Wasp* (18), and the thirty volunteers from the troopship *Dover* at Quebec. By October, Pring was left with only sixty-eight men under his command and in desperate need of more seamen.

Colonel Williams was able to have part of his command serve as seamen on temporary loan to Captain Pring. He then wrote to Prevost, alerting him to the situation that more than the stated maximum of marines were placed on the ships at Isle aux Noix, and that these marines needed to be replaced by seamen. The governor, however, had no more seamen to place on those ships, and therefore the marines had to stay.

Captain Pring had also corresponded with Sir James Yeo RN (Senior Royal Navy Officer on the Great Lakes), in attempts to have more seamen sent to his command. Yeo insisted that all replacements were more urgently required on Lake Ontario. Pring made other attempts to remedy his situation by travelling to Quebec himself to try to obtain volunteers from vessels there. The results were meagre at best, and the shortage of British seamen would persist from this point on.

Canada and Winter Warfare

The 1813 sailing season on Lake Champlain had been one of dominance by the Royal Navy, and now that additional Royal Marines were present at Ile aux Noix, a plan was devised by Colonel Williams and Captain Pring to raid the magazine and commissariat buildings on Cumberland Head.

A combined force of Royal Navy seamen, Royal Marines, and a number of Captain Parke's artillery company embarked on six gunboats and rowed and sailed southward down the west side of Lake Champlain, hiding in the bays and skirting the ice flows now forming on the lake, until the target was reached. The British report of the action stated, "The enemy magazines and stores were sacked and a large quantity of provisions, camp equipage and munitions, destroyed without interference from the Plattsburgh army, or the American flotilla, though these were only a short distance away."[6]

In contrast, an American report of the same incident stated, "Sir George (Prevost) was evidently misinformed as to the facts by the officer in command of the expedition. The extensive building lately erected at Plattsburgh as a depot magazine was a small shed near the lake shore at Champlain landing which had formerly been in public use, and the smoke from which gave the first information to Macdonough of the enemy's approach."[7] The British crews, having completed their mission, now had to row back, cutting their way through the ice, and arrived back at the naval base on December 5 without a shot being fired on either side. Commodore Macdonough USN, had dispatched four row galleys (gunboats) with a detachment of troops from his fleet. This force was under the command of Lieutenant Stephen Cassin USN, but the American row galleys turned back after a pursuit of three miles. Shortly after this event, Commodore Macdonough decided to move his fleet to Otter Creek, Vermont, the farthest point away from the British forces without leaving Lake Champlain.

December 1813 saw yet another British raid on New York soil. This time Royal Marines from the 2nd Battalion and other forces, including Lieutenant Stevens RMA, and some of his men, crossed the frozen St. Lawrence to the village of Hamilton (Now Waddington) and retrieved a quantity of captured British stores and other plunder that had been gathered at Hamilton. These were the gains of warfare in Upper Canada during 1813. The United States detachment at Hamilton was surprised and dispersed. The stores were carried back over the river, again with no casualties on either side.

On January 1 the Plattsburgh Republican newspaper published a statement from Captain Ezra Turner, cautioning the 36th regiment of New York Militia "To pay due attention to their arms and ammunition, that they may be found fit for service at a moment's warning for any emergency; for we know not at what hour the thief may come."

In February of 1814, the sick and near starving American army under General Wilkinson suddenly evacuated their winter quarter lines along the Salmon River at French Mills (Fort Covington) and broke up their camps to move back across the snow-covered country to Plattsburgh. This army had about 1,800 men ill with typhoid, pneumonia, dysentery, and atrophy of the limbs. Various newspaper reports told of infantry, dragoons, equipment, magazines and provisions all on the move. A British report stated, "A considerable quantity of useful military stores and war material was collected by our troops, which the enemy had abandoned, apparently not having sufficient transport to remove all in time."

March 2nd Major Benjamin Forsyth of the 1st US Rifle Regiment and 300 of his riflemen with a party of Dragoons were sent to the lines near Champlain to protect the frontier and break up an illicit intercourse with the enemy that had been carried out during the winter, while General Alexander Macomb and Colonel Isaac Clarke were sent to Vermont on a similar mission. General Wilkinson then moved the bulk of his forces northward, to the small border town of Champlain, on the 19th of March. In the meantime, the British had been aware of the American activity and had begun a reinforcement of their advanced post at La Colle Mill. They added two three-pounder cannons and an RMA detachment to service them. Other reinforcements were directed to Burtonville, Ile aux Noix, St. Jean, and Chambly. On the 26th of March the Plattsburgh Republican reported the hanging of a British spy. "Wm Baker a Sergeant of the British army (103rd Regiment of Infantry), was executed as a spy, on the sand ridge between Court and Brinkerhoff streets Plattsburgh."

The Battle of La Colle Mill

A council of war was held by General Wilkinson on March 29 at Champlain. Present were Brigadier Generals Macomb, Bissell, and Smith, Colonels Atkinson, Miller, and Cummings. Also in attendance were Majors Pitts and Totten. The meeting began with General Wilkinson giving a US

Canada and Winter Warfare

intelligence report, which advised that the British had 2,500 regulars at Ile aux Noix, with some 200 of these at the advance post of La Colle Mill. He stated his own force at 4,000 combatants, including 100 cavalry, 300 artillerists with eleven guns. He then asked his council, "Shall we attack the enemy?" The officers discussed the situation and expressed the opinion that light troops could probe the British position, and if favourable the whole army should move to support the light troops. They then approved Wilkinson's order of battle for the following day.

A general order was given requiring each man to be issued with sixty rounds of ammunition and four days' cooked provisions. The American high command issued an interesting order, to motivate, if not to intimidate, their men about to enter battle. "An officer will be posted on the right of each platoon, and a tried sergeant will form a supernumerary rank, and will instantly put to death any man who goes back." General Wilkinson addressed his troops directly. "Let every officer and every man make resolution to return victorious or not at all; for, with double the force of the enemy, this army must not give ground."[8]

In the early morning darkness of March 30 General Wilkinson's light troops, the 1st US Rifle Regiment, led by Major Benjamin Forsyth, reached Odelltown, a small hamlet on the Canadian side of the border. The entire region was heavily wooded, and the main road was covered with frozen slush and falling snow. The riflemen cautiously advanced into the eerie darkness. As soon as the houses of Odelltown were out of sight a large obstruction appeared ahead. It was a barricade of cut trees known as an abatis. This was the first of many such obstructions laid down by the British.

As soon as the riflemen passed the first obstacle a sudden volley of musketry from the woods broke the silence. Two riflemen fell dead, with another badly wounded. The small picket of Canadian Frontier Light Infantry were retreating in haste, raising Indian war whoops of victory in an attempt to further inhibit the American advance. The element of surprise was now lost. Soon the British officers at La Colle Mill would be informed of the presence of another invading army.

The sawmill on the La Colle River was the source of raw lumber used in the fortifications at Ile aux Noix and in part of the naval construction carried out in the shipyard. It had been attacked in 1812 and briefly captured by the American army. Since then the two-storey mill had been refortified.

29

Heavy logs had been used to double the eighteen-inch-thick stone walls. Other defensive measures, such as firing steps, loopholes in windows, and wide barbed bars, protected the windows from outside entry. A clearing of 150 yards around the two-storey mill gave an ample killing ground. Behind the mill a bridge extended back across the river, connecting it to a strong blockhouse built on a commanding bluff. The blockhouse occupants could observe the surrounding area and fire over the mill if under attack. Two more blockhouses and a defensive redoubt existed within musketshot of the mill. Both were located on Ash Island, which is a short distance from the mouth of the La Colle River. Fire from these positions would support the mill and also reach any vessels attempting to penetrate upriver.

The mill was under the command of Major Richard B. Handcock of the 13th Regiment. His force consisted of sixty officers and men of Captain Blake's company of the 13th, forty Frontier Light Infantry, and seventy Royal Marines commanded by Captain (Brevet Major) Robert B. Lynch RM, and Lieutenants Samuel Barton and William R. Caldwell RM. The RMA were also present in the form of a corporal's section of RMA gunners, manning the two small three-pounder guns. On hearing of the American army's approach, Major Handcock sent some of his junior officers with twenty men to hold the island blockhouses, in case of American gunboats supporting the land attack. Next he sent another officer with twenty more men to defend the hill blockhouse. He also sent a runner from the FLI to Colonel Williams to request reinforcements from the fort, as the enemy was reported crossing the frontier in large numbers.

After the initial skirmish that morning, the 1st US Rifle Regiment found a narrow footpath that gave a way to bypass the road and its obstructions. General Wilkinson now sent forward regiment after regiment, despite his own officers' advice to approach with caution. Soon the defenders inside the mill and blockhouses came under fire. More American troops arrived, and the encirclement of the British position became more and more complete. Forsyth's riflemen bypassed the mill and crossed the La Colle River, pushing on to infiltrate the woods on either side of the road to Ile aux Noix.

The US Army reserves under General Alexander Macomb were still filing past the British obstructions. Engineers were busy chopping and sawing through the tree branches to create a path for the heavier guns and equipment, only to find the heat of the day was turning the roadway into a slushy

Canada and Winter Warfare

quagmire. Artillery pieces and transport wagons sunk up to their axles in thawing mud. A few light guns were manhandled by large groups of soldiers, hauling and lifting them along the narrow footpath. Pack mules were used to transport the powder and ammunition for the guns. Eventually Captain Robert H. McPherson of the 1st US Light Artillery was able to set up two cannons and a five-inch howitzer and immediately began to bombard the mill.

The British Counterattack

On hearing the first news of the American attack, Colonel Williams advised the navy of the danger and to prepare for action. He then sent orders to Captain Edward Cartwright (formerly of the 41st Regiment) at Burtonville barracks to supply two companies of infantry to help relieve the mill. In addition, he had Captains Henry Ellard and Bennet Holgate form the flank companies of the 13th Regiment plus two battalion companies of Royal Marines as reinforcements for the mill. Once ferried to the mainland, the light company of the 13th led the way. Soon distant gunfire could be heard, and the force quickened the pace. About a mile north of the mill, Forsyth's riflemen ambushed the leading troops and severely wounded Captain Ellard. The relief force continued to fight in extended order (light infantry tactics) into the woods; however, they soon found themselves outnumbered and facing several US regiments. Barred from his objective, Captain Holgate ordered the gathering of the wounded and began a controlled retreat back to the fort at Ile aux Noix.

At the same time the second relief force from Burtonville was on its way to the mill. Captain Cartwright and his men were cautiously nearing the battle by crossing an ice-cold tributary of the La Colle River. Under the cover of heavy woods he found a gap in the American lines. Judging an appropriate time, when the American guns had just discharged and the smoke was thickest, Cartwright ordered a rush to the rear door of the mill and to the nearest blockhouse. A company of Canadian Voltigeurs and the Grenadier Company of the Canadian Fencibles successfully managed to pass through the US positions and gain entry to the mill, with no apparent casualties!

The British were elated. The two-storey thirty-five-foot-long mill was now positively crowded with defenders. Major Handcock held an officers meeting. The newly arrived troops now gave him the means to launch a counterattack. The American artillery posed the greatest threat. It was decided to attack and "spike" the guns.

Lieutenant Samuel Barton RM, volunteered to lead the "Forlorn Hope" sortie. His men consisted of volunteers from all units. Royal Marines, 13th Regiment, Voltigeurs, and Fencibles were all represented. Every musket and cannon in the mill was loaded and readied. Each volunteer fixed his bayonet; nails and hammers were distributed. At the given signal, the large mill doors swung open. A volley was fired from every loop hole and window, the small cannon firing canister shot. Out charged Barton at the head of his men. They raced across the clearing, heading for the enemy guns. The American infantry recovered quickly and began to fire at the British. Just as Barton reached the battery, the guns exploded into the group. The officer was seen to fall directly under the mouth of one gun. Now leaderless, the attack floundered, and the assault party retreated back to the mill, leaving Barton and others for dead.

After the failure of the sortie, Majors Lynch and Handcock decided to send a dispatch to Ile aux Noix. Lynch called for a volunteer to carry the message. Private J. Brown of the Royal Marines stood forward and said he was a good swimmer and would get through. The dispatch was written and sealed inside a lead sheath to keep it waterproof. If wounded or captured, Brown would merely release it, and it would sink to the bottom of the river. Private Brown, wearing only his shirt and trousers, slipped into the water and using a log to disguise his movements floated into the river with the dispatch firmly clenched between his teeth.

The nearest American infantry took some time to realize that the unnatural movements beside a floating log could be something other than river wildlife. Several rounds were fired at Brown, but none found its mark. Eventually floating out of range, Brown began to swim northward with the current towards Ile aux Noix. Swimming as far as he could in the near freezing water, he finally landed on the shore. He then ran to the boat dock opposite the island fort. He was then rowed over and taken to Colonel Williams, where he delivered the dispatch. Brown's verbal report and the written dispatch confirmed Williams' earlier intuition that naval vessels would be required for action. Colonel Williams thanked Private Brown for his gallant effort and promoted him to corporal in the next day's orders.

While Brown was proceeding with his journey, another sortie was being attempted against the US guns. Captain Blake of the 13th and

Canada and Winter Warfare

Captain Cartwright of the relief force led this second attempt. However, the result remained the same, and this sortie with casualties retreated back inside the mill.

Captain Daniel Pring RN had ensured his vessels were ice-free at the dockside, and his men had broken up the ice flows to reach the narrow stretch of open water in the Richelieu River. In addition his sailors had prepared the eleven-gun sloop HMS *Chubb* to slip its mooring and be towed out into the river. A number of gunboats had also been readied for action. At an officers' meeting, Colonel Williams arranged for a portion of Captain Parke's RM artillery company, Lieutenant Balchild's rocket half company, and a number of Royal Marine infantry to be embarked on *Chubb* and the gunboats.

The naval relief force under Captain Pring's command now left the island, the gunboats towing the larger vessel out towards open water. Here a light breeze assisted in filling its sails and sped it on its way southbound. The possible presence of US vessels was of great concern to the British. However, none were encountered. Commodore Macdonough of the US Navy had wisely declined to have any part of the attack into Lower Canada. This astute officer was wisely concentrating on building a stronger naval force to prevent British naval dominance of Lake Champlain in 1814.

By about 4 p.m. the American forces had seen the sloop and the gunboats approaching the mouth of the La Colle River. The US infantry opened fire on the British force. Captain Pring ordered a return fire from *Chubb's* carronades. This resulted in the shoreline and nearby woods being swept with grapeshot, causing the American infantry to fall back.

Shortly after this, the flotilla made sight of the battlefield. Lieutenant Balchild aimed his rocket apparatus and began to discharge rockets in the direction of the American flag and a group of officers, including General Wilkinson, who stood behind the infantry positions. Roaring over the heads of the infantry and detonating behind them, the rockets caused near panic to the US rank and file, who were kept in order by the threats of their officers to carry out the standing order to shoot any soldier attempting to run away.

As *Chubb* and the gunboats neared the battle site, the American artillery switched its guns to face the British vessels. The heavier, more numerous naval long guns soon outmatched them. The American artillerymen had suffered numerous casualties. The battery commander Captain McPherson had been wounded in the chin and thigh. Lieutenant Adam Larabee, the second in command, had been shot in the lungs, leaving a junior officer, Lieutenant Walter Sheldon, who had kept the battery functioning but now had to order its withdrawal. Captain Pring began to land his Royal Marines and Captain Parke's artillery unit. This put the American infantry in an untenable position, facing fire from two sides and now devoid of artillery support. A general retreat was ordered. The Royal Marine Artillery was able to discharge a few rounds to harass the departing Americans, but the time was near 6 p.m. and it was considered too hazardous to pursue the enemy through the darkening woods. Instead, the relief force was greeted with cheers from a much relieved group of defenders, who came out into the cold evening air to look for fallen comrades.

The wounded were gathered and were being attended to when a familiar figure was seen to rise and began to walk slowly towards his comrades. It was Lieutenant Barton. The young officer had been concussed by the discharge of cannon as he charged the battery and had lain unconscious from that moment on. Thinking he was dead, the American artillerymen had taken his sword, rank epaulette, gorget, and boots. However, apart from being a bit "shaky," he was visibly unhurt.

The following morning British patrols confirmed a complete withdrawal of all American forces. Later reports of this action placed the British casualties at eleven killed in action, forty-six wounded, four missing, plus one Indian warrior killed and one wounded. American casualties were thirteen killed in action, one hundred twenty-eight wounded, thirteen or possibly as many as thirty missing. Major General James Wilkinson later faced court martial, the results of which meant he never led American troops again. During testimony at the trial, General Daniel Bissell and Lieutenant Colonel Joseph G. Totten of the US Corps of Engineers said, "The British Company advanced against the guns with such resolution, that the artillerymen deserted them and were only saved from capture, by the powerful force of infantry behind them."9 Captain Robert H. McPherson, who commanded the 1st US Light Artillery, gave a similar testimony: "The conduct of the enemy that day was distinguished by desperate bravery. As an instance, one company made a charge at our artillery, and at the same instant received its fire and that of two brigades of infantry."10

Canada and Winter Warfare

Battle reports sent to England stated that the whole British force engaged did not exceed 600 at any one time against an army of 4,000. Several British officers were mentioned in dispatches: Major Handcock of the 13th, Captain Ritter of the Frontier Light Infantry, Captains Blake and Ellard of the 13th, Lieutenants Caldwell and Barton of the Royal Marines, Captain Pring RN, and Lieutenants Creswick and Hicks, also of the Royal Navy. With this battle over, the frontier returned to an atmosphere of fearful apprehension of what would take place next.

The spring mobilization would see armies on the march and warships setting sail, the only questions where and when. The new month of April would see an increased fervour of building of larger vessels in both navies. Wilkinson would be replaced by Major General George Izard as head of the Northern Army. This officer now began a rebuilding of his army after the abuses and defeats suffered under Wilkinson's leadership. He also tightened the anti-smuggling efforts in northern New York and Vermont. Likewise, Commodore Macdonough renewed the efforts of the US Navy to prevent contraband ship building materials from being smuggled into Canadian waters. He also was overseeing the work on the additions to his flotilla.

3

The Royal Navy's Offensive, 1814

The Royal Navy's Spring Offensive, 1814

The Royal Navy's spring offensive began with the Lake Ontario fleet emerging with a much enlarged squadron. Commodore Sir James Lucas Yeo RN, had added HMS *Prince Regent* (58) and HMS *Princess Charlotte* (42) in April. These new additions gave the British a superiority of force, which compelled the American Commodore Isaac Chauncey to quit open water for the time being and have his vessels take refuge under the batteries guarding Sackets Harbor. A new British commander appointed to Upper Canada, Lieutenant General Sir George Drummond, had consultations with Sir James Yeo in regards to an attack on Sackets Harbor, the home of Chauncey's fleet. To attempt an amphibious landing would require about 4,000 British regulars. A request was sent to Sir George Prevost, but this was refused. Drummond and Yeo turned their attention to the port town of Oswego, which was a weak point in the US supply route feeding into Sackets Harbor. A new plan was devised to attack Oswego to destroy or capture the materials in transit to Chauncey for his new vessels nearing completion at Sackets. The forces ready in Upper Canada were sent to embark at Kingston, and the British fleet set sail May 3. On board the British fleet were the 2nd Royal Marine Battalion, the RM Artillery company, six companies of the De Watteville Regiment, and a company of Glengarry Light Infantry.

Rockets, Bombs and Bayonets

The defences at Oswego consisted of Fort Ontario, first built in 1755, which had seen action during the French and Indian War and the War of the Revolution. The fort was situated on a precipitous height overlooking the town and the lake. It was assumed to be heavily defended and heavily gunned; this was incorrect. The recently arrived five companies of the 3rd US Artillery (trained and armed as infantry and artillery) were the only American regulars present, and they had to use five old cannons at the fort.

Lieutenant Colonel George E. Mitchell USA, had found the fort in disrepair and the guns without carriages and three without trunnions. Mitchell set his 290 regulars to work and had the local militia, numbering about 200, pitch their tents on the opposite side of the river to create the impression of a larger force than what he had under his command.

The British fleet arrived on the morning of May 5. The larger vessels began a bombardment of the fort while the landing boats were filled with troops. When ready, a number of gunboats led the landing force towards the shoreline. The American artillery held its fire until the gunboats came within range; then they opened up, with great effect. Two attempted landings were driven off. One gunboat was so badly damaged it was abandoned to the enemy. A further attempt was made at 8 p.m., but this was called off as a wind change required the British fleet to move farther out into the lake.

The following morning, May 6, 1814, the seven largest British ships moved closer to the shore and harbour and pounded Fort Ontario with cannon fire and rockets from the Royal Marine Artillery, under 1st Lieutenant John H. Stevens. The American artillery used hot shot and set fire to the rigging and sheets of the nearest vessels. The Americans were down to only four guns, as one had exploded the previous day. Meanwhile, the Royal Marines and the De Wattevilles secured a landing some 550 yards east of the fort. This landing was a near disaster, as the depth of the water was misjudged, and the overzealous officers, followed by their men, leapt into shoulder-high water. The following boats avoided the same fate and landed their men safely and with dry weapons.

Once landed, the attacking force came under heavy fire of grape and musketry from the woods and fort. Lieutenant Colonel Victor Fischer directed the British force. He sent Captain Alexander McMillan and his Glengarry Light Infantry to form the left flank and drive the American militia from the woods. The two flank companies of the De Watteville Regiment under Captain

The Royal Navy's Offensive, 1814

DeBersey formed the centre, and the 2nd Battalion Royal Marines under Major James Malcolm RM, secured the right flank. The Marines and De Wattevilles, with water still draining from their useless cartridge boxes, fixed bayonets and began the advance up the slope towards Fort Ontario. Captain William Mulcaster RN, with 200 British sailors armed with boarding pikes and cutlasses, landed directly below the fort, near the harbour mouth, and were accompanied by Drummond and Yeo and their staffs.

As the British advanced, Colonel Mitchell formed his men into a double rank line of battle. The American artillerymen fired repeated musket volleys, while moving back towards the fort's defensive ditch. A force of twenty-five US sailors under the command of Captain Melancthon Taylor Woolsey USN, and Lieutenant George Pearce USN, were manning the fort's guns. The Royal Marines and sailors swept over the rampart, overrunning the American battery, and a desperate struggle began to capture the fifteen-star American flag which had been nailed to the forts flagpole. It was musketshot against bayonet. Three British attackers were cut down while attempting to climb the flagpole. Lieutenant John Hewett RM, began his climb up the pole and was hit twice. A wounded American artilleryman raised his musket to shoot Hewitt again when Hewitt's first sergeant killed him with a bayonet thrust. The British officer cut down the flag with his sword; he then slid down and collapsed from blood loss. With the enemy inside the fort, Colonel Mitchell led a rapid withdrawal of his troops into the woods and along the road to Oswego Falls, in anticipation of further British action.

The main reason for the attack was to disrupt the flow of war supplies sent via the Mohawk River and across Lake Oneida to Oswego, and then on to the naval and army base at Sackets Harbor. The British captured 2,400 barrels of flour, pork, salt, and bread, and a large quantity of naval munitions and cordage. In addition the schooner USS *Growler* was raised containing seven heavy cannon; other small schooners, including USS *Penelope,* were also taken and used to bring back the spoils to Kingston.

The thirty-minute battle resulted in six American dead, including Lieutenant Daniel Blainey USA, thirty-eight wounded, and five missing. The British lost nineteen dead, including Captain William Holtoway RM, and seventy-three wounded, with some dying later. Captain Holtoway had a premonition of his own death and related this to Lieutenant John C. Morgan RM, whom he asked to look after his accounts. Morgan later recalled, "I complied with his desire, and endeavoured to rally his spirits; but it was to no avail, he felt assured of his fate and prepared to meet it as if it had been his inevitable doom."[11] British battle reports state that sixty American officers and men were captured, about half of these being severely wounded. The British buried the dead in two separate shallow mass graves near the fort, then set demolition charges and completely destroyed the fort and its buildings.

Commodore Yeo and General Drummond ordered the fleet to return to Kingston on the 6th of May, carrying off the American prisoners and bringing away the captured supplies, guns, and vessels. Yeo wrote, describing the attack in his report to the Admiralty,

> Our men had to climb a long and steep hill exposed to a destructive fire, but they gained the top, threw themselves into the ditch and stormed the ramparts. The Second Battalion of Royal Marines excited the admiration of all. They were led by the gallant Major Malcolm and suffered severely. Captain Holtoway fell gallantly at the head of his company.[12]

Commodore Yeo was slightly wounded in the heel, and another shot hit his hat. General Drummond's report made special mention of Lieutenant Stevens RMA, and his rocket company, who provided covering fire for the landings from gunboats. Also mentioned in dispatches were Lieutenant Hewett RM, and Lieutenant James Lawrie RM (Yeo's secretary), who was first into the fort, and Captain William H. Mulcaster RN, of HMS *Princess Charlotte*, who was severely wounded by grapeshot, from which he eventually lost his leg.

The return to Kingston on May 7 found a complete readjustment in Canada. The Quartermaster Generals Department had transferred all naval establishments, and control of all naval forces returned to the Admiralty. The 2nd Battalion was to be broken up for "Naval service on the lakes." The Royal Marine Artillery and Rocket Company with their guns and rockets were deployed with the army forces in Upper Canada, some stationed in forts along the St. Lawrence River, and others to service in the gunboats of Lakes Ontario and Champlain. Lieutenant Colonel Malcolm with his staff and a cadre of marines were to locate to Halifax and remain there to possibly reform another full battalion of Royal Marines if needed. Lieutenant

The Royal Navy's Offensive, 1814

General Prevost no longer commanded any part of the Royal Navy; he would now co-operate with Sir James Yeo on an equal basis if he needed naval support. The RMA units sent to the Niagara theatre were heavily involved in the Battle of Lundy's Lane on 25 July, where a sergeant and a gunner were captured and made prisoners. The R.M.A. were also present at the siege of Fort Erie where Lieutenant John Marsh RMA was killed on September 4.

Capture of the Fort at Oswego, May 6, 1814
From a coloured Aquatint in the Officers Mess, R.M.L.I., Chatham,
made from a contemporary drawing by Lieut. J. Hewett R.M.

Rockets, Bombs and Bayonets

Captain Pring's Otter Creek Raid

In November of 1813, Sir George Prevost ordered a "brig" to be constructed at Ile aux Noix by William Simons, a shipbuilder formerly of Greenock, Scotland. This vessel was completed and in service by April of 1814. Originally named *Niagara*, this was soon changed to HMS *Linnet*. It was rigged as a sloop of war, carrying sixteen guns.

Six weeks after the Battle of La Colle Mill, Lake Champlain was again free from ice. The British garrison at Ile aux Noix seized the offensive. Captain Pring took HMS *Linnet* and his smaller sloops, HMS *Chubb* (11) and *Finch* (11), with eight row galleys. Captain Robert B. Lynch and Lieutenants John Coulter and John Ashmore and 100 Royal Marines were on board *Linnet*, with Lieutenants John A. Phillips and Fortescue Grahame with 116 Royal Marines on the gunboats. Lieutenant Balchild and his rocket half company were also embarked on several of the vessels. Another vessel was an improvised shallow-draught bomb-vessel, armed with a light mortar. This was manned by a detachment of Royal Marines Artillery. The British fleet sailed southward on the Richelieu River on the 8th of May. The only hindrance to their progress was the northerly current and a persistent head wind. Even before leaving Canadian waters, the flotilla was under observation by Americans, both military and civilian.

While American troops on both sides of Lake Champlain kept watch for any sighting of the British ships, the local newspapers were printing warnings and raising the alarm, as no one knew for certain what target the British were after. The American spy Peter Sailly reported to Commodore Macdonough that the British were taking every vessel they could find, with the intent to block the mouth of Otter Creek and seal in the American fleet. The farther south the British came, the more obvious the British goal of Otter Creek was. By the evening of May 13, Pring's flotilla was reported to be at Split Rock Point, three miles north of the mouth of Otter Creek.

In December of 1813, Commodore Macdonough had concentrated most of the American fleet in Otter Creek, with the exception of a few guard boats. He had wisely decided not to participate in the La Colle Mill fiasco. Instead he had been working tirelessly on ensuring that his new vessel, a corvette USS *Saratoga* (26), would be complete and armed ready for action in the forthcoming season. He had also purchased a second vessel, which was

The Royal Navy's Offensive, 1814

intended to be a commercial steamboat. This second vessel was rigged as a schooner and was launched May 15 as USS *Ticonderoga* (17). These new acquisitions would provide Macdonough with the naval superiority needed to beat the British in any forthcoming engagement.

While his vessels were near completion, Macdonough's nearly insurmountable problem was the lack of seamen, trained or otherwise, to man his ships. He had exhausted all avenues of acquiring seamen, even to the point of acquiring 250 soldiers on temporary loan from General Izard. His officer complement was also deficient in numbers. The US Navy would not emerge into Lake Champlain till May 25.

Captain Pring's flotilla proceeded to the mouth of Otter Creek on the morning of May 14, only to find four American gunboats ready for action under Lieutenant Stephen Casin USN, and a newly constructed battery of seven heavy guns commanded by Captain Arthur W. Thornton of the US Light Artillery. These guns had been mounted on the cliff overlooking the creek. In addition a brigade of 1,000 Vermont militia turned out to defend the Vergennes dockyard.

A two-hour artillery duel ensued, providing no appreciable damage on either side. The British bomb vessel delivered a number of high angle shells and bombs, all to no avail. A brief attempt to land 150 Royal Marines was aborted owing to large numbers of Vermont militia firing at the boats. Commodore Macdonough and his military partners had prepared for just such an attack and won the day. Macdonough had complete control of his ships and was able to decide when and where he would fight. His ships would not enter into battle in an unready state.

The British flotilla now retired northward back to Canada, with the loss of one seaman killed and three wounded. On the return journey several row galleys entered the Bouquet River in an attempt to seize U.S. government flour known to be in the grist mill at Willsboro Falls. On the return to the lake, a party of Essex county militia under General Daniel Wright fired on the rearmost galley and caused an estimated thirty-three British casualties. A return of fire allowed the rescue of the now drifting rear galley. Only one Essex militia man, by the name of Job Stafford, was wounded.

The British fleet anchored for the night near the islands of Four Brothers. Here they buried their dead and in the morning resumed their journey back to Ile aux Noix, arriving on May 16th. Captain Pring later wrote to a friend describing the action, "Every tree on the lake shore seems to have a Jonathan stationed behind it."

During Pring's absence from the naval station, orders had been given by the Admiralty to begin a 1,200 ton vessel, to be constructed at Ile aux Noix. The vessel was so large that it required the removal of the northeast redoubt from the fort's defences to give room to build it. Post Captain Peter Fisher RN, was transferred by Sir James Yeo to assume command of the base and of the new ship, a 5th rate frigate HMS *Confiance*. (This was a salute to Sir James Yeo, RN, the senior Royal Navy officer commanding the Great Lakes Squadron.) Once the frigate was completed it would be the largest warship to sail on Lake Champlain's waters.

The warm weather saw a number of minor actions and occurrences on the lakes and border regions. Commodore Sir James Yeo continued to dominate Lake Ontario by patrolling the waters, searching for opportunities to raid. One such instance was Pultneyville, New York, on May 15. Yeo's fleet intimidated the local militia commandant, Brigadier General John Swift of the New York Volunteers, to negotiate under a flag of truce; he agreed to let the British remove all government stores without hindrance, providing no civil property was taken. A dispute took place as the British were leaving, and they were fired upon while still under a flag of truce. Captain James Short RM, and several of his men were wounded. Two U.S. citizens were killed and three wounded; a further two were taken prisoner and sent to Halifax. Brigadier Swift was later killed near Newark, Upper Canada, on July 12, 1814.

The British Loss at Big Sandy Creek

Another incident of serious consequence to the Royal Navy on Lake Ontario was the Battle of Big Sandy Creek. Part of Yeo's fleet was monitoring the mouth of the Oswego River for any American boat activity trying to resume the flow of naval cannon and other war supplies to Sackets Harbor. On May 28, 1814, at dusk, a convoy of nineteen unarmed canal boats carrying naval supplies left Oswego commanded by Captain Melancthon Woolsey USN, accompanied by Major Daniel Appling and 150 riflemen of the 1st US Rifle Regiment. The convoy carried a load of thirty-five cannons and large heavy cables, all desperately needed to complete the war vessels waiting at Sackets Harbor. Lying in close to the shoreline to avoid British patrols, Woolsey and Appling went ashore to rendezvous with 130 Oneida

The Royal Navy's Offensive, 1814

Indians friendly to the U.S. cause. These native allies would run on land parallel to the canal boats providing flank protection. None of the boat crews knew of this arrangement.

The following morning one of the canal boats became lost in the fog and was captured by the British. This capture of the American vessel may have been the work of a British spy by the name of Curley, who was piloting the boat. The significance of half the crew being armed US regular army riflemen did not dawn on the British interrogators. Commodore Yeo sent out a search party to find the convoy. Yeo had two gunboats, two cutters, a ship's gig, and a complement of 210 Royal Navy and Royal Marines officers and men. Commanding this flotilla was Captain Stephen Popham RN, of HMS *Montreal* (21) and Captain Francis B. Spilsbury RN, of HMS *Niagara* (20). After a fruitless day of searching on the 29th no signs of the American flotilla were found.

The following morning Popham learned from a local woman that the convoy was up the Big Sandy Creek. Ignoring the warning given by Commodore Yeo "not to enter creeks or rivers," Popham and Spilsbury saw the masts of Captain Woolsey's flotilla and signalled *Montreal* and *Niagara* to land field artillery. These guns and the long guns of each ship were to provide a covering bombardment while the British flotilla went up the Big Sandy.

Captain Woolsey and Major Appling had called out the local militia on their arrival at the Big Sandy wharves. This location was a small commercial port in 1814, with houses, barns, and storehouses, which connected Lake Ontario to the local area and its road system. The Ellisburg detachment of the 55th New York Militia turned out but was sadly deficient in arms, many having no flints for their muskets and some armed with pitchforks! However, Woolsey and Appling set them to work unloading the naval supplies and obtaining every cart and wagon in the area to move these supplies northward to Sackets Harbor. Runners were also sent to Sackets and Oswego to obtain reinforcements from the troops at each location.

General Edmond P. Gaines USA, sent Major McIntosh and his squadron of US Dragoons and Captain George W. Melvin of the 2nd Light Artillery with two six-pounder guns, and a detachment of US Marines under Captain Richard Smith USMC (all of whom arrived just before the action, and all held reserve positions out of sight of the British). Woolsey's aide, Lieutenant Pearce USN, had been sent to see if any enemy were near. He returned at

5 p.m. with news that British gunboats were at the mouth of the Big Sandy and larger warships were nearby. Appling, Woolsey, and their officers now devised a plan of entrapment if the British came after their boats and cargo.

At 8 a.m. on the 30th the British began a bombardment of the wharf area in which movement could still be seen. Appling had dispersed his riflemen on the north side of the creek. Chief Adam Skenadore and the Oneida warriors lay hidden and dispersed throughout the field and wetlands on the south side. With the Oneida force was Appling's liaison officer, 2nd Lieutenant Josiah Hill of the 1st Rifle Regiment.

The British boats entered the sixty-foot-wide Big Sandy Creek. The area surrounding the waterway is mainly wetlands full of swamp vegetation, marsh grass, and ponds. Very soon it became evident that the New York Militia was forming near a wooded area on the north side of the creek. The British naval and field artillery directed their fire towards them, but that seemed to make no impact. The militia commanding officer, Captain Gad Ackley, could be seen riding his horse up and down the line. Popham's boats found the creek very winding, with many blind bends. Eventually he spied the enemy militia and brought the twenty-four-pounder of the first gunboat to bear. Unfortunately, the gun could not be depressed far enough to fire accurately, so with little effort the gunboat swung round 180 degrees and presented its other gun, a sixty-eight-pound carronade, towards the militia.

The large-calibre carronade fired alternately round shot and then canister. The other boats in the flotilla joined in. This fire from a new and closer direction caused Ackley's militiamen to retire out of sight and into the woods. Unseen from the British positions, these militiamen filed back to reinforce Appling's riflemen. Popham and his officers spied out the countryside for any other U.S. forces and decided to proceed, as no other opposition had been sighted; the unwitting British were now entering the trap.

As the British boats came closer to the American vessels the bombardment ceased. Popham ordered his protection force to disembark on to either side of the creek. The north side was 1st. Lieutenant Thomas S. Cox RM, and Master's Mate Charles Hoare RN, with about forty Royal Marines. On the south shore, Captain Spilsbury and 2nd Lieutenant Patrick McVeagh RM, had about twenty Royal Marines and twenty seamen. This party also carried a loaded small brass mortar known as a cohorn.

The Royal Navy's Offensive, 1814

Once assembled on firm land as well as water, the British force proceeded slowly and with utmost caution up the narrowing creek, finally rounding Signal Pole Bend, which left them in full view of the rearmost American vessels. It was seen that the American dock workers and boatmen ran from the wharf, abandoning unloaded cargo, the canal boats, and their lifting pry-pole shear legs and tackle.

The British adjusted the aim on the large carronade as the gunboat rounded the bend. The gun misfired and was being worked on as the other boats behind started to fire towards the landing area. The foot soldiers halted, fixed bayonets, and waited for the order to advance. Unknown to the attackers they had sailed and marched past the Oneida force and were now in the sights of the American riflemen, who were now being reinforced by the militia.

When the British were only sixty feet away, Major Appling stepped out from behind a tree, aimed his pistol directly at the thickest assembly of redcoats, and fired. Immediately, this signal shot released a volley of 150 rifle bullets, which smashed into the marines on the north shore. Master's Mate Hoare fell dead with no less than eleven bullets in his chest. Lieutenant Cox also fell mortally wounded. In an instant numerous others fell dead and wounded. One American soldier by the name of J. M. Sturdevant later wrote that "The redcoats dropped to the ground like apples shaken from a tree in October."[13]

Popham had his boats return fire as quickly as they could. However, the targeted American riflemen in their green uniforms seemed to disappear into the brush and trees. Canister shot hit only one rifleman, by the name of Pvt. Simon Johnson from Lieutenant Lewis Armistead's company. The smoke now prevented the British from seeing their enemy, and despite the best efforts of the marine NCOs to form ranks and return fire, most of their musketry was ineffective.

On the south side of the creek Captain Spilsbury and Lieutenant McVeagh deployed their men in support of the north shore. The cohorn was fired, but the ball went high. Like much of the British bombardment the ball buried itself harmlessly in the wet ground. Skenador and Lieutenant Hill signalled the Oneida warriors to commence firing. The effect was devastating. McVeagh fell with what would become a fatal wound. Spilsbury continued to rally the Royal Marines and seamen and led them back to the safety of the boats, where they returned fire on the Indians. This too met with little success, as the Oneidas were well hidden in the marsh grass. Only one Indian was wounded.

Rockets, Bombs and Bayonets

The rearmost vessels in Popham's flotilla began to back out of the fight, only to find the Oneida warriors had crossed the creek and were firing into the boats. Once they realized the British were surrounded, the warriors rose up, waving tomahawks and yelling war cries, and began to charge the boats. Observing the Oneida's aggressive move Major Appling ordered a "bayonet charge" on the British. This was carried out by his riflemen using their long rifles, which had no bayonets. They raced towards the British boats. Popham, realizing the situation was hopeless, lowered his flag in surrender. Appling and his officers were quick enough to get across the creek and between the warriors and the now defeated flotilla. Even Captain Gad Ackley of the militia rode his horse in front of the warriors. This effort was to ensure that no massacre of British prisoners would take place.

Two incidents of note happened at the conclusion of the battle. An unnamed tall black seaman had been detailed to throw overboard all armaments in the event of capture to deny them to the Americans. This he did, and he was in the act of heaving a brass cannon over the side of his boat when ordered to stop at gunpoint by a party of Appling's riflemen. The seaman's reply was "The dammed Yankees shall not have that."[14] And with another heave the brass gun was overboard, as twelve riflemen fired. This brave sailor had stayed true to his duty.

The other incident involved a young Royal Navy lieutenant by the name of James Rowe, who was renowned as a vain, well-groomed, good-looking "dandy" by his fellow officers. After all of his men had been either killed or wounded, Rowe attempted to escape, but he was captured by a tomahawk-wielding Oneida. The warrior dragged Rowe back by his hair while Rowe screamed hysterically, "This Indian is going to scalp me!"[15] The reality is that the Oneida Nation did not scalp during the war of 1812. It was contrary to their rules of warfare. Lieutenant Rowe had read too many fictionalized novels or believed exaggerated accounts of the actions of indigenous Americans.

The battle casualties were one American rifleman (Pvt. Simon Johnson), who died of wounds on June 3, 1814, and One Oneida warrior (Jim Chrisjohn) wounded. The British had one Royal Navy officer killed outright, Master's Mate Hoare, and two Royal Marines officers, Cox and McVeagh, died of wounds. At least fourteen Royal Marines and seamen were killed outright and forty-three seriously wounded, most dying within days. Two more bodies were found days later in the creek. Twenty-seven Royal

The Royal Navy's Offensive, 1814

Marines and 106 sailors were prisoners. Popham, Spilsbury, and nine other Royal Navy officers were all marched off into captivity. Many of these men, including Popham and Spilsbury, were less seriously wounded and would be treated at Sackets Harbor. The officers were eventually sent to Cheshire, MA. The officers were allowed parole while they waited to be exchanged. The rank and file were all sent to a prison camp at East Greenbush, NY.

Master's Mate Hoare and the thirteen other sailors and marines killed in action were all buried on a hillside near the battle site at 5 p.m. on the day of the battle. Full military honours were given to Hoare but not to the rank and file, as per the custom of the day.

The severely wounded prisoners were taken into the private homes of Otis and McKie and other local families. Here while under guard they were attended to for many weeks by the ladies of the village, who used sheets and pillowcases to make bandages and applied "home remedies," as there were no local doctors. It took some time before General Gaines sent Dr. Samuel Eli to help heal the wounded. The care was given mainly by Mrs. Otis, Mrs. McKie, and Mrs. Ward. Mrs. Otis and her infant daughter had fled their home during the bombardment. Returning a day after the battle she found her main floor filled with dead British soldiers. She had to step over the bodies to reach her bedroom. In her bed she found a dying officer (Lt. Cox). His blood had soaked through the bed and had run across the floor. The bloodstains remained for years, despite many attempts to wash them away. Lieutenant Cox and the others who died at the house were buried in an apple orchard behind the home, which was later named "the hospital."

In the McKie home the severely wounded Lieutenant McVeagh was greatly concerned about the lack of a doctor for his men and himself. He wrote a letter on June 10 to Sir James Yeo, requesting that Dr. McActland, his personal friend and trusted physician, be sent to treat his men and his own wounds. Yeo denied the request on June 12. McVeagh, realizing he would soon die, entrusted his wedding ring to Mrs. McKie and asked her to send it to his wife. He was buried in the orchard with full military honours beside Lieutenant Cox and their men.

The prisoners who had survived their wounds endeared themselves to the American ladies. One lady described them as the handsomest men she ever saw. Mrs. Harriet Ward said, "They [the British] never took anything they did not pay for. They seemed much nicer than the Americans, who stole everything they could lay their hands on. They [the Americans] even stole the straps off McKie's harness while the British paid for everything they got."[16] When fit to leave, the prisoners were sent to Sackets Harbor and then onward to Greenbush, NY.

It was not unusual for correspondence to be exchanged between the adversaries. This was usually done under a flag of truce. The US vessel *Lady O' the Lake* carried a letter from Commodore Chauncey to Sir James Yeo on June 4, stating,

> Agreeably to your request I do myself the honour to forward by a flag of truce two thousand and seventy five dollars in Canadian notes collected from the seamen and marines late of your squadron and for which I paid Captain Popham the same amount in Bank Notes of this State—this money was not counted by myself but collected counted and sealed by Captain Popham before he left this place. You can at your convenience return me the same amount. I regret that it becomes my painful task to inform you of the death of Lieut Cox of the Royal Marines. He died of his wounds on the evening of the 1st and was buried with the Honours of War.[17]

It may be of some interest that Lieutenant Thomas Sherlock Cox was a native of Ireland and died at twenty-four years of age. He had been severely wounded and taken prisoner by the French in the East Indies when HMS *Nereide* surrendered on August 23, 1810. Cox was reputed to be a favourite of Sir James Yeo's.

The result of this American victory was that Commodore Chauncey was able to complete USS *Superior* (64) and USS *Mohawk* (42) with armament and cables and in July leave Sackets Harbor with a more dominant fleet to blockade Kingston's harbour. This lasted until October, when Sir James Yeo launched the first-rate ship of the line HMS *St. Lawrence* (102), returning dominance of Lake Ontario back to the Royal Navy.

Another interesting part of the Big Sandy Creek battle is the co-operation of civilians and militia in Jefferson County by the lifting and carrying of one of the heaviest cables from the landing site at Big Sandy to Sackets Harbor. A force of 300 to 450 men, working in relays, lifted and carried the 600-foot long, 7-inch diameter, 9,600-pound cable and carried it twenty miles over three days march to reach the US fleet at Sackets Harbor.

4

Britons Strike Home! John Bull on Capitol Hill

The Greater War and Preparations for Battle

April and May saw a subtle change in Royal Navy activity on the Atlantic seaboard. Vice- Admiral Sir Alexander F. I. Cochrane RN, had replaced Admiral Warren as commander of the North Atlantic fleet. This aggressive Scotsman was particularly vengeful towards the United States, having lost his brother, Major Charles Cochrane, at Yorktown and another relative, Major John Pitcairn of the marines, at Bunker Hill. This latter officer is of particular note, being the commanding officer of the British light troops at the battle of Lexington and Concord in 1775.

Cochrane increased the blockade of all the New England ports north of Cape Cod on the 25th of April. The blockade was further extended on May 30, indicating a new British strategy, which would lead to the occupation of northern Maine in June. He also ordered his subordinate, Rear Admiral Sir George Cockburn, to continue aggressively attacking American shipping and any U.S. government targets he could find in the Chesapeake. He wrote to Cockburn with words such as "You are at perfect liberty as soon as you can muster a sufficient force, to act with the utmost hostility against the shores of the United States." The "sufficient force" was to include a third Royal Marines battalion commanded by Major George Lewis RM, which had been serving in Holland. On reaching Tangier Island this latest battalion was met by Colonel James Malcolm with his staff and cadre from Upper Canada.

Malcolm split the new arrivals into two separate units, A reconstituted 2nd battalion under himself and a 3rd battalion under Major George Lewis.

Both battalions now numbered about 300 effectives plus a small RMA gun and rocket detachment. A further addition to bring both units up to strength was 300 Colonial Marines to each battalion. The Colonial Marines were a battalion of former slaves. These men were now uniformed and had been fully trained at Tangier Island by Sergeant William Hammond RM, the senior sergeant of HMS *Albion*, promoted ensign and adjutant by Rear Admiral Cockburn for his zeal and ability in training these black soldiers. Hammond and a small number of white officers of the West India Regiment would serve as Colonial Marines company officers within the RM Battalions. Admiral Cockburn also had his 400 ships marines with 200 sailors "fully trained to small arms" who had been operational within the Chesapeake region.

During this period to the end of the war, a journal on the operations of the 3rd Battalion Royal Marines was kept. Unfortunately it never named the officer who wrote it.

> 18 July, 1814. At ten at night the Battalion being embarked in the boats of the fleet proceeded up Leonard's Creek to attack a town of that name; landed at half past-three next morning, about seven miles below it, and moving parallel to the boats up the creek entered the town by its right, without opposition, found it evacuated by the enemy; after completely plundering and embarking all the tobacco, flour, and other stores. The Battalion quietly returned the following night to their respective ships. One sergeant, two privates accidentally wounded.
>
> 20 July, At 2:30 p.m., proceeded in the boats up the river Nominy the town of which was taken possession of, plundered and afterwards burned, a strong picquet in advance during the night on the main road, across which was constructed a chevaux-de frise and a 5.5 inch howitzer being got on shore was brought up; at daylight the Battalion moved forward with it about two miles, covering the embarkation of the stores, etc., which being completed re-embarked in the boats, and moved down the river; about half-way the skirmishers landed and exchanged some shots with the enemy;

Britons Strike Home! John Bull on Capitol Hill

the house occupied by the enemy burned instantly. Occasional firing with the enemy while in this river—and at this post a sergeant badly wounded. Near the mouth of the river the whole Battalion landed again in rear of a large house, belonging to a Major Lewis, reported to be occupied by 400 Militia and several field-pieces. The enemy retired but the house burnt and Battalion returned to the ships in the afternoon. Two schooners taken above Nominy (a Militia post), one laden with silk and dry goods. Poison being found at Nominy in some spirits—induced the Admiral (Cockburn) to destroy by fire every house on both sides of the river going back.

23 July. At daylight entered a small creek in Clements Bay and brought out four schooners. Exchanged a few harmless shots with the enemy during the day and burnt a house returning, from which a boat had been fired on going up.

26 July. At one o'clock in the morning left the ships for Machodic creek. Battalion landed a few miles up from this entrance with a 6-pounder, and marched to a ferry two miles higher up. The boats went on and destroyed six schooners—a slight skirmish with the enemy—who retired, brought off about 100 head of cattle, returned to the ships about half past six in the evening.

30 July. Entered the town of Chaptico on the River Wycomico, found it abandoned by the enemy, brought off seventy hogsheads of tobacco, forage, etc., returned to the ships, the Battalion having been two nights in the boats.

3 August. At two o'clock in the morning left the ships for the River Yocomico—a battery commenced a sharp fire at the entrance of the river, landed under the guns instantly, which being well horsed, were drawn from their position, and rapidly pursued by the whole Battalion; one of the field-pieces abandoned about seven miles from the battery; moved on with the Battalion about three miles further to the headquarters of the enemy, which was burned, with several other houses on the road; returning to the boats at the battery, three companies turned off to the left and captured the town of Kinsale, brought off four schooners, eighty hogsheads of tobacco, twenty barrels of flour, returned after dark to the ships—one killed, one wounded.

7th August. Having observed the enemy busy the evening preceding with an entrenchment near the entrance of the River Caan, moved towards it so as to find ourselves close in at daylight when the enemy opened a brisk fire from three field-pieces, dashed at them directly but being obliged to wade some distance through the water from the boats to the shore, the enemy gained sufficient time to secure the guns and only left a little powder and shot behind them, which with the battery was instantly destroyed. Captured four schooners, destroyed three and brought off twenty hogsheads of tobacco. Lt. Col. Malcolm joined and took the command from Major Lewis.
12th August. Made successful forage on both banks of the River St. Mary.
14th August. The Commander-in-Chief, Sir Alexander Cochrane, joined us in the Potomack, with General Ross' Division from France consisting of the 4th, 21st, 44th and 85th (Lt. Infy.) Regts.[18]

The journal of the 3rd Battalion continues right through to the conclusion of the war, with the arrival of the news of the Treaty of Ghent. The continuance of these events is covered in a more general manner.

The end of the war in Europe allowed the British to send thousands of Wellington's veteran troops to the North American theatre. Admiral Sir Plutney Malcolm RN, and his fleet reinforced the North American squadron. The troopships carried four regiments of infantry under the leadership of Major General Robert Ross. The regiments were the 4th, 44th, 85th and the 21st. The latter regiment was newly recruited and had been doing garrison duties in the Mediterranean. The total landing force numbered 4,500 men, including marines and sailors.

HMS *Tonnant,* the eighty-gun flagship of Vice Admiral Alexander Cochrane, was the location where Major General Ross met Rear Admiral Cockburn for the first time. The forthcoming campaign was discussed amongst the three officers. Cochrane had hoped for a larger force of 13,000 soldiers to reinforce his "extended operation at a distance from the coast." Both Cochrane and Ross had great doubts about the practicality of achieving Cockburn's ultimate goal, the capture of Washington.

Cockburn was quite unwilling to see his goal being forgotten. He befriended General Ross. After he showed him the ease with which British

Britons Strike Home! John Bull on Capitol Hill

troops could be transported and landed almost at will, with negligible resistance from American forces, Ross became his ally.

Fifty-five-year-old Commodore Joshua Barney USN, had provided the only significant federal response to the Royal Navy's reign of terror in the Chesapeake. The news that Barney's gunboat flotilla was in the Patuxent River gave Admiral Cockburn the excuse to pursue the little band of gunboats.

Admiral Cochrane agreed on the need to capture or destroy Barney's unit. The British fleet now numbered over fifty large warships flying the pennants of three admirals, together with troop transports and numerous smaller craft. This armada entered the Patuxent River and sailed as far as Point Patience, where the largest ships anchored. The wisdom of Cockburn in having a great part of the Chesapeake Bay surveyed was now bearing fruit. Captain Joseph Nourse RN, of the frigate HMS *Severn* (38) had carried out much of this work.

A small squadron of war vessels entered the Potomac River led by the frigate HMS *Seahorse* (38) under the one-legged Captain James Alexander Gordon RN. This squadron was tasked with destroying fortifications along the Potomac River, creating a diversion as far as Alexandria to distract U.S. troops from the main expedition in the Patuxent. The convoy included the frigate HMS *Euryalus* (36), rocket ship HMS *Erebus,* bomb vessels HMS *Aetna, Meteor, Devastation,* and *Manly,* and a dispatch boat named *Auna-Maria.* This squadron suffered a number of groundings at Kettle Bottom shoals, but once past that obstacle the ships reached Fort Warburton (Fort Washington), where they opened fire on August 27. The immediate reaction of the commander of the fort was to spike the guns and abandon the fortification in great haste. The British continued to bombard the fort until the magazine blew up. A naval and marine detachment landed to ensure the entire destruction of the fort.

The next port of call was the town of Alexandria on the 28th, where Gordon's ships destroyed the barracks, forcing the garrison to flee and landing parties to destroy the public works. Gordon wrote to the common council of Alexandria, proposing his terms: the giving up of all naval and ordinance stores, both public and private; the giving up of all vessels, including sunken vessels, to be returned to their previous condition, complete with all fittings and cargo. British officers would oversee that all these conditions were in compliance; plus, all refreshments required would be paid for in British bills at market price. In return for these services the safety of the town would be maintained, providing no hostile action was taken against the British.

The ship HMS *Fairy* (18) arrived with orders for Gordon to rejoin the main fleet under Cochrane. *Fairy* had encountered a battery of five American guns and a large military force on its approach to Alexandria. Captain Gordon decided to return by warping his vessels down the river. This slow and difficult journey took several days, with his twenty-one prizes and original vessels being under fire most of the journey. The Americans sent three fire vessels against the British ships, which were easily towed away.

Later the US Militia forces opened up on the British convoy. This was answered by a bombardment from *Meteor*, assisted by the carronades of HMS *Fairy* and a number of ships' boats. Eventually rocket fire from *Erebus* and gunfire from *Seahorse* and *Euryalus* scattered the American force and caused a retreat, despite the enemy having enlarged their battery to eleven guns. These guns were spiked by a landing party of marines and seamen. There were no further actions, and Gordon's ships and prizes rejoined Admiral Cochrane's fleet prior to the attack on Baltimore. The British loss from September 1 to 5 was seven killed and thirty-five wounded.

Another squadron, led by Captain Sir Peter Parker RN, in HMS *Menelaus* (38) left the main armada at sunset on August 17 and were to sail up the Chesapeake above Baltimore and interrupt communications with Philadelphia and New York. No action was seen by this squadron.

Britons Strike Home! John Bull on Capitol Hill

Vice Admiral Sir Alexander F. I. Cochrane KCB, commander of a fifty-vessel armada of British ships, observed the transfer of thousands of British army soldiers, Royal Marines and Colonial Marines to the smaller vessels of his fleet at Point Patience. Cochrane shifted his flag to HMS *Iphigenia* (35), a fifth-rate frigate, to enable his own observations of the fleet proceeding farther up the Patuxent River.

On August 18 the fleet reached St. Leonard's Creek. More vessels anchored as their draft was too large to allow them to proceed; more cross-decking of the troops was carried out. The fleet headed farther upriver and resembled a regatta, with ships tacking across each other to combat adverse wind and tide. Unseen by the British a number of mounted American scouts were relaying their movements back to President Madison's staff in

Britons Strike Home! John Bull on Capitol Hill

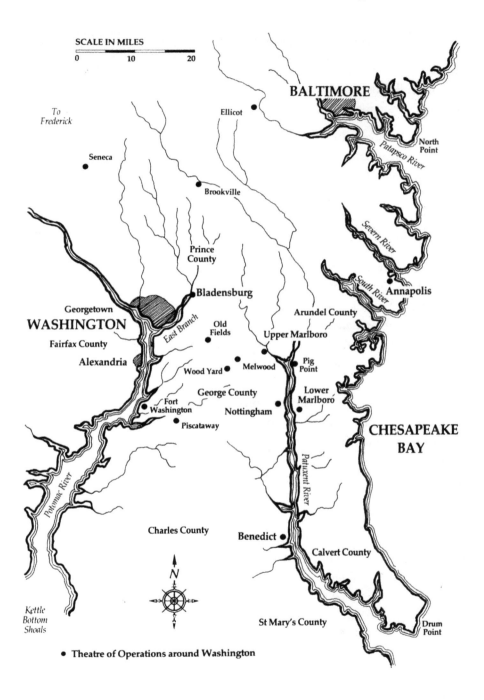

• Theatre of Operations around Washington

Washington. Their perception was that the British could strike at Benedict, Lower Marlborough, possibly Annapolis or even Baltimore. It seemed unlikely that Washington would be the target.

General Ross's assistant adjutant, Captain Henry G. W. Smith, later described the passage this way:

> It was resolved the force should sail up the serpentine and wooded Patxuent in frigates and smaller vessels. This we did and it was one of the most beautiful sights the eye could behold. The course of the large river was very torturous, the country covered with immense forest trees; thus to look back, the appearance was that of a large fleet stalking through a wood.[19]

As they drew nearer to the town of Benedict, the British vessels were required to move forward in single file. By nightfall the lead ships were anchored at Benedict, with a trail of vessels extending ten miles downriver.

Commodore Barney had moved his flotilla further upriver, away from the oncoming British. He soon received orders from Washington to destroy his boats and return with his guns to help defend the capital if the city was threatened.

August 19 saw the British fleet consolidate at Benedict. Admiral Cockburn with a number of smaller boats continued after Barney while the army began to disembark and prepare for mass movement by land. General Ross and his commanders assembled the infantry battalions, artillery and rocket units, camp supplies and tents. The following morning the troops were issued with rations for three days route march. They began their northward trek to Nottingham with a flotilla of small craft on the river supporting their flank.

The excessive heat and humidity plus the inactivity of the troops who had spent weeks at sea began to take a toll; men were dropping like flies with heat exhaustion. General Ross halted the column after six miles. An overnight camp was set up, but an intense thunderstorm did little to rest the men. Reveille was at 5 a.m. on the 21st.

Ross's army reached Nottingham later on the 21st to find Cockburn making plans for his ships' marines to further pursue Barney, who was now at Pig Point. On approach to Pig Point they could see the masts of the American vessels in the distance.

Britons Strike Home! John Bull on Capitol Hill

Admiral Cockburn ordered Captain John Robyns RM, to land the marines at a location named Leon on the 22nd, where a minor exchange took place with local militia. Moving on, Robyns and his men encircled Pig Point and again entered into a firefight with a number of Barney's seamen; these were overcome and captured. The vessels of Barney's flotilla, including his sloop, were on fire and began to be "blown to atoms." Only a single gunboat was taken as a prize. Once the American opposition ended, Cockburn and his vessels arrived. The British now took several small craft and a quantity of tobacco and returned downriver with their prisoners and prizes. Cockburn sent his ADC, Lieutenant Scott, back to Admiral Cochrane with news of the destruction of Barney's flotilla.

Commodore Joshua Barney and about 400 of his sailors had departed Pig Point with a number of large cannons in wagons, as ordered by his superiors in Washington, to reinforce the defence of that town. Admiral Cockburn rode over to Upper Marlborough to confer with General Ross on their future combined operations. Ross and Cockburn agreed to advance the army to Melwood and camp there.

Melwood is the location where Cockburn finally convinced General Ross that the advance to Washington was now not only feasible but entirely possible! As chance would have it, Lieutenant Scott returned from giving the news of Pig Point to Cochrane, bearing a reply letter suggesting—not ordering—a return of the army to Benedict. Cockburn and Ross decided to disregard the letter and carry out the attack on Washington.

The morning of August 24 was very hot and oppressive. After breakfast, the British force began a long hard march from Melwood to the village of Bladensburg. The British force was divided into three brigades, the first consisting of the 85th Bucks Light Infantry with the light companies of the other three regiments and the 3rd Battalion of Royal Marines.

Eighteen-year-old Lieutenant George Gleig of the 85th could see dust clouds half an hour before seeing the "Yankees drawn up on the heights above the village." Gleig was ready to drop, like all the other British soldiers marching in furnace-like weather. Eighteen of their number lay dead from heat exhaustion. The brigade commander, Colonel William Thornton of the 85th, from the saddle of his charger urged his men forward. They were the light brigade and would be the first into action.

Rockets, Bombs and Bayonets

General Ross spied out the enemy massing on Bladensburg heights. He noticed that the town seemed to have no barricades or any sign of defence works; likewise the bridge leading to the heights was also unmanned. The American force consisted of 6,000 militia, 300 regular US infantry, 120 US Dragoons, and twenty six-pounder guns manned by militia artillerymen. Six eighteen-pounder guns manned by 300 seamen and US Marines under Commodore Barney were late in arriving. The troops were deployed in three defensive lines, one at the base of the hill near the bridge, another midway up the hill, and the third at the top. General William H. Windler was in charge, having been appointed by the president. Windler was a politically appointed leader recently exchanged from being a British prisoner of war. An unexpected arrival was that of U.S. President and Commander-in-Chief James Madison with his political entourage, including Secretary of State Monroe and Secretary of War Armstrong.

The heights of Bladensburg contained the "dueling ground" of Washington; President Madison came suitably armed with a pair of dueling pistols in his belt. Without the knowledge of General Windler, Madison and Monroe began to reposition some of the troops. President Madison at one point even took command of a battery.

Colonel Thornton was ordered by General Ross to attack and take the village and bridge at the far end. Thornton sent out advance parties from the 85th and formed the remainder of his division into columns of route and ordered "Quick march." The advance parties flitted from house to house and found no resistance whatsoever. They did find the home of the British envoy, who gave them a great welcome. The light brigade reformed in the shade of an orchard, piled their packs, and fixed bayonets.

The first frontal assault took place on the command of "Double quick march." The bridge would allow only three men abreast as the British troops took the bridge almost at a run. All three tiers of American defenders opened up with muskets, rifles, and cannon. A number of redcoats fell, but soon they occupied the first entrenchment beyond the river. Most of the militia ran in the face of bayonets. A few were killed, and the British force took the emplacement. The light company of the 21st lost Lieutenant James Gracie, along with eleven rank and file wounded.

Once the British cleared out the militia, a heavy fire developed, and in particular, officers, including Colonel Thornton, were hit by rifle fire. There

Britons Strike Home! John Bull on Capitol Hill

was no American counterattack. General Ross had sent word to the 2nd and 3rd Brigade commanders to rush their men forward. The column also contained four light guns being dragged by sailors and a detachment of Royal Marine Artillery, commanded by Captain James H. Harrison RMA, a rocket battery, and some support troops. Once in range of the American positions the British artillery started a supporting fire over the heads of the 1st Brigade. The rocket apparatus was also set up, and Admiral Cockburn directed the marine artillery fire at the heights. Cockburn, dressed in his naval uniform and riding a white horse, was the target for American sharpshooters; one shot cut his stirrup leather. While dismounted, a Royal Marine standing at his side was killed by round shot.

Ross sent both brigades to the flank of the hill where, despite being exhausted, they deployed in linear formation two ranks deep. The American reply was to switch some of their artillery units to fire on the new target. They did not deploy their Dragoons or shift any of their infantry formations. Commodore Barney now had his eighteen-pounders in action from the top of Bladensburg Hill. Ross had his horse shot from beneath him. He recovered and mounted another animal and carried on the attack.

Ross gave the order for the 2nd Brigade to advance at the "high port." The steady, swift advance of a line of shining bayonets was unnerving to many of the inexperienced militia. Rockets screamed overhead and exploded in the rear of the American lines. The veterans of Napoleon's War showed no fear, no emotion; they just kept coming onward. Each shot fired seemed to be absorbed into the red line. Every gap was filled immediately. It seemed that cannons and muskets wouldn't stop the advance; indeed, they didn't seem to slow the British at all.

Maryland Militia Private Henry Fulford described the scene as the British were under fire: "They took no notice of it; their men moved like clockwork, the instant part of a platoon was cut down, it was filled up by men in the rear without the least noise and confusion whatever."[20]

Suddenly the British line halted. On the order to "prepare to fire" a ripple of muskets switched to shoulder height in an instant. The loud single command "Fire" sent a cloud of foul sulphur-smelling smoke along the red line, blotting out the shape of the soldiers behind it. Hundreds of musketballs ripped into the American lines. Before the smoke cleared the British were reloaded and listening for their next command. It came almost instantly—"Charge"—and the British surged forward up the hill. More rockets exploded nearby. For many of the U.S. militiamen the experience was too much to take, and they broke ranks and ran.

General Windler's pre-engagement instructions were "When you retreat, take notice you must retreat by the Georgetown road."[21] His officers were unable to stop their men from running in all directions. The hope was that the American army could regroup and mount a second defence before reaching Washington. However, the American army simply disintegrated, with the exception of a few units, such as Commodore Barney's sailors and marines, who kept up a fire on the British till the ammunition ran out. General Windler realized the American army was out of control. He rode over to President Madison and advised him and his group to leave with haste as their capture was imminent. The retreat was so rapid and complete it has become known as the "Bladensburg races." Madison rode back to Washington through the city and across the bridge to Virginia.

On reaching the top of the hill the British made prisoners of the remaining defenders, many of whom were wounded. Commodore Barney was severely wounded and refused to surrender to anyone other than a senior officer. Finally he formally surrendered to Admiral Cockburn, who immediately placed Barney on parole and had some of Barney's own officers take him for treatment of his wounds.

The British army was so exhausted that a pursuit of the enemy was out of the question. Ross allowed his men to remain resting till evening, when the dead were buried and the army recovered enough to carry on. During the respite General Ross ordered the signal for parley, a loud long roll on the drums. No reply of any kind was given from the American forces. The British loss was 64 killed and 185 wounded. The U.S. loss was numbered as 26 killed with 51 wounded.

As evening arrived the 3rd Brigade, containing the 21st Regiment and the 2nd Royal Marines, formed up and led the army towards Washington. At various points Ross called for parley with a large flag of truce clearly visible, but no reply was made. On entering Washington, Ross, Cockburn, and their staffs plus a small protection party neared the Capitol building and were suddenly fired on by a volley from the Capitol and by crossfire from houses on either side of the road.

Britons Strike Home! John Bull on Capitol Hill

Ross had a second horse shot from under him. Cockburn took charge, having been subject to this type of ambush in his Chesapeake raids. He ordered an immediate return of fire and an assault on the buildings, but their assailants had left. Cockburn had always tried to respect private property; however, when armed resistance had been encountered or hidden arms found, he did not hesitate to destroy buildings being used as fortifications or armouries. He had the buildings burned using Congreve rockets.

As evening turned to night, the British army enveloped Washington, eventually reaching the President's mansion. Here Ross, Cockburn, and their senior officers sat down and ate the "victory" dinner set out to celebrate a British demise. General Ross wrote in his journal,

> The fare, however; which was intended for *Jonathan* was voraciously devoured by *John Bull;* and the health of the Prince Regent and success to His Majesty's arms by sea and land, was drunk in the best wines. Madison, having taken to his heels and ensured his safety on the opposite bank of the river by causing the bridge to be burnt down.[22]

Since no military officer or government official of the United States had availed themselves of the opportunity to discuss terms on the capture of Washington, it was decided to destroy all United States government property. The order was given to set fire to all government buildings. The British popular song "Britons, Strike Home!" was now a fact, and the second stanza, "Revenge, revenge your countries woes," was now an achievement of military and naval arms.[23]

The orders to burn were carried out with only two federal buildings being missed. The naval dockyard had already been burned by Captain Thomas Tingey USN, who destroyed a number of ships under construction and all of the naval supplies, preventing the British from taking them as prizes. The British destroyed 20,000 stands of arms, all the munitions that could be found, and numerous cannons by discharging a smaller bore cannon into the barrel of a larger gun, blowing its breech out. The destruction went on for a full day while Cockburn made civilian property off limits. The British estimated cost of the destruction was two million pounds sterling! He did destroy the newspaper office of the *National Intelligencer,* which had been particularly offensive to him. He ordered all the Cs destroyed, "So that the rascals can have no further means of abusing my name."

The burning of Washington was meant as a psychological blow to American morale and as a retaliatory strike for the burning of Canadian towns, including York and Port Dover. General Prevost had written to Admiral Cochrane in June asking that the Royal Navy take such action whenever possible. Captain of the Fleet Edward Codrington RN, wrote a letter to his wife: "President Madison, by letting his Generals burn villages in Canada, has been trying to excite terror but....the terror and suffering will probably be brought home to the doors of his fellow citizens. I am fully convinced that this is the true way to end this Yankee war." Codrington was one of Admiral Cochrane's main advisors.[24]

That night a severe thunderstorm broke over the city, providing perfect cover for the British to depart. Several sightings of American troops in the nearby hills had made the decision to return to the fleet an easy one. The expedition returned to Benedict unmolested. The fleet returned to sea, continuing the blockade, while Admirals Cochrane, Cockburn and Malcolm and General Ross planned for attacking that "nest of pirates at Baltimore."

Taking the news to Britain was Captain John Wainwright RN, of HMS *Tonnant* (80). This was seen as a rebuke to Cockburn for ignoring Admiral Cochrane's letter to return to Benedict. Cochrane was more interested in capturing the prizes at Baltimore than risking the army to attack Washington.

The victory at Bladensburg and the capture of Washington were so overwhelmingly rejoiced in Britain that General Ross was now to be known as Ross of Bladensburg. The army regiments and the Royal Marines were immediately granted the battle honour "Bladensburg," and Admiral Cockburn was eventually rewarded as a Knight Commander of the Order of the Bath for his service in America.

5

Plattsburgh, The Land Invasion Begins

Plattsburgh, The Next Battle

The Royal Navy in May of 1814 assumed responsibility for all naval activities on Lake Ontario and Lake Champlain. An order on July 13 called for the disbandment of the 1st Battalion Royal Marines under Lieutenant Colonel Williams "For Naval service on the great lakes," their place at Ile aux Noix being taken by three companies of the 13th Regiment and the Light Company of the 49th Regiment. It is highly likely the Royal Marines were now required in Kingston to make up for the loss of manpower in Yeo's squadron after the Battle of Big Sandy Creek. Colonel Williams and a number of his officers were to return to Halifax with any of his men who were unfit for further service. The rest of the 1st Battalion was broken up as follows: three captains, two each 1st and 2nd lieutenants, with 324 rank and file to Lake Ontario, with one captain, three 1st lieutenants, and 178 rank and file to Lake Champlain. Williams carried out his orders to the letter, and within three days the marines had all been dispatched. He did, however, use his discretion in allowing his officers to choose their own destiny. He held a lottery where each officer in seniority blindly picked his own assignment. The results were that Captain Alexander Anderson, 1st Lieutenant John Ashmore, 2nd Lieutenants Glassen Calwell, and Joseph Childs would remain with the Royal Navy at Ile aux Noix.

Rockets, Bombs and Bayonets

Other officers of the 1st Battalion remaining in Canada were 1st Lieutenant John Fennell, who since February 25th had held the position of staff adjutant of the township's militia, after being wounded during his service with the sleigh establishment. Another was 1st Lieutenant John E. Jones, who remained at Ile aux Noix as fort major until October 1, 1814, when replaced by 1st Lieutenant Thomas Triphook of the 13th Regiment. Neither of these Royal Marine officers took part in the Plattsburgh campaign.

Anderson and his subordinates now began an upgrade in training their marines on boat service. Training alongside the Royal Navy officers and men, the marines would work the heavy sweeps (oars) and sails, most boats using the square "lug" or triangular lateen types. The Royal Marine Artillery had one or two gunners on each boat to man the heavy guns with the crew's help. Soon the marines were as efficient as any in boat handling. It was not unusual for boat crews to race each other, turning hard work into a recreational sport.

At this time the small group of Royal Marine officers would have shared stories of past service and loved ones at home. Captain Anderson was first commissioned in 1796 and had served at the Battle of Algeciras Bay against the Spanish and French fleets in 1801. In that battle he served on board HMS *Pompee* (74). When his superior officer, Captain Samuel Middleton RM, was wounded, he took command of the marine detachment mid-battle. HMS *Pompee* was so badly damaged it had to be towed to the dry dock in Gibraltar. He later served at the Chatham division and joined the 1st Battalion in 1810. On the personal side, he was a widower with a seven-year-old son, also named Alexander. The boy was in the care of his mother's family. His uncle and cousin also currently served as Royal Marines officers.

First Lieutenant Ashmore had been commissioned in 1805 and had seen action against the French on three different frigates before joining the 1st Battalion in 1813. He was unmarried at this time.

Second Lieutenant Joseph Childs was commissioned into the corps at age twenty-two. He first served on board HMS *Gibraltar* (80) blockading the French coast. He frequently served in boats cutting out French coasters. He volunteered to serve on the Chesapeake in February of 1813. He also was unmarried.

Second Lieutenant Glassen Caldwell gained his commission in May of 1810 under the name of William Robert Caldwell. By 1814 he had changed

Plattsburgh, The Land Invasion Begins

his name. He went directly to the 1st Battalion and saw service in Portugal, Spain, and the present war. He was inside the mill at the Battle of La Colle, where he gained a "Mention in Dispatches" for his service with the Royal Marines detachment. He too was a single man.

As the building of the large frigate progressed, Anderson also prepared his men for the very real possibility of shipboard service. Using the larger vessels at Ile aux Noix, he again combined his officers and marines with the seamen and trained them in "fighting" the guns. The heaviest guns available were the twenty-four-pounders, mounted on HMS *Linnet*. Here the naval gun crews practiced all the steps of loading, running out the gun, and firing, cleaning the bore and reloading, without actually discharging the guns. The Royal Marines often took positions as rope men, powder monkeys, or crewmen with hand spikes shifting the heavy cumbersome guns, which weighed over a ton. The work was so strenuous it was referred to as "fighting the guns." The marines also provided guards for the naval base, and some were posted to the guard ships and gunboats, constantly watching for Macdonough's fleet and also providing protection for smugglers inside Canadian waters.

Captain Peter Fisher RN, took command of the Ile aux Noix naval station in July of 1814. The Admiralty required the leadership of an officer superior in rank to Captain Pring, owing to the size of the new British frigate HMS *Confiance*. The captain of that vessel would command and be responsible for the entire British squadron.

From early May the practice of smuggling masts, spars, tar and other naval supplies to the British naval base had been increasing. So too was the US Navy activity in stopping the practice. More than five thousand dollars worth of contraband was seized and diverted to American naval use at Vergennes.

In addition, Commodore Macdonough planned a clandestine attack on stores destined for HMS *Confiance*. Midshipman Joel Abbot USN, volunteered for the hazardous duty. When asked by Macdonough if he was ready to die for his country, Abbot replied, "Certainly, sir; that is what I came into the service for." The midshipman entered the Richelieu River after dark with a crewed launch, rowing by night and hiding by day. The vessel neared the location of the British store. Abbot then, impersonating a Royal Navy officer (the British and U.S. uniforms were nearly identical), bluffed his way past British sentries and located the store full of yards. He then returned to his hidden launch, and later, under cover of darkness and using muffled oars, he and his crew returned to the store and successfully destroyed the spars. They then returned safely to Lake Champlain. Had he been caught, Abbot would undoubtedly had been shot as a spy. He later took part in the Battle of Cumberland Bay, where he gave excellent service. Abbot was promoted to lieutenant and awarded a sword of honour by the U.S. Congress for both of these actions.

The large frigate *Confiance* would not now be ready till mid-September; the master shipbuilder William Simons was behind in construction, owing to a lack of skilled workmen. He had only six carpenters. The rest were pioneers, sappers, and general labourers from the army, navy, and local inhabitants. He also contended with the shortage of spars, masts, and yards. Even the very hardware needed for the ship had to travel from British factories, as did the guns, cannonballs, anchors, and cables. All had to travel well over 3,000 miles to reach their destination.

Any fifth-rate British frigate of thirty-six guns would have a crew of about 232 sailors and 45 Royal Marines, including officers. The available seamen and marines were dispersed throughout the Lake Champlain squadron, including the gunboats, leaving a great gap in manpower required for *Confiance*. Captain Fisher would have to find many more seamen. Like Pring before him he found himself on the short end of his frantic efforts to obtain seamen from Commodore Yeo. A draft of 400 seamen and officers had been sent to Yeo's squadron in Kingston from the fifteen naval transports now vacant at Quebec. Yeo did not send any to Fisher's command. The relationship between these officers became untenable, and Yeo finally replaced Fisher on August 25, 1814, the same day the frigate HMS *Confiance* was launched into the Richelieu River.

It is about this time when Lieutenant General Prevost sent a letter to Rear Admiral Edward Griffith, commander of the Halifax naval squadron, advising him that HMS *Confiance* at Ile aux Noix was very undermanned, and more officers and seamen would be needed to crew this ship. Griffith emptied his ships' brigs to obtain 161 seamen (of very poor quality), guarded by 26 Royal Marines, and 10 Royal Navy officers with 5 assistant surgeons to proceed to the Champlain squadron as reinforcements for that flotilla.

Plattsburgh, The Land Invasion Begins

The Land Invasion Begins

During this same period of May to August, Prevost was receiving the numerous army regiments from Bordeaux, France, promised by Earl Bathurst in his secret dispatch of June 3. These regiments under Lord Wellington had defeated Napoleon's best soldiers. Additional regiments with newly trained recruits sailed from England and Ireland. Other regiments sailed from the Caribbean Islands, where they were stationed as local garrisons.

Prevost inspected his regiments on arrival before locating them at bases such as Chambly, St. Jean, and Montreal and throughout Lower Canada. After inspecting the peninsular regiments from France and Spain, Prevost issued a general order directing the commanding officers to ensure proper dress amongst their officers and troops. Those comments only served to make him more unpopular with the newly arrived officers of the army. Sir James Yeo had been unhappy with Sir George's actions since the battle of Sackets Harbor in 1813, where Prevost had managed to turn victory into defeat. Prevost had tried to claim the victory at Chateauguay as his doing, thus alienating Lieutenant Colonel Charles-Michel De Salaberry, the officer who engineered this success and won the battle. Now, this latest alienation of Wellington's veterans drew unhappy comments from junior officers such as Lieutenant William Gratton of the 88th Regiment (Connaught Rangers), who saw the orders as petty and detrimental to good discipline. Even Lord Wellington said that Prevost "had gone to war about trifles with the General Officers I sent him, which are certainly the best of their rank in the army." Prevost had also given cause for displeasure amongst the four major generals now under his command. He promoted his secretary, Adjutant General Edward Baynes, to the rank of major general so that he would be of equal rank to the newly arrived generals, and he named himself as commander in chief, with the fifty-seven-year-old Major General Francis De Rottenburg as second in command of the army.

Despite the uncomfortable relationship with their commander, the British army prepared for an arduous campaign. Provisions and supplies arrived from Britain. Troops practiced their field manoeuvres often under the inspection of high ranking officers, and then they were on the move to advanced positions on the border. The main army in Lower Canada now included the reformed Royal Marine Artillery companies under Captain

Parke (newly returned from the Niagara campaign) and Lieutenant Balchild, rearmed and now attached to the Royal Artillery as a heavy artillery unit. Commissariat officers obtained wagons, carts, and beasts of burden to move the army forward towards the American border. Smuggled cattle and other foodstuffs arrived from the south in ever increasing volume, despite US General Izard's efforts to halt the practice. In his reports to Washington, Izard wrote that the smuggled cattle "were like herds of Buffaloes who press through the forests, making paths for themselves. Were it not for these supplies, the British forces in Canada would be suffering from famine."[25] Prevost in his dispatches to Lord Bathurst wrote, "Two thirds of the army in Canada live on beef provided by American contractors drawn principally from the States of Vermont and New York."

By the end of August the British army was ready to strike. Prevost had sent Major General James Kemp's brigade of the 9th, 37th, 57th and 81st regiments towards Cornwall and Kingston to threaten Commodore Chauncey's fleet at Sackets Harbor and to try to draw away a portion of Izard's forces. Ultimately this force returned to Montreal and remained as an army reserve.

On the 29th of August, the bulk of the American forces under General Izard moved west towards Sackets Harbor. Izard had been ordered to do so by Secretary of Defence Armstrong, despite the invasion warnings he had given. No retraction of the order was received, so he reluctantly moved 4,000 of his best troops slowly away, hoping to be recalled if Armstrong finally recognized the danger. At Plattsburgh, General Alexander Macomb was left with 3,400 men on the army roll: 1,500 were effective and able soldiers; the rest were either sick or about to follow Izard or men posted to the fleet as marines under Commodore Macdonough.

On the next day advance units from the Major General Brisbane's Light Division began to infiltrate the border near Champlain, NY. These were local border units such as the Canadian Chasseurs, Voltigeurs, and Frontier Light Infantry, with 200 Kanesatake Mohawk warriors, all of whom were familiar with this area of New York. The news of this incursion prompted General Macomb to order Major General Benjamin Mooers to call out the New York Militia of the five nearest counties. Macomb also sent an appeal for the Vermont militia to join him at Plattsburgh.

On September 1 the three infantry brigades of the British army advanced southward. Prevost had placed Major General De Rottenburg in

Plattsburgh, The Land Invasion Begins

overall command. The 1st Brigade consisted of 2,495, all ranks of 3/27th Inniskillings, 39th Dorsetshire, 76th Hindoostan Regiment, and the 88th Connaught Rangers, under the command of fifty-year-old Major General Frederick P. Robinson.

Robinson, a United Empire Loyalist, was born in northern Virginia. In the first American war he had been wounded and captured by American forces under General Wayne. Eventually released, he returned to the British army. He and his family lost all their American holdings in that war, leaving him with a very personal interest in the success of the forthcoming campaign.

The 2nd Brigade, led by Major General Thomas Brisbane, numbered 3,785 British regulars and Canadian militia, consisting of the Light Division, (already at Champlain), the Neuchatel Regiment De Meuron, 2/8th Kings, 13th Somersetshire, and 49th Herefordshire Regiments.

Major General Manley Power's 3rd Brigade, of 3,226 all ranks, consisted of the 3rd The Buffs, 5th Northumberland, 1/27th Inniskillings, and the 58th Rutlandshire Regiments.

Each brigade had an attached Royal Artillery brigade of five six-pounder guns and one 5.5 inch howitzer manned by a total 536 officers and other ranks. In addition were the 19th Light Dragoons with 309 officers and troopers, 75 men of the 4th company 4th battalion, Royal Sappers and Miners under Lieutenant Joshua Jebb RE.

Another large part of Prevost's army was the large commissariat train of wagons and carts of all sizes, driven by locally hired drivers and accompanied by the army's camp followers, who in the main were wives and children of the soldiers, needed to wash and cook and look after the domestic chores of such a large assemblage of men. Many of the peninsula veterans, wives, and children had been left behind in Europe, which meant many of these soldiers were extremely unhappy about serving so far from them in this present campaign. The vehicles were pulled by draft horses, oxen, and even mules. The cargo was all that the army would need—ammunition of all kinds, tents, blankets, clothing, medical supplies, cooking pots, food for the men and fodder for the animals, plus all the necessities required by the officer corps while on campaign. The heaviest items required by the army—heavy guns, mortars, and their ammunition—were being sent by bateaux to Chazy. September 1st is also the day that two Royal Navy officers, Captain George

Downie RN, and his aide, Lieutenant James Robertson RN, arrived at Ile aux Noix naval station.

The American capital city had fallen to the British on the 25th of August. Shortly after this the news had reached Plattsburgh. General Macomb had several reports of the strength of the British army facing him, 10,000 to 25,000 men. He needed more information as to the disposition of Prevost's army. Knowing the news would soon reach the British advance camp at Odelltown he decided to send to Major General Brisbane an "intelligent officer, bearing a flag, with his compliments and the newspapers of the day, together with an extra containing an account of the Capture." By doing this, he was able to learn more about the British strength and positions. It also presented his attitude of sangfroid to the "affair in Washington as a mere ordinary occurrence of war, and not as a disheartening augury of further defeat."[26]

It was the first of many such cordial exchanges between the two generals, lasting through to the departure of Brisbane in 1815. It was also the beginning of General Macomb using espionage tactics to manipulate the British general staff into making bad decisions.

The British were at Champlain in force by September 3. Prevost decided to leave an unusually large reserve at this location. These lines of communication troops were to protect the rear of his column. In this reserve were the officers and men of the heavy artillery, including the RMA Company. When at Champlain, Prevost ordered the handing over of wagons and teams from the local populace. These new acquisitions were to be used to transport the heavy artillery guns and mortars, which were being sent by lake boat from Ile aux Noix to Chazy. The British army occupied Chazy with its lakeside landing. Captain Pring arrived with a flotilla of gunboats off the western shore of Ile la Motte. Here he set up and provisioned a land battery of three eighteen-pounder long guns. Pring's gunboats also covered the lake and landward area of Chazy Landing.

On September 4, the British army, now numbering 8,200, marched forward to the hamlet of Chazy. Here Prevost's column met the first signs of resistance by American forces. A series of destroyed bridges and abatis blocked roads; these obstacles temporarily delayed the advance. However, bridges were easily forded with help from the Royal Sappers and Miners. The pioneers from the ranks of the leading regiments quickly cut down the wooden obstructions with their large axes. These strong, bearded soldiers in

Plattsburgh, The Land Invasion Begins

their tan leather aprons numbered about ten to a regiment and were vital to the army for rapid movement in wooded areas.

These delaying tactics had been ordered by General Macomb and were carried out by a company of 110 riflemen of the 1st US Rifle Regiment under their new commander, the victor of Big Sandy Creek, Lieutenant Colonel Daniel Appling, replacing Lieutenant Colonel Benjamin Forsyth of the Rifles who had been killed in a border skirmish on the 23rd of June. The riflemen were assisted by 200 infantrymen of the 13th US Infantry, commanded by Captain John Sproul, and a troop of New York State cavalry. General Prevost began written communication to Captain Downie with a letter written by Adjutant General Edward Baynes in which he advised that Major General Robinson would be at Little Chazy with three battalions "instructed to co-operate with the execution of your [Downie's] plans."

The next day, September 5, Major General Robinson left behind the light company of the 39th as lines of communication troops and as a guard of the stockpile of supplies at Chazy Landing. The British army split into two wings as they left Chazy. Major General Brisbane led the left brigade or Lake Road column, and Major General Power's brigade plus General Robinson's demi-brigade and four companies of light troops were on the right or Beekmantown Road column.

The American preparation of the defence of Plattsburgh was still underway. Brigadier General Macomb now directed Major John E. Wool with 250 men to support the 700 militia covering the Beekmantown Road. A further reinforcement was sent in the form of Captain Luther Leonard with two guns and crews of the US Light Artillery.

Macomb was also working with Major Joseph G. Totten of the US Engineers on improvements to the three defensive redoubts: Forts Moreau, Brown and Scott. The bulk of Plattsburgh's populace had left as the progress of the British army became more evident. Macomb used his troops working day and night to erect the defences. He sent Dr. James Mann with one assistant, together with approximately 900 sick and invalid troops, to Crab Island, as the existing hospital would be in the direct line of fire between the two armies. From Chazy General Robinson wrote to Captain Downie to "request you will inform me in what way I can most usefully co-operate with you."

Tuesday, September 6, saw the first serious skirmish between the leading element of the British troops, led by Major General Manley Power and

Major Wool's regulars and militia. First blood went to the British forces, as an advance party surprised and fired on a group of US militia attempting to remove planking from a bridge. Militiamen Goodspeed and Jay were both wounded and captured. Shortly after this Major Wool's force opened a brisk discharge on the main column of British, killing a number and severely wounding about twenty men of the 3rd Buffs, including Lieutenant John West. Wool's men continued firing controlled volleys and gradually withdrew towards Culver Hill. However, many of the militia under fire for the first time lost their nerve and fell back in disorder.

At Culver Hill the militia was reformed and stood with the US regulars. A brief exchange of musketry took place, leaving Captain (Brevet Lieutenant Colonel) James Willington and Ensign John Chapman of the Buffs regiment both killed outright and Captain John L. Westropp of the 58th Rutlandshire Regiment severely wounded. He survived and was made a deputy assistant quartermaster general on November 29th, 1814. A number of rank and file redcoats were also wounded or killed. The British skirmishers again deployed, and the main column marched on undeterred.

The New York cavalry officered by Captain Gilead Sperry, Lieutenant Hiram Stafford, and Coronet Matthew M. Standish appeared on the hillside north of the American militia. This cavalry unit, dressed in red tunics and light cavalry helmets, looked to the militia like another British force about to outflank them. Many of the militia broke and ran despite their officers' attempts to halt the panic. Major Wool's regulars covered the retreat, firing disciplined volleys at the front of the relentless British column.

At Halsey's Corners the British saw a detachment of US regular infantry lined up across the roadway in the open and apparently ready to volley fire. As the leading redcoats came into musket range, the American troops advanced to the cover of a stone wall, revealing the light artillery detachment under Captain Luther Leonard. The American guns immediately gave three rapid discharges and combined with the fire from the US regulars and militia; dozens of British soldiers were cut down, some killed outright, and others, including officers, wounded. The leading regiments dropped packs, fixed their bayonets, and charged the American position.

A rapid withdrawal from the wall saw the militia in full flight and Leonard's artillerymen rapidly retiring towards the bridge leading into Plattsburgh. Wool's regulars again withdrew in an orderly fashion but did

Plattsburgh, The Land Invasion Begins

not dally in the face of British bayonets. Crossing the Saranac's lower bridge, Leonard set up his battery again to cover the last of the American troops and the bridge itself. During this latter action Lieutenant Robert Kingsbury of the 3rd Buffs was mortally wounded; he died at Isaac Platt's farmhouse.

Now in full view of Plattsburgh, General Power deployed his force along the river, looking for other American forces, and awaited further orders from Prevost or De Rottenburg.

Brisbane and Robinson's Lake Road column of troops made heavy going owing to the poor road conditions. Near Dead Creek, Appling's and Sproul's men were manning a large abatis road obstruction. The sounds of distant battle could be heard from north of this position, and then the news of the British army at the banks of the Saranac caused a fallback to a defensive position at a ravine close to the Saranac River. Commodore Macdonough, at General Macomb's request, had sent gunboats to support Appling's Dead Creek position. As the leading British troops reached the road obstruction, none observed the gunboats silently waiting nearby. The British pioneers were cutting down the obstruction, and then the gunboats opened fire, smashing and scattering the lead troops. The British quickly brought up their light artillery and Royal Artillery rocket troops.

A bloody exchange followed, resulting in several killed and wounded US sailors. Third Lieutenant Silas Duncan USN, was severely wounded in the shoulder by a cannonball. Duncan was serving on board *Saratoga* when sent by Macdonough to retrieve the gunboats, which were in danger of loss to the British. (Duncan survived his wound but lost the use of his arm. He was later officially thanked by Congress.)

Once beyond Dead Creek the British army advanced to the town limits. Here General Robinson inspected the view of Plattsburgh, the Saranac River, its bridges without planking, the US fleet in the bay, and most importantly the enemy redoubts, blockhouses, trenches, guns and troops. His mind would have been racing through all the best possible attack scenarios. A report was made by Lieutenant John Lang of the 19th Light Dragoons that the American forts were not built "within established rules": they were incomplete, weak, and without shelters from bombardment.

One of General Prevost's senior staff members, Sir Thomas Sydney Beckwith (quartermaster general of the British forces), asked Robinson if the troops could attack if packs were removed for easier mobility.

Robinson asked if the American territory had been reconnoitred. Beckwith replied that it had not. General Prevost had withheld all the Secret Service money from his generals, which was to be used to pay spies, deserters, and others who gave information on the American defence of northern New York. Robinson would later write in his journal and cite Prevost's actions and sentiments. "The army moved without a clear plan and with no effort to gather intelligence." Prevost had stated, "It was throwing money away to attempt it."[27]

Robinson conceded that the advance into Plattsburgh should be halted. His men had marched all day without food, and intelligence on the best fording places was needed in order to continue the battle.

Firing from within the town was heard, as some elements of the British force had separated from their column and entered the village. The Swiss Neuchatel Regiment De Meuron, part of General Brisbane's light troops, had entered Plattsburgh along the shore road. This regiment of mercenaries was dressed exactly like the majority of Prevost's army, while being the most unorthodox of all the British troops engaged. The only visible distinctions were the light blue facings on their uniforms and the unusual colouring of their regimental flag, yellow, green, and black, with a cross stating "Fidelitas & Honor, Terra & Mare," the British Union Flag in the top left canton next to the spear-pointed flagpole. The soldiers of this regiment were Swiss, German, Polish, Dutch, Alsatians, Spanish, and Italians, all of whom were willing to fight against Britain's enemies for pay.

The American rearguard of Appling's riflemen and other soldiers were in the act of removing planking from the bridge when the British opened fire. A slow retreat began back to the wooden forts. When the American force was seen to be far enough from the redcoats, the gunboats of Macdonough's fleet opened fire with grapeshot. The fortress guns also opened fire on the De Meurons, which caused some casualties.

By late afternoon, Lieutenant Colonel Francois–Henri De Meuron-Bayard sent an orderly to advise General Prevost that his regiment was in position to storm and capture the "citadel" (Fort Moreau), which was incomplete and would fall to an immediate attack. Prevost failed to order the attack; instead he ordered De Meuron-Bayard to maintain his position as best he could and under the cover of darkness prepare a defensive position to accommodate heavy siege artillery. The regiment spent the next six days

Plattsburgh, The Land Invasion Begins

under constant fire from the forts and gunboats. Prevost sent a brigade of Royal Artillery to support the Swiss with counter battery fire and other British troops to help repair the bridge and construct the gun emplacements. The fire was so intense and destructive that the De Meurons hid behind walls and inside houses, where Subaltern Frederic De Graffenreid and his men found provisions, to which they helped themselves, and the officer enjoyed "the excellent cigars that I found there."

The De Meuron Regiment kept up its harassing fire at the American forts, attempting to slow down their construction work. De Graffenreid later wrote of the American bombardment, "They didn't seem to worry much about their own houses, which they doused liberally with both cannon and grape shot, although without causing us much damage."

General Macomb ordered the use of "hot shot" to be fired at the British troops firing from windows and balconies of the houses in the lower town. This set a number of buildings on fire. Twenty-seven-year-old James Humphries Wood, a 1st Lieutenant in the Royal Artillery, recorded in his diary, "A flag of truce was sent in, proposing to extinguish it, which they declined, and kept up their fire, warmer than before."28

While both armies in the lower town were occupied with the constant exchange of musketry and cannon fire, the bulk of the British army was establishing tented camps, constructing scaling ladders, and preparing three additional gun emplacements for the heavy artillery batteries that had been ordered forward to Plattsburgh by Prevost. Only darkness reduced the volume of firing, giving both sides an opportunity to consolidate and strengthen their positions.

Early morning of September 7 saw a party of British troops from General Power's brigade locating a crossing point near Wait's Mill some five miles west of Plattsburgh. When attempting to cross they were ambushed by a company of New York Militia under Captain Daniel Vaughan, who killed two and wounded several others, which forced the British back to their lines. On the same day Lieutenant George W. Runk of the 6th US Infantry was seriously wounded by musket fire and had to be removed to the Crab Island hospital, where he died of his wounds a day later.

September 8 saw continued bombardment from the American forts. The British light guns were also in action but too light to inflict serious damage to the wooden forts. General Prevost had ordered his heavy siege artillery to the front line. One of Prevost's aide de camps, Major John Sutherland Sinclair of the Royal Artillery, had set the dispositions of the batteries to take the larger twenty-four-pounder guns and heavy siege mortars. The day was one of busy construction and constant firing, the British still probing for a way to encircle the Plattsburgh defences and still meeting heavy fire from an unseen enemy.

General Macomb began to receive his volunteers from Vermont. They arrived by the hundreds, steadily wearing away the numerical advantage held by the British. The British in turn were receiving the first of the heavy twenty-four-pounder siege guns and more reserve infantry from Chateauguay.

That night a superb attack took place, directed by Captain George McGlassin with fifty men from the 15th US Infantry regiment. Under cover of darkness, at 2 a.m. on the morning of September 9, the party crossed over the Saranac River near Fort Brown. McGlassin ordered the men to remove the flints from their weapons and fix bayonets and form two separate parties. Next they mounted the bank and worked their way forward to the sand-bagged gun emplacements. On seeing the British work party unaware of their approach and the British guns lightly guarded, McGlassin yelled the order to attack "on the front and rear." His fifty infantrymen yelling at the tops of their voices chased the confused and unprepared British from the battery at bayonet point, then into the tented encampment, where more fighting took place, leaving several dead and wounded redcoats. The British guns were spiked, and the American party returned without loss or even firing a shot. McGlassin was promoted to Brevet Major by President Madison for his gallantry.

The Royal Marine heavy gun battery of two twenty-four-pounders and two eight-inch mortars was the unit that fired from Sailly's Point at Macdonough's fleet without damaging any vessel, but it caused the American flotilla to shift its berths farther out into Cumberland Bay. By September 9 the RMA were repositioned in a new battery opposite the American forts, which they engaged as part of the overall bombardment of the American positions. Captain Parke commanded the long guns, having recently commanded a battery at the bombardment of Fort Erie, and Lieutenant Balchild commanded the mortars. Balchild had a great deal of experience in the use of mortars, having served on bomb vessels HMS *Discovery* and HMS *Meteor*. Both vessels carried ten-inch and thirteen-inch mortars. He served against the French and the Turkish in the Dardanelles and at Constantinople, where he had been severely wounded.

Plattsburgh, The Land Invasion Begins

September 9 and 10 saw continued firing of all arms from each side. The British had constructed seven batteries and were replacing the infantry support cannons (six-pounders and 5.5-inch howitzers) with the much heavier twenty-four-pounder field guns and eight-inch mortars. The Royal Artillery light guns had been firing mostly uphill and without much penetration on the American forts. Now the heavier British weapons were beginning to make an impact, particularly the exploding mortar bombs and the rockets, which inflicted few casualties but were highly unnerving to the American infantry. This resulted in an even more vigorous response from the American artillery.

Major John S. Sinclair, the highest ranking Royal Artillery officer, with over twenty years service, was overseeing his units when he observed that Captain Frederic Gordon's battery had two twenty-four-pounder guns disabled and a number of his men wounded. Major Sinclair ordered Gordon to retire his guns, as his battery was "exposed to an overpowering and in some degree plunging fire." Sinclair then ordered another "Light Half Brigade" to continue firing while, in his own words, "I directed Captain Gordon to place his men under cover, and retire his guns behind the Merlons, until circumstances should admit of using them to a greater advantage."[29] "The Merlons" is a reference to a higher, more solid part of the parapet. Captain Gordon had been present at the capture of USS *Growler* and *Eagle* in March of 1813, where he was mentioned in dispatches as having "contributed greatly to the capture of the enemy."

While the British forces had been increasing the pressure on the American forces in Plattsburgh, General Macomb had been working diligently to supply misinformation to the British high command. It had been observed that two men working on the Plattsburgh defences had been acting strangely by asking questions of the troops near them. Macomb decided to feed them erroneous stories of reinforcements on the way to Plattsburgh: 5,000 volunteers under Martin Chittenden from Vermont, General Izard's force of 4,000 on the way back, and further troops coming from Albany. That night the two men were observed secretively crossing the Saranac to the British lines and probably went straight to Prevost's headquarters with the news.

The following morning the warring factions in Plattsburgh hardly noticed the series of intermittent cannon fire from just north of Cumberland Head. It was Sunday, September 11. The British fleet had just delivered the signal for British army co-operation to begin before rounding Cumberland Head.

Commodore Macdonough USN, and his officers, together with many officers of both armies, were training their telescopes on the tip of Cumberland Point. They could see clearly the sails of warships entering Cumberland Bay. The Royal Navy had arrived, flying their battle ensigns.

Woolwich—Rocket Practice, 1813
From Colonel Congreve's Book, *The Rocket System*

6

The Battle of Cumberland Bay

The Royal Navy's Lake Champlain Flotilla

On September 1, Ile aux Noix was one of the hubs of activity supporting the British army's recent move into New York. The small island held numerous freight barges containing the supplies and provisions needed to sustain an army of several thousands, for not only a campaign but a complete occupation of an undetermined area of territory for an unknown period of time.

Thirty-six-year-old Post Captain George Downie RN, recently dispatched from the Kingston Naval station in Upper Canada, arrived amidst great confusion to assume command of not only the new frigate but the entire flotilla and naval base. He assumed command on the 3rd of September.

Captain Downie was accompanied by his aide, Lieutenant James Robertson RN. While not generally known at the time, Downie and Robertson were distant cousins, related to each other through Downie's maternal great grandfather, Sir Donald Bayne of Tulloch, part of the Clan MacKenzie. Robertson's mother was the daughter of John Mackenzie of Ross, another senior member of Clan MacKenzie. Both officers were part of the landed gentry of Scottish society. Downie had served at the 1797 Battle of Camperdown against the Dutch and later saw action against the Spanish, Turkish, and French. He was promoted to captain in January 1813 and was appointed to HMS *Montreal* (20) on Lake Ontario and took part in the attack on Oswego before being sent to HMS *Confiance* at Ile aux Noix.

...nant Robertson, as a teenager, served in merchant ships before ...ng the Royal Navy in 1801. His first naval action was as a midshipman, serving under Vice Admiral Lord Viscount Nelson KB RN, on board HMS *Victory* (100) at the Battle of Trafalgar in 1805. He next saw action in 1809 against costal batteries and two French frigates at Guadeloupe. As the 1st lieutenant of HMS *Hazard* (16), he took command of the ship when Captain Hugh Cameron RN, was killed. He later served in the Baltic, on HMS *Antelope* (50) and HMS *Vigo* (74); both were flagship vessels. In February of 1814 he was sent out to North America for lake service.

When Captain Downie assumed command of the naval base on Ile aux Noix, he would have received a salute of seven guns, fired from HMS *Linnet*, in formal greeting to him as the new post captain and commodore of the Royal Navy's Lake Champlain flotilla. He and Captain Pring would have inspected the Royal Marine guard of honour, led by Captain Anderson RM.

Downie and Robertson would then have been introduced to a number of junior naval officers, now under Downie's command, and army officers in charge of the supplies being transported to General Provost's forces, now marching to Champlain and Chazy. Both of the newly arrived officers would soon be assessing the state of readiness of the fleet, and in particular the state of HMS *Confiance*.

Downie also had a duty to support and expedite the supply line to General Prevost's army. He would have been put on his guard against Prevost by Sir James Yeo RN. Both Yeo and Prevost had held a proper but distant relationship since the affair at Sackets Harbor in 1813. Downie, therefore, sent Captain Pring with six gunboats to secure the dockside at Chazy and permit the flow of supplies to the land troops.

Next, Downie would get to grips with the delay in completing *Confiance*. The ship was busy, with seamen working high on the masts and spars, hauling up the large canvas sails into position and securing them. Each sail was made from Lieth or navy duck canvas, in 22" horizontal strips sewn together and braced with vertical and additional horizontal strips for strength. *Confiance* carried about thirty different sails. Other sailors were working on preparing the ship's cordage, hawsers, and cables of large size for the anchors and for heavy lifting of spars and yards into place, as well as smaller size ropes for the rigging and gun ropes, all needed to complete this gigantic vessel. Master shipbuilder William Simons went through the lists of incomplete

The Battle of Cumberland Bay

work with Downie, and then both men walked the length and breadth of the ship to inspect the work done and in progress above and below decks. They discussed lack of skilled men and the uncertainty of obtaining suitable spars and masts from the American smugglers; even hardware was difficult to obtain. These were all reasons for *Confiance* to not be ready. The naval base at Ile aux Noix held a smaller, less sophisticated shipyard than Kingston or Sackets Harbor. Also, the British did not have the luxury of an onsite industrial complex like the US shipyard at Vergennes. Finally Downie accepted that the completion date of September 15 would still stand, but Simons and his workmen would do all possible to move up that date.

Anecdotally, a Royal Marines officer by the name of David James Ballingall serving at the Royal Navy base at Kingston from 1841 to 1842 made a comparison study of the United States and British navies in the war of 1812. Here is an extract from his observations:

> The conduct of an enterprising enemy should always be narrowly observed and a countervailing power be prepared commensurate to the means of aggression. The Americans build their ships faster than we did on this side of the lake, and for this reason, strength is the chief object with them, and if that be obtained they care little about beauty of model or elegance of finishing, in fact they received no other polish than what was given by the Axe and Adze, which on the other hand we employed as much time upon our ships as we should in the Dockyard at home. They were as strong as the Americans, Handsomer and much better finished, but they were far more expensive, and did not endure so long a period. Ours as I have already stated after crumbling to pieces, have been broken up, some sold as old timbers, and others sunk while those of the Americans are still to the fore, and with (Better) little Expense be made available for service.[30]

Captain Ballingall by coincidence was the nephew of Captain Alexander Anderson RM.

Next, Captain Downie pursued the urgent problem of finding suitable gun locks for the main armament. It appeared from all investigations that the thirty new cannons sent from the Board of Ordinance at Woolwich had no gun locks supplied with them. "The want of gun locks as well as the other necessary appointments not to be procured in this country" is how Captain Pring later described the discrepancy.

By trial and error, it was found that the new guns could be fired using the type of lock from a larger carronade and by securing it into position with copper hoops. This was a better solution than the quill tube igniters or the firing of a blank charge from a pistol into the vent, as happened in the Battle of Lake Erie.

The stores at Ile aux Noix did not hold any of the required locks. Downie wrote to the ordinance storekeeper at Quebec, "In a few days she [*Confiance*] will be before the enemy and the want of locks may be seriously injourious in the action." Finally suitable locks were located on warships near Quebec, HMS *Junon* (38) and *Ajax* (74). Captain Clotworthy Upton RN, of *Junon* demanded that paperwork to "borrow" these locks be completed before the components were dispatched at great haste to Ile aux Noix.

On September 3, the 202 officers and men destined for HMS *Confiance* left the various warships and transports in the St. Lawrence River, fifty-eight from HMS *Leopard* (50) and another forty-eight from HMS *Ajax*, *Warspite* (74), and transport HMS *Ceylon*. Lieutenant Robertson of the *Confiance* described them as men "sent to the Lakes against their inclination" and "chiefly men who were in disgrace." Robertson did concede that several men had volunteered and were excellent seamen; most, however, were not. At least forty seamen were newly impressed merchantmen with no gunnery skills whatsoever.

As the days quickly passed, Downie and Robertson would have checked that nothing was being left to chance. The letters from General Prevost were becoming a daily occurrence, each one more demanding than the last. It must have seemed that Prevost had no concept of the unready state of the fleet, despite being advised that it would not be ready till mid-September.

September 7, from his head quarters at Plattsburgh, General Prevost next wrote to Captain Downie,

> The enemy's force in the Bay consists of a ship, inferior to the *Confiance,* a Brig—a large schooner, a sloop, and seven or eight Gun boats. When the Gun boats are manned the remaining craft appear to have but few men left on board. If you feel that the vessels under your command are equal to a contest with those I have described,

The Battle of Cumberland Bay

you will find the present moment offers many advantages which may not again occur. As my ulterior movements depend on your decision, you will have the goodness to favour me with it, with all possible promptitude.[31]

He then added a P.S. "In the event of you coming forward immediately, you will furnish conveyance for the two 8-inch mortars ordered from Ile aux Noix with their stores, provided you can do so without delaying the sailing of your squadron."

Captain Downie's reply showed he was "off Ash Island and was still two days away from being ready to sail to Chazy."

On September 8, 1814, General Prevost's letter to Captain Downie said,

I only wait your arrival to proceed against General Macomb's last position on the South Bank of the Saranac. Your share in the operation in the first instance, will be to destroy or capture the Enemy's Squadron if it should wait for a contest, and afterwards cooperate with this Division of the Army, but if it should run away and get out of your reach, we must meet here to consult on ulterior movements.

Captain Downie's reply read,

To, Lieutenant General Sir George Prevost Bt. September 8th 1814. I stated to you that the ship was not ready—She is not ready now, and until she is ready, it is my duty not to hazard the squadron before an Enemy who will even then be considerably superior in force. Signed, Your Obedient Servant, Downie.[32]

Captain Downie now decided to move the frigate and the rest of his fleet to Chazy. The workmen were still busy on the half-finished magazine and numerous other works, such as fitting breaching bolts, cleats, belaying pins, and installing the bilge pumps. Sailors too were busy scraping the decks to remove tar and smoothing out uneven boards on the deck. *Confiance* cleared the defensive barriers around Ile aux Noix under tow by several gunboats, the ship trailing its explosives behind it in a covered boat.

The gunboats of the fleet and even the larger vessels had many empty berths. Downie was still waiting for the last of his seamen to arrive. In the evening the fleet arrived at Chazy. Much depended on manpower and the frigate's fitness for battle. At least Chazy offered the prospect of help from the army.

On September 9, General Prevost's latest letter to Captain Downie at Chazy Landing read, "I need not dwell with you upon the Evils resulting to both services from delay, Capt. Watson of the Provincial Cavalry is directed to remain at the Chazy until you are preparing to get under way, when he is instantly to return to this place with the intelligence." The twenty-four-year-old Canadian Captain William Watson was an energetic young officer who raised the Dorchester Provincial Light Dragoons and was later rewarded by the Prince Regent with a land grant for war services.

Downie wrote his return dispatch to Prevost:

> I have the Honour to communicate to Your Excel'cy that it is my intention to weigh and proceed from this anchorage about midnight, in the expectation of rounding into the Bay of Plattsburgh about dawn of day, & commence an immediate attack upon the Enemy, if they should be found anchored in a position that offer a chance of success. I rely on any assistance you can afford the Squadron. In manning the Flotilla & ships, finding we are many short, I have made application to the Officer Commanding at Chazy for a company of the 39th Regt. I have the honour of Your Excelly's letter of this morning to which the proceeding is a full answer.[33]

Sealing the reply, Downie handed it to Captain Watson, who immediately rode back to Prevost's head quarters.

An informal invitation was sent to the senior army officers of the troops present at Chazy to join Downie for a luncheon and libation. In short, this was a recruiting invitation, and as with all such exercises, the benefits—such as prize money and a share in the glory—of serving the king in the upcoming lake battle were stressed. The risks were minimized. It was here that Downie made the remark "that *Confiance* alone, can beat the American fleet." In theory at least, this was true on paper, but in reality he was desperate to fill the empty seats in the gunboats and provide willing hands on undermanned ships. The 39th agreed to provide a company officered by Lieutenant Fitzpatrick and Ensign Bond, and the Canadian militia provided

The Battle of Cumberland Bay

approximately 150 men under the command of Captain Raumzie and Lieutenant Oliver. A few gunners were also spared from both the Royal Marine Artillery and Royal Artillery units at Chazy.

Downie returned to his ship to find that the last of the seamen transferring to his command had arrived. Once assigned a hammock space, the seamen began learning gun drills. The guns were found to be hard to move owing to the tar and the difficult uneven surface of the deck. More scraping of the decks would be needed. The distribution of officers and men amongst the gunboats and larger vessels was worked out by Downie late into the evening.

On Sept 10, 1814, Prevost wrote to Downie,

> I received at twelve last night your letter acquainting me with your determination to get under weigh about that time in the expectation of rounding Cumberland Head at dawn of day; in consequence, the troops have been held in readiness since six o' clock this morning to storm the enemy's works at nearly the same moment as the naval action should commence in the Bay. I ascribe the disappointment I have experienced to the unfortunate change of wind and shall rejoice to learn that my reasonable expectations have been frustrated by no other means.[34]

In order to jack up the pressure on Downie, Prevost sent the letter via a higher ranking officer and aide de camp, Major Foster Lechmere Coore. The thirty-four-year-old Coore was a graduate of Eaton School and had served in the 15th Dragoons for six years before becoming a staff officer in North America in 1809. He later served with the 3rd West India Regiment, where he met Prevost, who, latterly as governor general of the Canadas, engaged him as part of his staff. Coore was the officer entrusted with the dispatches sent to England announcing the British capture of Detroit in August of 1812.

Major Coore and Captain Downie discussed and agreed that the British army would storm the American works to assist the Royal Navy squadron when it attacked the American fleet. Captain Pring later stated in writing that he was present in person at that agreement and that the signal of scaling of *Confiance*'s guns by the naval squadron was "that they might know when their co-operation was wanted."

When Coore left, the fleet got underway from Little Chazy. However, as stated by Captain Pring, "but in consequence of unfavourable wind, we could make but little progress, and we were obliged to anchor again nearly in the same spot from which we weighed. The next morning however the wind veered to the Northward, and we set sail for the Bay of Plattsburgh."

The day was spent on teaching the new seamen gun drills while the carpenters continued their work. The guns were still heavy and sluggish to handle, owing to the tar and unevenness of the decks. The officers then ordered the decks to be scoured by crewmen using soft sandstone blocks. These were often referred to as Bibles or holy stones, with smaller stones called prayer books. The crewmen on their knees scouring the decks looked like men in the act of praying.

The full force of the Royal Navy's Lake Champlain flotilla was now present for the first time. The strength of the four major vessels amounted to 15 officers, 257 junior officers, 440 seamen, and 110 Royal Marines, in all 822 all ranks. The gunboats and tender vessel *Icicle* (4) held a total of 420 officers and men, both naval and military, for a total numerical strength of 1,242. Downie decided to keep the existing officers in charge of the larger vessels while consulting with Captain Pring on who should lead the gunboats.

Lieutenant Mark Raynham RN, formerly of HMS *Ceylon*, being the most senior naval officer was given overall command of the gunboats. The second senior officer was Lieutenant Thomas Duell RN, commanding the gunboat *General Drummond*. The other officers were mostly midshipmen, also transferred from the ships at Quebec, except for Royal Marines Lieutenants Ashmore and Caldwell and Midshipman Christopher James Bell RN. These officers were respectively given command of the gun vessels: *Sir George Prevost* (2), *Sir Sydney Beckwith* (2), and *Colonel Murray* (1).

The next day, Sunday, September 11, 1814, in the early morning half light, the ship's gig of HMS *Confiance* pulled away from the ship's side. On board were Captain Downie and Sailing Master Robert Anderson Bryden, with a small crew of oarsmen and a protection party of Royal Marines. On rounding Cumberland Head, Downie and Bryden studied the line of American warships moored in line of battle and noted the numerous spring lines holding them firmly in place as floating batteries. This was a classic harbour defence strategy, similar to that used at the battles of Copenhagen and the Nile, where Admiral Nelson's ships had attacked and crossed the "T," destroying enemy warships at anchor to win each battle.

The Battle of Cumberland Bay

Downie now had his own attack strategy formed in his mind and so ordered the gig returned to Chazy. On his arrival, he found the officers of the fleet assembled on the afterdeck of *Confiance,* as he had ordered. He advised them that the fleet would form as two separate elements. *Chubb, Linnet,* and *Confiance* would round Cumberland Head as sharply as possible and head straight for the northernmost American vessels, *Eagle* and flagship *Saratoga. Chubb* and *Linnet* would concentrate their fire on *Eagle,* while *Confiance* would head for the gap between *Eagle* and *Saratoga* and, when there, broadside both as it crossed between them, then if needed go on to dispatch *Ticonderoga* and *Preble.*

The other division of the flotilla, consisting of *Finch* and all the gunboats, were to take a wider swing around Cumberland Head and attack *Preble* and *Ticonderoga.* Supported by fire from *Finch,* the gunboat crews would attack "with the greatest expedition, fire once and then board the schooner *Ticonderoga*" and then concentrate on *Preble.*

General Provost's emissary Major Coore had agreed that when signalled the British army would advance and capture the enemy fortifications in support of the naval action. Downie wanted all his officers to understand the plan, in case of signalling being obscured by smoke or the loss of any key personnel in battle.

As September 11 was a Sunday, Downie also had a responsibility to hold a church service. The "Divine Service" pennant was run up to the gaff position, above the Union Flag; this alerted the entire fleet that church services were beginning. He then assembled his officers and the ship's company and would have held a brief but pertinent service using the Book of Common Prayer. Captain Downie himself, being no stranger to the Bible, would have read the Scriptures; his father, brother, and brother-in-law were all ministers of the church in Scotland.

The next task was to disembark all the officers to their respective vessels and transport the noncombatants to the transport and hospital ship, *Icicle.* Those leaving were mainly the shipbuilding crew, including master shipbuilder William Simons, who had been helping ship's carpenter Henry Cox to finish building the frigate's second bilge pump.

The orders were now given to get the British fleet underway. Royal Marines not on guard duty were ordered to remove coats, store their arms, and "standby the guns." There would be no Royal Marine marksmen firing down from the ships "tops," all of them needed as gun crews. The only red coats would be those of Captain Anderson and Lieutenant Childs, plus the duty guard. The seamen brought up their hammocks and bound them to the netting across the ships rail along both sides; these would help retard the splintering of the wooden wall when hit by cannon balls. Other preparation involved the running of a spring line around the ship to the best bower anchor. The galley fires were extinguished and the embers thrown overboard; as a rule British warships never went into battle with a fire on board.

On nearing Cumberland Head, Downie ordered the scaling of his new cannon. One by one the blank charges were fired, cleaning out the scale and, more importantly, heralding their approach. All eyes above deck on the British vessels were peering where water meets land and forest at Cumberland Point, everyone looking for their first view of the American Fleet.

Once around the point USS *Saratoga* was seen, clearly displaying Commodore Macdonough's message to his men: "Impressed seamen call on every man to do his duty." After rounding Cumberland Head, Downie spoke to the crew, as later recalled by Sailing Master Bryden, and said, "There are the Enemy's ships. Our army are to storm the Enemy's works at the moment we engage, and mind, don't let us be behind."[35]

Very quickly Downie found the wind had shifted from the north to westerly. Now, instead of having a useful crosswind, his ships faced a headwind. He entered the bay close-hauled to the shore of Cumberland Head. He soon found the breeze light and fitful. The three British shallow draft vessels found it increasingly difficult to attack in the desired formation. The wind also forced the *Confiance* to sail towards the American line much more slowly than desired. With its topgallant sails set and jib and spanker out, *Confiance,* along with *Linnet* and *Chubb,* went into action.

Part of the British strategy was to hold fire until the enemy fired first. It was the Royal Navy's form of psychological warfare. Only the most experienced officers and men of both sides would have had any idea of the devastation that was about to break about them.

As the British came even closer with sails looming larger, Master Commandant Robert Henley USN, of USS *Eagle* would be the first to lose his nerve. Henley began the firing with a broadside of *Eagle's* long eighteen-pounders, which fell well short of the target. The British vessels close-hauled on a starboard tack and continued on towards the Americans. Commodore

The Battle of Cumberland Bay

Macdonough waited for the big British frigate to come closer into range of his main armament, the carronades. He personally sighted one of his long twenty-four-pounders, and when *Confiance* was in range he ordered the gun to be fired.

The ball entered *Confiance*'s hawse hole and ranged the whole of the deck, killing and maiming several British seamen and smashing the ship's wheel, damaging the vessel's steering system. Macdonough then ordered the signal flags for "close action" to be raised. The American gunboats all advanced forward of the line and with *Saratoga* unleashed what Pring called "a heavy and galling fire" at *Confiance,* which it could not return because the vessel had no (bow chaser) guns to fire directly forward. Having discharged their first shot, the American gunboats retired behind the larger US vessels, which continued their bombardment of *Confiance.*

The initial bombardment from *Saratoga* and the gunboats immediately affected Downie's flagship, which finally halted due to lack of wind. *Confiance* had lost its sheet anchor and bower anchor, and when it dropped its best bower, the spring was shot away. The loss of these large anchors and of the spring line contributed significantly to the battle's eventual outcome. The British gun crews, now experiencing casualties, quickly replaced the missing gunners and anxiously waited for orders to fight. The wounded were carried below decks to the surgeon, while other seamen were ordered to remove the dead by throwing the bodies overboard, followed by the dismembered body parts of the poor unfortunates; this was standard practise in the Royal Navy. *Confiance* now found itself 300 yards away from the beam of *Saratoga* with little ability to fire at the *Eagle* but still absorbing heavy fire from both.

Linnet took its station abeam *Eagle* and engaged it. The cutter *Chubb* passed behind *Linnet* and sailed directly into *Eagle's* range. Before *Chubb* could seriously contribute to the action, two broadsides from *Eagle* left it with sails shot away and much of its standing rigging cut. Soon the foresail was smashed and fell into the water over its lee bow. Having received such a devastating shower of shot, the cutter was now uncontrollable. *Chubb's* captain, Lieutenant James McGhie RN, was wounded by a splinter in his thigh plus the loss of the tips of two fingers. He went below decks for medical attention. Two soldiers of the 39th were killed and one soldier wounded. Seven other infantrymen of the 39th, plus two Royal Marines, named Newton and Barnet, and one seaman, John Shenfield, fled their posts and went below. The command was taken over by Midshipman John Bodell RN, who now had only about six seamen and marines working with him on deck. Each time he ordered the sweeps out to bring it into position, the oars were shot away.

Chubb drifted in the current between the two flagships and was subjected to the fire intended for *Confiance,* plus a fusillade from *Saratoga*'s marines. Finally Bodell asked for and received Lieutenant McGhie's permission to lower the tattered red battle ensign. An American gunboat quickly towed the devastated *Chubb* out of the action. The British had lost one of their four main vessels before their flagship had even fired its first shot. Downie watched *Chubb*'s demise and carried on the struggle to get *Confiance* into position to broadside *Saratoga*.

The earlier order to double shot *Confiance*'s guns was now increased to add a canister shot to each gun's load. Downie's first barrage took place at approximately 9:30 a.m., with one terrific roar and fifteen bright flashes, sending thirty twenty-four-pound iron spheres and a hail of canister shot blasting forward, smashing and splintering *Saratoga* with a tremendous force. Both ships were now momentarily curtained from each other in clouds of acrid billowing smoke. The American flagship shuddered from bow to stern; the impact threw over half the crew to the deck.

Despite all the flying wood and metal, casualties were light, and the wounded were passed below. The dead were dragged over to the larboard side of the main gun deck. This done, the American sailors returned to their guns and continued to fight. Amongst the dead was Lieutenant Peter Gamble USN, killed in the act of sighting his gun. Macdonough and Downie now had the same unenviable situation of having on board a very junior officer as their second in command. The American gunnery was proving superior to the British because of Macdonough's insistence on live fire practice and because his ships were solidly anchored, giving his gun crews a perfect condition to keep up a high rate of fire.

Shortly after *Confiance* fired its first broadside, Downie stood behind one of the guns, watching by telescope for General Prevost's land attack. An American shot hit the artillery piece on the flat face of the cannon, throwing it backward off the carriage, crushing and killing Downie instantly. In less than fifteen minutes into the battle, the Royal Navy had lost its most senior officer.

The Battle of Cumberland Bay

Lieutenant Robertson immediately took command of *Confiance*. This was the second time in his career he had to take over command of a ship in battle. Downie's body was removed to the captain's cabin. Robertson now had to notify Captain Pring that command of the squadron was now his. In the confusion of Downie's death, no one could find the signal book, and the message could not be made. Robertson, unable to signal his superior officer, tried to send over a message to *Linnet* by boat. However, all of the frigate's boats were damaged and unable to float.

The battle raged on with Captain Pring unaware of Downie's death and the British command and control system in total disarray. Near the time of Downie's demise, *Confiance* discharged a second broadside. A shot hit the spanker boom of *Saratoga*, driving the spar against Macdonough and knocking him out. The crew saw him arise after a few minutes, regain his composure, and continue working the guns like a common sailor. In a separate incident, a shot took off the head of a gun crewman and sent it flying against Macdonough with such a force that it knocked him down between two guns. His uniform was soaked with blood and brains; he again recovered and resumed command of *Saratoga*.

Commodore Macdonough was not the only officer to receive such a grisly experience. Sailing Master and Acting Lieutenant Elie A. F. Vallette USN, who was placed in charge of the 1st and 2nd divisions of guns on board *Saratoga*, was also hit by the decapitated head of one of his gun crewmen. He also had a cannonball cut a semicircular hole in the crown and side of his hat! The experience of the battle saw him off on a career where he would rise to the rank of rear admiral, USN.

HMS *Linnet*, having Captain Pring's seasoned and skilful crew, kept up a constant and heavy fire against USS *Eagle*, which was manned, much like *Confiance*, with less seasoned seamen, soldiers, and men released from detention. Eventually the spring lines of *Eagle* were shot away, and it retired behind *Saratoga*. *Linnet* now turned its attention to *Saratoga* and began a heavy fire at it.

Saratoga, now facing cannon fire from two directions, suffered two separate fires breaking out on board, in addition to the cannonballs and the torrent of splinters. The fires were attributed by Commodore Macdonough to "Hot Shot" being fired at it by *Confiance*. The fires were most likely caused by the flames of *Saratoga's* own carronades, which tended to get excessively hot and which were shorter than long guns and therefore had more discharge flame inboard. Many such instances of fires during battle on board men-o'-war have been recorded by the Royal Navy. All of the US officers, including the commodore, had never been exposed to such heavy and constant bombardment, whereas the Royal Navy had endured the collective experience of dozens of such intense battles at sea, none of which involved a hot shot oven.

On each of the four vessels, all aboard could hear the screams of the wounded and dying, the deafening roar of cannon, the whizzing sound of the enemy's shot passing overhead, or a crashing sound of cannon shot as it hit the vessel's side, sending showers of sharp-pointed splinters flying through sails, hammocks, and human flesh. There was the sight and smell of smoke and the feel of blood under bare feet as men slid in trying to haul on a rope. Torrents of blood were on the deck; bodies, bones, and body parts lay strewn everywhere. The horror was most intense on these four vessels, but the battle was nearly as intense at the other end of the American defensive line.

Ticonderoga and *Preble* Under Attack

The 350-ton *Ticonderoga* and the 80-ton *Preble* were anxiously waiting at the south end of the American line for the British gunboats and *Finch* to come into range. The action began about 9:40 a.m. as the British gunboats advanced in line behind HMS *Finch* towards *Ticonderoga*, looking like flotilla of Barbary pirates with their "Lug" sails, and sweeps lashing through the water. The lead gunboat was *Sir James L. Yeo* (2), commanded by Lieutenant Raynham. *Yeo* and gunboat *Provost* both had twenty-four-pounder long guns, which could easily outrange the four eighteen-pounders and eight twelve-pounders on *Ticonderoga* and the seven twelve-pounders on *Commodore Preble*. But as with the other American vessels they had more stable gun platforms, and their ships were more sturdily built than those of their opponents. In addition, Stephen Cassin's *Ticonderoga* mounted five thirty-two-pounder carronades, which by far represented a more violent threat to any gunboat approaching at close range to this vessel.

The gunboats advanced in line toward *Ticonderoga*, led by Raynham's *Yeo*. At approximately five hundred yards from the target Raynham hoisted the signal for close action and boarding, but instead of leading the rest of the gunboats in the race for *Ticonderoga*, he promptly withdrew *Yeo* from the action. Raynham would later claim that the touch-hole on his long gun was

The Battle of Cumberland Bay

clogged, but no rational reason was given when it was pointed out that his boat also had a thirty-two-pounder carronade, a more suitable weapon at close range, and lesser boats were armed only with a single carronade.

The retreat of *Yeo* was observed by several of the closer gunboats, giving rise to confusion amongst the officers of these other boats and contributing greatly to the refusal of many of the Canadian militia to press on. Indeed, the gunboats entry into the action had been delayed by a lack of zeal from the same source.

The American ships opened fire when the British closed to about 500 yards. The inexperienced midshipmen called for return fire from their gunners, but more experienced heads waited for closer range. One report states a Royal Marine Artillery gunner refusing to obey the order to fire, saying, "Not near enough." However, when reaching "within about half a musket shot" he fired to some purpose. "Not a shot he afterwards directed could fail to do tremendous execution." The boat was claimed to be *General Simcoe*, which reportedly lost two of the 39th privates George Abernathy and James Reid, "The same shot cutting them asunder." *Simcoe* was commanded by thirty-year-old Midshipman Charles E. D. P. Houghton RN. Interestingly, another report states that *Simcoe* was manned by thirty-one Canadians, three seamen, and a single gunner; a further report states *Simcoe* did not actively participate in the close action.

At the height of the battle, a number of British boats entered within grapeshot range of *Ticonderoga's* carronades—*Marshal Beresford, Blucher, Sir Hope Popham, Lord Wellington,* and the fifty-foot gunboat *Colonel Murray.* This last boat was commanded by nineteen-year-old Midshipman Christopher James Bell RN, who was wounded by a grapeshot ball in the foot, and then a second wound took his right leg completely off and damaged the boat. Bell was the officer who later verbalized the conduct of the major part of the Canadian infantrymen in the boats, stating, "The Captain of Militia (Raumzie) and a number of his men (Canadians) twenty three of whom I had in the boat, the major part with the Captain lay down in the bottom, with the exception of Lieutenant Oliver of the Canadian Militia." Bell and Olliver tried to motivate the troops to row the boat closer, but when Bell was wounded a second time, the boat retired back toward *Icicle,* the fleet hospital tender. It has been claimed that the Canadian Infantry were on board to become a boarding party and not to man the guns.[36] While it is understandable that this type of warfare was new to the Canadians, it is, however, the very act of not swiftly rowing the boats forward that enabled the Americans to inflict such a high number of casualties in those boats.

The men of the 39th, who had also volunteered for this service, had no such problems or complaints. The Quebecois volunteers suffered nine killed and three wounded in the gunboat action. As for Midshipman Bell, he was promoted to Lieutenant on March 1, 1815, and was present on board HMS *Gladiator* for the courts martial of the officers and men of the Lake Champlain Squadron. He and most of the other officers were cleared, having "Conducted themselves with great zeal, bravery and ability during the action." Bell was given a pension of five shillings (one dollar) per diem "For wounds received in the service." In 1817 he immigrated to Upper Canada and received a grant of 800 acres. He went into business in the logging industry, created a village named Castleford, in Renfrew County, became a magistrate, commissioner of the court of requests, land agent, and postmaster.

At one point the American gunboat *Borer*, commanded by Midshipman Thomas Conover USN, came forward in support of *Ticonderoga* and was fired on by the British boat *Colonel Murray*, killing two men and wounding another, forcing *Borer* to withdraw. By battle's end, *Borer* reported three killed, purser's steward Arthur W. Smith, boy Thomas Gill, and marine James Day. Wounded was corporal of marines Ebenezer Cobb.

The remaining US gunboats were more occupied with the fighting at the north end of the bay. The attack on *Ticonderoga* was so intense that Midshipman Hiram Pauling USN, resorted to firing the cannon by using his pistol. The British gunboats came so close that Pauling and the US infantry were able to fire their weapons directly into the boats. The British did not make it close enough to use boat hooks or climb aboard. Lieutenant Stephen Cassin had also been able to shift his cables from time to time, enabling him to direct fire at *Finch*, which received several hits, shredding its rigging, and hulled the smaller cutter several times.

Other casualties to the British were Midshipman Pym of *Wellington*. He was slightly wounded twice, once in the arm by grapeshot. He also was hit in the shoulder by the flat of a grapeshot charge. His boat also had one of the Canadian militiamen killed on board.

Midshipman James Robertson RN, commanding *Marshal Beresford* was slightly wounded by grapeshot. Midshipman William Allen RN, of *Sir Hope*

The Battle of Cumberland Bay

Popham was also closely engaged with *Ticonderoga* but appeared not to have received any catastrophic damage to the boat or wounds to his men.

The other British gunboats seem to have engaged *Ticonderoga* and *Commodore Preble* from greater distances. HMS *Finch*, a seven-gun cutter, also appeared to have held back. Lieutenant Hicks had had several problems with some of the crew on board. The pilot, Simpson, was constantly "dodging when shot came over." Hicks also stated the pilot "was of no use to him." In another incident, Hicks had seen a crewman deliberately lower the ship's colours. Hicks raised his pistol at the seaman and threatened "to blow his brains out," whereupon the seaman rehoisted the colours and returned to his station. *Finch* sailed so far to the leeward that it focused its attack on *Preble*, not on *Ticonderoga*. Acting Lieutenant William Hicks RN, *Finch's* commander, later argued that his orders were only "to lead the gunboats in and support them." This meant that the five close combatant gunboats were badly outgunned and driven off under a heavy fire from *Ticonderoga*.

Lieutenant Charles Budd USN, commanding USS *Preble*, failed to demonstrate the fighting spirit that Macdonough expected of him or his ship. By 9:45 a.m. *Preble* and *Finch* were within half a gunshot of each other. After an exchange of fire for over three-quarters of an hour, Lieutenant Budd slipped his vessel's cable and sailed off toward the safety of the guns covering the Plattsburgh shore. The British claimed *Preble* lowered its colours as if in defeat but raised them again later. Commodore Macdonough excused Lieutenant Budd's conduct as necessary to avoid capture by the gunboats.

With *Preble* out of reach, Hicks turned his attention to the seventeen-gun *Ticonderoga* about the same time that the American schooner chased off the gunboats. Soon *Finch* had its forestay cut away, its main boom nearly cut through, and its mainmast severely hit. Its rudder became unserviceable, and over three feet of water filled its hold. Desperately trying to stay afloat and fighting, Hicks found *Finch* was drifting toward Crab Island. He tried to steer his ship to avoid the stony reef. However, before this could be accomplished the cutter struck ground. From this grounded position Hicks fought off *Ticonderoga* on the one side and two six-pounder field guns manned by invalids from the Crab Island hospital on the other. These land guns were soon cleared, and the surviving invalids were then ordered back to the tented hospital by Dr. James Mann, who wished to prevent enemy cannonfire from reaching his patients.

Hicks tried to refloat his vessel by unloading weaponry and excess ammunition. Now desperate to get off the shoal, he tried to get lines out to four of the British gunboats. The boats responding were *Beckwith,* commanded by Lieutenant Glassen Caldwell RM, *General Brock* under Midshipman William H. Dickman RN, *Blucher,* commanded by the wounded Midshipman Pym, and lastly the damaged *Wellington,* under Sailing Master Robert Wemyss RN. It was all in vain. With his ship aground and taking on water, Hicks kept up his fire until after the gunboats had fled under a heavy fire from *Ticonderoga,* and he saw *Confiance* and *Linnet* struck before doing the same with *Finch's* colours.

Winding *Saratoga*

Saratoga and *Confiance,* and *Eagle* and *Linnet* engaged each other in an intense, continual struggle. On board the four vessels, gun crews heaved, sweated, and groaned; flintlocks sparked; cannons roared and smoke billowed; men were wounded and some died. The rate of fire declined as more and more weapons became disabled. Shots were now discharged singly, the disciplined broadside firing was now gone and reduced to the isolated world of each gun crew: the deafening noise, shouted commands, swabbing out, loading, running out the gun, and firing, all the time hoping if not praying that this world of blinding smoke, noise, and extreme toil would not suddenly explode into the hereafter.

The effective fire of *Confiance* declined quickly and dramatically. The gun crews unfamiliar with the new twenty-four-pounder Congreve long guns failed to notice that each time they fired the recoil caused the wooden quoin to slip backwards, thereby elevating the muzzle of the gun. Each new round flew higher than the previous one. In the heat of battle, with smoke obscuring the target, the frigate's gun captains failed to notice that they were hitting the masts and rigging and not the *Saratoga's* hull and deck.

The more accurate American gunfire had hit the wooden wall of *Confiance* regularly. It had twelve large holes between wind and water, all close to its waterline. Several holes were below the waterline, which admitted water faster than the carpenter, Cox, and his crew could plug them. One shot drove out a seven-foot plank, and the water gushed in. The seamen on both pumps found themselves working at a failing effort; constant bailing through the main hatch was all that kept it afloat. The wounded men had to

The Battle of Cumberland Bay

be moved higher to keep them from drowning. Most of the frigate's masts were disabled, and much of its sails and rigging were shot away. Still, with all the defects, Lieutenant Robertson and his men fought on.

Linnet too had been badly mauled. The water inside its hull rose nearly a foot over the lower deck, and its wounded crewmen had to be shifted to the tops of chests and cables to keep them from drowning in the rising water. Captain Pring had the most experienced and best trained crew of all the British vessels. Despite his forcing of *Eagle* out of the line, he was now facing the unused side of that same vessel in an even heavier bombardment. Lieutenant Cassin's *Ticonderoga* was now supporting *Saratoga* and *Eagle* by firing at *Confiance,* in addition to its quarterdeck guns still engaging *Finch.* No communication of any kind had been given to Captain Pring by *Confiance.* He sent over a boat with Lieutenant William Drew RN, to find out the status of the battle from Captain Downie. On the return of Drew, Captain Pring first learned of Downie's death and that the flagship was in such a bad way.

At this time the last serviceable carronade on *Saratoga's* starboard side was disabled. Commodore Macdonough ordered the winding of the American flagship set into motion. He had deliberately sent below all men who had their guns disabled. These men now streamed onto *Saratoga's* deck, exposed again to the British cannon fire while under orders to cut certain cables and to wind in others. One man, Sailing Master Brum, had all of his clothing blown off by flying splinters; he remained unhurt and carried on directing the seamen under his charge. As *Saratoga* began to swing around, its stern castle became more exposed and received a fair blasting from *Linnet.* Lieutenant Robertson of *Confiance* observed *Saratoga's* move and attempted to wind his ship in a similar fashion. Lieutenants Charles Creswick and William Hornby, Sailing Master Bryden, and Master's Mate Simmonds with other officers managed to get a spring line bent to the only anchor cable in place. A number of crewmen began hauling on the spring line, and while veering the cable, all of them came under a devastating and raking fire from *Saratoga,* which killed and wounded several men. The winding was slow and incomplete. The early loss of the frigate's main anchors was now costing it dearly.

The American flagship began to slide around; soon the carronades on its larboard side began to line up on *Confiance* and began a rolling broadside, which smashed up the big vessel even more. Once fully in place another of *Saratoga's* devastating broadsides was driven home. Robertson, with his officers in agreement, conceded the contest in the interest of saving lives. He ordered the lowering of the red and white Royal Navy battle ensign. *Confiance* surrendered, with nearly every living person on board wounded or hurt in some manner. The time was 11:30 a.m.

The fight, however, was not over. Captain Pring kept the gun crews of *Linnet* working despite the fire from *Eagle* and *Ticonderoga,* plus the intermittent fire from US gunboats, which had been a constant annoyance throughout the battle. On seeing *Confiance* surrender, he knew he would now be battling virtually the entire American fleet, including *Saratoga*. The British gunboats were now seen by him to be distant from his area of battle, so with no support *Linnet* fired a last couple of broadsides and survived a further fifteen minutes amidst a virtual hail of canister and cannonballs. Pring then gave the orders to lower the ship's blue battle ensign at 11:45 a.m. In the distance Pring would have watched as the last shots were fired at the grounded HMS *Finch,* still struggling to refloat herself. In turn it lowered its colours at about 12:15 p.m., completing an overwhelming American naval victory.

The Aftermath of the Naval Battle

Pring, Robertson, and Hicks, each on their respective vessels, sent their gun crews to the aid of the wounded below decks. Soon many had been released from the dark interior of the hull and placed more comfortably on the deck, while the dead were separately placed and covered over.

HMS *Confiance* had three and a half feet of water inside the hull and was near sinking. In order to prevent this, Robertson ordered the larboard guns run inward, making the ship heel over to the starboard. The enemy shot holes were now mostly above water. The frigate was kept afloat only by continual pumping and bailing. The seamen working hard at the bilge pumps now had replacements to help with the strenuous toil of working pumps that could each deliver a volume of water to service a town of some 7,000 persons, and the surgeons and their assistants knew that the stream of blood-soaked casualties would soon end. In the captain's cabin of *Confiance* three bodies now lay side by side, wrapped in sailcloth shrouds: Captain Downie RN, an early casualty; Captain Alexander Anderson RM; and Midshipman

The Battle of Cumberland Bay

William Gunn RN. Little is known of the details of the deaths of Anderson and Gunn other than that they were both gun captains during the battle. Amongst the dead was the wife of the frigate's steward, killed at the side of the surgeon while in the act of nursing the wounded.

Onboard *Linnet*, the bodies of Acting Lieutenant William Paul RN, and Boatswain Francis Jackson RN, were also shrouded in sailcloth and placed aside from the other dead seamen. An accounting of all the British casualties was never accurately given, either in numbers or severity of wounds. Since the ship's log of *Confiance* was never found, the following is a general estimate.

Vessel	Officers	Seamen, Royal Marines and 39th Regiment
HMS *Confiance*	3 KIA, 6 wounded	38 KIA, 34 wounded
HMS *Linnet*	2 KIA, 1 wounded	8 KIA, 13 wounded
HMS *Finch*	0 KIA, 0 wounded	0 KIA, 2 wounded
HMS *Chub*	0 KIA, 1 wounded	6 KIA, 15 wounded

Figures of 27 officers and 340 other ranks captured were stated in after-battle reports by Commodore Macdonough.

Strangely, none of the ships' logs from the four British vessels were found. This was probably an intentional act to deny intelligence to the US Navy. However, what was found was the ship's log of HMS *Wolfe*, which Downie had captained on Lake Ontario. This is now believed to be in the Library of Congress.

The escaped British gunboats had three wounded officers and an undetermined number of other ranks wounded, plus several killed. The wounded were transferred to *Icicle* and returned to Ile aux Noix. Some of the dead were reportedly buried at Chazy, while others were discharged overboard. The lake would give up the dead combatants for days after the battle.

The termination of the lake battle was heralded by loud cheers from all the American sailors and soldiers on Macdonough's fleet. The cheers were so loud they interrupted the cannonade between both land forces and conveyed a very disturbing message to the British high command.

To Commodore Macdonough, it must have sounded like music to his ears. He had not only won a battle; he had struck a blow for sailors' rights, and on a more personal level he had used his knowledge, instinct, hard work and seamanship to outwit and ultimately defeat the enemy, which had terrorized the lake from Ile La Motte to Vergennes and had been a constant threat to lake commerce and activity of both the US Navy and army.

Macdonough now began the immediate tasks of the victor, to preserve the lives of all his men and the British prisoners now under his charge, and to inform his superiors of his complete victory. His gunboats had ventured out in pursuit of the now distant British boats. The Commodore ordered a signal that returned his boats to the task of securing the surrendered enemy and to secure the prizes to prevent recapture by the British forces now bombarding Plattsburgh.

Shortly after the naval battle ended, the four surviving Royal Navy commanders were taken by boat to Commodore Macdonough, who met them on the shattered quarterdeck of USS *Saratoga*. Captain Pring presented his officers, Lieutenants Robertson, McGhie, and Hicks. In front of the assembled American crew the British officers drew their swords and holding them by their blades offered them to Commodore Macdonough in a symbolic act of surrender. The swords were graciously declined by Macdonough, saying, "Gentlemen, your gallant conduct makes you worthy to wear your weapons; return them to their scabbards." This was the true character of an officer and gentleman of the highest calibre by placing his vanquished enemy at ease.

With the full co-operation of the British officers Macdonough had all of the wounded from both fleets transferred to the hospital on Crab Island. Dr. Mann and his assistants, which now included the British surgeons, worked on the wounded from both antagonists.

Many American civilians had observed the battle. Benajah Phelps, a fourteen-year-old farm boy, watched from Sawyer's Hill on South Hero Island. He had an excellent view of the battle, including the fall of the British colours. He gave an interview in November of 1901 to the *Outlook* periodical, which recorded his words:

> "Well, that [the surrender] was about twelve o' clock. Pretty soon I saw two or three pushin' out a boat down in Rockwell's Bay…I was bound to go on board the ships, so I run down and jumped in. It was a four oared boat, and we rowed out to the big British ship. She was a fine ship, I tell ye…The plankin' was white oak six-inches thick. The small balls did not go through these planks. They were just stuck solid full of balls…It seemed as if you couldn't git any

The Battle of Cumberland Bay

more balls in. The grape-shot and rifle-balls pooty nearly covered the plankin' all over. The riggin' was all cut to pieces. There wasn't any of it left...The decks was the most awful sight I ever saw. It was—it was Awful!...Blood, blood was everywhere! The decks was covered with arms and legs and heads, and pieces of hands and bodies all torn to pieces! I never see anything in this world like it! Seemed as everybody had been killed! They must have fought terribly before they hauled down the flag. It 'most made me sick!"

Later in the afternoon other visitors arrived on board *Saratoga*. Judge Julius C. Hubbel and Judge Scott congratulated Commodore Macdonough on his victory. Hubbel described the scene as "The dead all packed up in order here" and the decks having been "Cleaned up." but he could clearly see blood in the seams of the planking, the torn hull, and the devastation to masts and spars, which told the story. From *Saratoga* the group went to *Confiance,* and here Hubbel and Scott found a "horrible sight."

The vessel was absolutely torn to pieces, the decks were strewn with mutilated bodies lying in all directions and everything was covered in blood. It was the most fearful sight I ever beheld or ever expect to, and one I shall never forget. One poor fellow whom I had seen before—a pilot named Brown—lay groaning on the deck, his head swathed up with a bloody shirt. He recognised me, but when I returned to him a few moments after words he was dead. I went below and saw the body of Commodore Downie lying in his state room. He was a large fair looking man, and the surgeons could find no mark upon him, but on examination concluded that he must have been killed by a spent shot.[37]

Commodore Macdonough in an effort to help the wounded offered parole to Captain Pring and to those severely wounded prisoners who would survive a return boat trip to Canada. Pring accepted on both accounts. Pring on the 12th, while still on *Saratoga,* wrote his after-action report, detailing the loss of the British squadron to his superior Sir James L. Yeo at the naval base in Kingston.

The British and American wounded on Crab Island intermingled and assisted each other in any way possible. Both redcoats and bluecoats stood their turn at guard. The severely wounded Lieutenant Richard Lee RN, wrote in a letter home to his brother describing the battle,

> The havoc on both sides is dreadful. I don't think there are more than five of our men, out of three hundred, but what are killed or wounded. Never was a shower of hail so thick as the shot whistling about our ears. Were you to see my jacket, waistcoat, and trowsers, you would be astonished how I escaped as I did, for they are literally torn all to rags with shot and splinters; the upper part of my hat was also shot away. There is one of our marines who was in the Trafalgar action with Lord Nelson, who says it was a mere flea bite in comparison with this.[38]

By September 12, the wounded had all been transferred to the Crab Island hospital. A US militiaman, Simeon Doty, would later relate his account of the transfer of the dead. "The boats landed on the North end of the Island next to Cumberland Head and the hospital tents were located just south of the landing in the bushes. These tents were built of boards and canvass and were ranged from East to West. A sentry, who wore a red coat and was a British prisoner, was pacing up and down between the tents and keeping guard."[39]

Doty saw that many of the bodies were terribly mutilated when they were brought ashore. In some cases only dismembered limbs and other portions had been found, and he recollected seeing human entrails and other parts, which, as he supposed, had been thrown overboard from the vessels, floating up to the shore at the landing.

Inside the tents the scene was a terrible one: shrieks from the wounded soldiers who were undergoing operations at the hands of the surgeons, others crying and begging relief from their sufferings, while dead men were carried out on rude briers made of poles to the burial yard south of the hospital tents.

Here Doty saw trenches dug, ranging from north to south, into which the bodies were placed. Some of them were rolled up in blankets and others had only their ordinary clothing on. Their heads were placed to the west and their faces downward. The Americans and British were buried indiscriminately together, probably to the number of at least one hundred in his estimation.

Eventually the owner of Crab Island, Caleb Nichols, sent a bill for damages to the United States government. Amongst the itemized entries was $150 to cover burying 150 men on the island.

The Battle of Cumberland Bay

On September 14, with distant gunfire from the north and west, the American gunboats collected the British officers, both dead and surviving, along with the American officers and their dead. They assembled at the dockside and marched in a funerary procession to Riverside Cemetery in Plattsburgh. Here they lay to rest the officers of both sides in a shaded area with full military honours. At a later time additional British army officers were also interred in the same plot.

British prisoners, numbering some 26 officers, 340 seamen, Royal Marines, and 39th Regiment, all departed Plattsburgh on board a steamship destined for Greenbush, NY, on September 15. The American guard was commanded by Captain White Youngs of the 15th Regiment, US Army. Captain Pring wrote his full official admiralty after-action reports, defining the loss of ships and casualties and his perception of why the loss had taken place. This was done in the certain knowledge that he and the other officers of the British fleet would face a future admiralty court martial in the loss of His Majesty's vessels. He also ordered the arrest of Lieutenant Mark Raynham RN, on charges pertaining to his conduct during the battle. On the way back to Kingston, Upper Canada, Raynham escaped custody and was never heard from again.

The British Army Retires from Plattsburgh

On September 6 the eastern column of the British army had encountered the gunboats of Macdonough's fleet. The sharp action between these two forces influenced General Prevost into insisting that his army could not advance farther south without the elimination of the American navy.

In consequence Prevost halted the army and forbade the De Meuron Regiment from assaulting the American Fort Moreau, leaving that unit under constant bombardment for several days. He completely lost the army's momentum by building heavy artillery battery positions. Over the next several days Prevost had corresponded with Captain Downie in an increasingly confrontational manner, in effect an act of bullying a much junior officer into premature action. Prevost expected nothing less than a quick and complete Royal Navy victory over an equally sized American fleet, while he himself balked at attacking an American army of a quarter of his strength.

Prevost also went against the advice of three of his most experienced generals, who favoured an immediate assault on what they knew was an incomplete and weak series of defenceworks. He had also denied them the secret service monies to pay informers to gain intelligence. Instead he had the Quartermaster Generals Department provide intelligence, which on the day of advance proved to be defective and caused an hour's delay in launching the army's attack.

Prevost's timid and tentative approach to the land battle was greatly influenced by his erroneous belief that he was about to face the return of General Izard's army. In short, he believed the misinformation put out by General Macomb's spy network. His inaction allowed an uninterrupted buildup of American forces, mainly Vermont militia, to a point of numerical equality by September 11 and allowed the strengthening of the enemy's defensive works.

The scaling of *Confiance's* guns had signalled the Royal Navy's presence to the land forces. We know that General Robinson was called to Provost's headquarters, where he and the other field commanders were advised of Prevost's plan of attack once the naval battle started. Firstly a bombardment of the American works would begin; General Brisbane's division would engage the American ground troops across the Saranac at both bridges, "To create a diversion in favour of the column under General Robinson." The Quartermaster Generals Department would lead the British troops to cross the Saranac at the ford near Pike's Cantonment and be in a position to attack Macomb's unfinished fortifications from the rear.

The staff meeting took about an hour and ended as the British fleet rounded the tip of Cumberland Head. General Robinson would later quote Prevost as saying, "It is now nine o'clock, march off at ten."[40] This is in direct contradiction to Prevost telling Lord Bathurst that he immediately ordered the troops to advance upon seeing the British fleet entering the bay.

Robinson, like so many others, watched as naval battle began. "Before I left the spot I could perceive showers of grape shot falling about the '*Confiance*' in every direction." From his distant hilltop position he further concluded that "Two thirds of her guns on the larboard side were either dismounted or disabled."[41]

It was 9:30 a.m. when Robinson's troops marched towards the crossing place on the Saranac. Brisbane's force in two columns advanced towards the two bridges in the town near the entrenched American positions. This move precipitated a barrage from the American guns. "When they arrived at the

The Battle of Cumberland Bay

brink of the river, they were saluted with such a storm of shot and grape from our battery, as to compel them to fall back, and make their way into the houses, shops, barns and ditches," as recorded by Eleazer Williams, a U.S. government agent who was present during the battle and was severely wounded. In the burned-out buildings of Plattsburgh, the De Meuron Regiment were reinforced by their reserve battalion, the grey uniformed light infantry of the Canadian Chasseurs. Both regiments had a front row view of the naval action while enduring the American maelstrom.

The Royal Artillery batteries opened up with cannon and rocket fire on the American fortifications. The combined gunfire from both land and lake was so intense that civilian observers watching the battles from Cumberland Head reported that "the ground shook beneath their feet."

Brisbane's efforts at the Plattsburgh bridges were a mere rouse to draw away attention from the battalions under Generals Robinson and Manley Power, who were about to attempt encirclement of the three American forts. General Macomb, the American commander, had long anticipated an encircling manoeuvre from his enemies. He and Major Totten of the US Engineers had both experienced firsthand the delaying tactics used by the British at the Battle of La Colle Mill. They decided on a similar defensive move to slow the enemy forces. Working mostly at night, the US Engineers altered the roads at the ford to Pike's Cantonment by moving trees and undergrowth to block out the genuine road and created false roads, which led away from the shallow ford on the Saranac and into the wilderness.

Initially the British troops were guided by officers from the Quartermaster Generals Department, who believed they had located the ford to Pike's Cantonment. General Macomb's tactics had worked, and the British were led off in the wrong direction, away from the river and the ford, up a series of cart roads leading into the thick woods. Prevost's unwillingness to pay for local guides was now to have dire results. It took an hour of marching and countermarching before the column was placed in the correct direction by Major Nathaniel Thorn of the 3rd Buffs, serving as an assistant quartermaster general, who had found another deeper ford that led to the road leading to the Salmon River settlement.

The exercise was later described by Ensign John Mackenzie Kennedy of the 76th Foot: "They were conducted by a circuitous route, by the guide, to find a ford of the Saranac, which though very deep, they succeeded in crossing without much opposition by the enemy."[42]

The British column had eight light companies of various regiments in the van. These troops were the best suited for skirmishing in the heavy woods and were led by Brevet Lieutenant Colonel Patrick Lindesay of the 39th Dorsetshire Regiment. The battalion and grenadier companies of each regiment followed in column of route, with the usual display of colours and the fife and drum bands playing traditional marching tunes. Two squadrons of the 19th Light Dragoons and a brigade of light six-pounder guns under the command of Brevet Major William Greene, RA, as well as a number of wagons carrying ladders gathered from farms and homes throughout the area, formed part of the column.

Robinson and Manley Power ordered the light companies to wade across the ford, only to be met by musket volleys from the estimated 400 Clinton and Essex militia hidden in the woods. The red-coated light companies rushed to the shore and deployed into the trees and began skirmishing. The New York militiamen quickly retired, not wishing to face the British regulars at close quarters.

Robinson stated in his report that the British troops "dashed down a very steep and high bank and forded the river like so many fox hounds, driving the Doodles before them."

Another observation came from Ensign J. M. Kennedy of the 76th Foot. He described the cool professionalism of a British regular: "An orderly bugler was sounding a call in the middle of the river, when a shot knocked off his head-dress, which was carried down the stream. This accident, however, did not disturb him, for, still continuing to sound; he employed one of his hands in disengaging his forage cap from the strap of his knapsack, and placed it on his head as if nothing had happened."[43]

The brigade now marched over the Saranac and crested the hill, where General Robinson and his staff came into sight of the smoke and fire at Plattsburgh. They could also see the American regulars defending the bridges in Plattsburgh. The 76th and 27th regiments were partly across the river, with two of the six-pounder guns and a number of artillerymen in the process of marching towards the Plattsburgh fortifications. The time was close to 1 p.m. At this moment General Prevost's ADC. Brevet Major William Cochrane of the 103rd Regiment rode up and delivered the handwritten order for retiring.

The Battle of Cumberland Bay

Robinson and Manley Powers were both utterly astounded with the order signed by Adjutant General Baynes. "Equally astonished" was how Robinson would later recall this incident. However, both generals, like their troops, were well disciplined and followed their orders, however distasteful to themselves.

The orders were given to recall the light infantry companies. Instantly the bugles sounded the "retire." The main column was given the order to "about-face," then "quick march" This began its retirement from the field. The ordinary soldiers in these battalions were still carrying the same load in their muskets, not having fired a shot in anger, and many would return to Canada wondering why they had not been allowed to carry the fight to the enemy.

Before hearing the bugles calling out the signal to retire, Captain John Purchas of the 76th's light company spotted a lightly defended American artillery piece in the road. He decided to capture the gun and led a charge into the open roadway, only to find the gun was the bait in a cleverly designed trap. Once out in the open Purchas and his men came under heavy fire from both the Vermont volunteers on the far side of the road and the New York militiamen on the near side. The British had a number of men hit and had to take cover. The "retire" signal was being blown repeatedly, ordering all the light companies back to the main body of British troops.

Captain Purchas now realized that he and his men were surrounded and would soon be wiped out, so he quickly prepared a surrender signal by removing his scarlet coat and white waistcoat. Thrusting his sword through the buttonholes, he fashioned a makeshift white flag of surrender, which he waved frantically. The American troops kept firing until their officers ordered a halt, realizing the small British force was finished. By this time the British main column was seen to be marching back over the rise and possibly to another direction of attack.

The isolated officers and men of the 76th's light company, out in the open area between the two American militia forces, were taken into custody. The count was three officers, Lieutenants George Hatch, George Ogalvie, and Edward Hethrington, and twenty-seven men as prisoners with an undetermined number of soldiers dead, including Captain Purchas.

The American militia were led by Generals Mooers and Wright from New York and General Samuel Strong from Vermont. They quickly reformed their troops along with the two field guns of the US light artillery under Lieutenant Sumpter. The Americans began to follow the British main force back towards the Saranac River. When cresting the hill they encountered the British light troops drawn up in line as a rearguard, with Major Greene's artillery at the ready. The British fired a volley, which quickly drove the Americans back into the woods for shelter. The volley was then replaced by the artillery pieces firing repeatedly into the woods. This process was repeated each time the American force was nearing the British lines. Skirmishing between both forces took place along the Saranac close to the ford, as the bulk of the British regulars marched back to their start point, this time with their colours furled and encased. There was no music; only the rhythmic tap…tap…tap of the drummers kept the troops in step.

General Brisbane's troops were also ordered back to their campgrounds. Brisbane himself rode over to General Prevost's headquarters and demanded to know why the action had been stopped so abruptly. Here he found the headquarter staff preparing for imminent departure. General De Rottenburg informed Brisbane that the loss of the British fleet negated the need to capture Plattsburgh, as the British army could not be sustained without naval support. General Prevost had decided to order the army to retire, and that order would stand. Brisbane had no option but to comply with the order and went about the business of organizing an orderly withdrawal.

The army would move back in stages, covered by the De Meuron Regiment and the Canadian light troops, who were still heavily engaged with the Americans. The Royal Artillery would increase and continue bombarding the enemy with rockets, mortar shells, and continual cannon fire, in some cases using double shot, owing to the large supply of those munitions.

The artillery duel between both sides intensified greatly despite the heavy rains. The American gunners under the leadership of Captain Alexander Brooks US Artillery, were firing from all of the three forts. The British infantry with their baggage train vacated their lines out of range of the American guns. Major Sinclair RA, slowly withdrew each battery in turn. By now the rain was heavy, making movement difficult. The process continued until dusk. When only one last battery remained, he left the area.

The last battery was the Royal Marine Artillery. Captain Parke had his three long twenty-fours taken away in virtual darkness while his second in

The Battle of Cumberland Bay

command, Lieutenant Balchild RMA, continued firing with his three mortars. Once the last round of Balchild's mortar ammunition was fired, the battery was installed on their wagons and then proceeded to join with the rear of the British column.

Royal Artillery diarist J. H. Wood, when describing the bitter disappointment and amazement of the whole force, noted "the unnecessary precipitancy of our retreat, or more properly speaking, our flight…is spoken of with disgust and indignation."[44] The heavy rains that had begun in the afternoon did not stop the movement of troops. It did slow them down, and much in the way of spades, axes, tents, foodstuff, even gunpowder and artillery shells, had to be abandoned or hidden, as not all could be transported. Several wagons got underway but broke down under the excessive weight of their contents. These were destroyed on the spot. An American report stated, "Scattered equipage, broken carriages, abandoned baggage wagons, deserted magazines, and straggling plunderers alone marked the field."

Another incident of note occurred as the bulk of General Prevost's high ranking staff rode past the De Meuron Regiment and the Canadian Chasseurs. The De Meurons merely stood to attention but did not salute by presenting arms. The Canadian Chasseurs reportedly booed and jeered, after four days of being under continual bombardment and being held back, then told to retreat. The frustration of these men was entirely understandable.

The Canadian Chasseurs and the De Meuron Regiment finally left the environs of Plattsburgh by midday of September 12. Their loss in men was relatively light until they reached the Dead Creek, where once again the gunboats of Macdonough's fleet found targets amongst the last of Prevost's invading force. An estimated twenty-two men of the Swiss regiment were killed.

By the time the British rearguard reached Chazy, the De Meuron Regiment had been in continual contact with the American forces from September 6 to 14. The Canadian Chasseurs under Captain Frederic Matthey (De Meuron Regiment) were across Dead Creek ahead of the De Meuron Regiment. They also had an undetermined number of casualties caused by the gunboats, and Lieutenant Edouard Vignau of the Chasseurs was amongst the missing in action.

General Brisbane in his reminiscences of the retreat described another unusual incident. "Destroyed the bridge of communication over Dead Creek. Here I found an old English twenty-four-pounder, which had fallen into the enemy's hands at the end of the American war, at the surrender of Burgoyne at Saratoga, and which I tumbled over the bridge into the creek."[45]

Macomb's troops were understandably cautious of following the British army. They too were finding that the rain had turned roads into quagmires. A quick about-face by Prevost's troops at any time could see the American force caught out in the open with Plattsburgh undefended. A few minor skirmishes took place, and a number of casualties and captures were made on both sides. The British were later described as losing large numbers by desertion. During the advance, no desertions were recorded. When the retreat was completed, the number of British desertions was recorded at 234, amongst which were 161 men of the De Meuron Regiment. These soldiers were all professional mercenaries and would be loyal until the next paymaster's parade. Many, if not all, would have been aware of the benefits of deserting to the American side. The possibility of all the foreign regiments being disbanded and returned to Europe was very likely after this American war ended. So self-preservation, rather than questionable loyalty, drove many to the decision of desertion.

At Chazy both British columns converged, and much of the heavy equipment and supplies were loaded onto barges to be transported northward. General Baynes ordered the 1st Brigade under Robinson to Chambly and La Prairie, the 2nd under Brisbane to La Colle, Ile aux Noix, and St. Jean, and Manley-Power's 3rd Brigade to Odelltown.

The British sick and wounded at Plattsburgh who could not march had all been left behind under the care of a British surgeon aided by local nuns at the Dunham house in Plattsburgh. General Prevost was reminded of them when he arrived at Chazy. There he wrote a note to General Macomb, requesting information regarding the wounded and killed; also he requested that the wounded be humanely treated. The letter was sent under a flag of truce through the advancing American force to Macomb, who by return letter promised casualty details from the naval battle and also gave a positive response to Prevost's request for humane treatment of those left behind.

General Prevost wrote his after-battle report, mostly blaming the Royal Navy for his retreat; he then returned to his Montreal headquarters. He carried on with his duties as before, thinking the war would continue for some

The Battle of Cumberland Bay

time. He anticipated that the Royal Navy would rebuild a fleet to take Lake Champlain, and the British government would continue to send troops as they had been doing. In October he went to Kingston, to be present at the launch of the first-rate ship of the line HMS *St. Lawrence* (112). This vessel was now the most powerful on Lake Ontario. Its presence forced Commodore Chauncey to retire his fleet to Sackets Harbor for protection. The expected movements of *St. Lawrence* also disrupted General Izard's supply line to his forces on the Niagara frontier, forcing him to retire his army back to U.S. territory.

Prevost's enemies, both civil and military, sent a storm of complaints about him. Letters to the newspapers in Canada and the United Kingdom castigated him for his performance at Plattsburgh and before. Complaints were even sent to the Prince Regent. Sir James Yeo sent a report to the Lords of the Admiralty, blaming Prevost for his part in goading Captain Downie into premature action and then not supporting the naval attack in Cumberland Bay.

During the fall of 1814 the British army regrouped along the border area of northern New York. The commander of the Left Division, Major General Baron De Rottenburg, returned to Britain. His place was taken over by Major General Thomas Brisbane. Other changes saw the departure of Major General Sir James Kemp and his ADC, Lieutenant Charles Gore of the 43rd Regiment. Both returned to Britain and were present at Quatre Bras and Waterloo.

Amongst the other officers returning to Britain were Lieutenants Balchild and Stevens of the Royal Marines Artillery Rocket Companies. These officers were required by the Admiralty to report of the effectiveness of the rocket weapon in conjunction with the Royal Marines battalions. On their arrival in England they were subject to an order for mobilization of all officers on leave or on half pay, recalling them for active service against Napoleon. This saw Lieutenant Balchild being sent to Antwerp to take over part of the artillery defending that city. However, Napoleon's army did not make it that far.

General Brisbane found the border skirmishing with the Americans under General Macomb quite disturbing. In his memoirs he described the problems and his solution in this way:

> I found every possible atrocity committed on both sides. The sentries were frequently attacked, and a number of isolated individuals

murdered. This system was so opposite to what I had been accustomed to in the Duke of Wellington's army that I immediately wrote to General Macomb, to propose that we should carry on the warfare on the same system as was followed by the European armies. I received a very polite reply from the General, stating that if I would give the orders to my troops, he would undertake to see them enforced on the part of those of the United States.

Brisbane also commented on a further incident:

The American commander, General Macomb, asked leave to carry away for burial the dead body of one their officers. I at once granted leave, and continued standing beside the Americans while at least 700 Indians stood behind me. They would have otherwise have fallen on the enemy and foully murdered them. From that date I am glad that I can freely state that regulation was most faithfully observed on both sides. So satisfactory and honourable was the communication established between us, that though we never spoke together, yet on the peace being proclaimed, the General actually sent me various letters of introduction to General officers in the United States, and Governors of State. I regret that I never had an opportunity to avail myself of these advantages.[46]

Brisbane, besides being a major general and an old personal friend of the Iron Duke, was also an astronomer of some note. Every time his troops stopped for a break while on the march, he would use his pocket sextant, chronometer, and artificial horizon "to take actitudes of the sun and obtain the true time." In this way Brisbane kept the time for the British army during the peninsular and American campaigns.

Brisbane also kept his mind on the military situation on the border. Early in 1815 the Scotsman presented General Prevost with a proposal for a winter campaign. He had created a detailed plan, complete with three maps based on reports of enemy troop movements, their strength and location. His plan would see 7,000 British troops advance on Plattsburgh once again and follow on through to reach the American fleet at Whitehall and destroy it. The plan did not require British naval superiority!

The Battle of Cumberland Bay

General Prevost was very interested in the plan and was in the process of sanctioning it when news arrived of the Treaty of Ghent. The plan was of course scrapped. The next day Prevost received word of his recall to London on March 15, delivered by Sir George Murray, a much junior officer. This Prevost took as an unfair slight on his efforts and reputation. Prevost was eventually replaced by Sir John Coape Sherbrooke.

Epitaph for the British dead at Crab Island

'Our white bones lie
'Neath the cloudless sky
Of the summer islands fair.
And there's never a bay
In North lad grey
But our British dead are there.'
–Anon.

Royal Marine private's
shoulder-belt plate

Captain's, commander's,
and lieutenant's button

Royal Marine
officer's button

Royal Marine
officer's gorget

7

Actions in Maine, North Point, and Baltimore

The British Occupation of Penobscot

From August 1814 to February 1815, the war had intensified on the eastern seaboard with the capture of a large area of Maine. Sir John C. Sherbrooke, Governor General of Nova Scotia, had been given a similar mandate to that given to General Prevost by the British government. Sherbrooke was given 3,000 regulars from Europe (29th, 60th, 62nd, 98th regiments and a company of Royal Artillery) under Major General Gerard Gosselin, along with a squadron of ships under Rear Admiral Edward Grifith RN. The navy supplied Royal Marines landing parties to supplement the army. Working together they forced the scuttling of USS *Adams* (28) at Hampden, then went on to capture and occupy the entire Penobscot region of Maine.

Royal Marines 2nd Lieutenant George Thomas Welshman of HMS *Tendos* (38) was awarded an honourable mention in dispatches for the capture of three cannons in the expedition against Machias. The cost of capturing Penobscot was two men killed, one missing, Captain Thomas Gell of the 29th, and seven men wounded. The officials from the region, who had been anti-war from the outset, agreed to work with the British authorities and returned to a peaceful trade relationship and even paid taxes and duties on the import and export of goods and materials. These taxes became known as the "Castine fund," which would later finance Nova Scotia's Dalhousie University and the Cambridge Military Library.

The uniforms of the American militia were seized and sent to Halifax as clothing for the refugee former slaves liberated by the Royal Navy incursions into slave-holding states. The American prisoners of war from this area were set free to return home. The occupation of Penobscot lasted until April 26, 1815.

The Battle of North Point

The British forces were now intent on seizing Baltimore, the third largest city in the republic, which in British eyes had become a "Nest of Pirates," describing American privateers, who had cost much loss to British commerce and were greatly detested by the Royal Navy. Within three weeks, an even larger assemblage of Royal Navy ships sailed into the Patapsco River. It was September 11, 1814.

When assembled, the reinforced British fleet flew the pennants of three admirals, Cochrane, Cockburn, and Plutney Malcolm (brother of Major James Malcolm, commanding the 2nd Battalion Royal Marines). There were over fifty major warships, including ten ships of the line, carrying a total of 736 guns. The rest of the fleet contained frigates, sloops, brigs, bomb ships, and rocket ships. Six troop ships, carrying the same regiments that were present at Bladensburg, all formed part of the combined attacking force.

The largest vessels with the deepest draft formed the North Point Squadron. These, with the troop ships and some smaller craft, sailed into Old Roads Bay. Admiral Cockburn switched his role to that of colonel of Royal Marines and joined the launches, barges, cutters, and pinnacles filled with soldiers, Royal and Colonial Marines, plus 600 sailors, a total of 4,500 men under the joint command of Cockburn and Ross.

The attacking British were apprehensive on landing; the closeness of trees and abundant cover could easily contain hundreds of armed Americans. They were indeed under observation by a screen of riflemen and cavalry. The main force of 3,200 Americans under Brigadier General John Stricker USA, were waiting at a "choke" point where Bread and Cheese Creek and Bear Creek had only a narrow strip of land between them, near a wood called Maiden's Choice. The American force was placed across the North Point Road. Six field guns of Captain Montgomery's Union Artillery, flanked by the 27th and the 5th Maryland militia regiments with riflemen, posted towards Bear Creek. In reserve were the 39th and 51st regiments, with a further reserve of the 6th regiment at Cook's Tavern.

Actions in Maine, North Point, and Baltimore

Under the protection of naval guns in the squadron and the carronades in the landing boats, the British soldiers and marines assembled on landing and quickly set up a defensive perimeter, but no opposition was encountered. The troops were issued with twenty additional cartridges to augment the usual sixty carried in an attack; they also carried a blanket, spare shirt, and a spare pair of boots as their only field equipment. This was planned to be a quick, decisive assault.

As the bulk of the landing force arrived with their field guns and rockets, the first light troops set out on the North Point Road to Baltimore. The officers' breakfast was taken at the Gorsuch House, where three captured cavalrymen of the 1st Baltimore Hussars were interrogated. The information obtained was on the main defences at Baltimore with the large proportion of militia units. Ross commented that he didn't care "if it rains militia." The closeness of General Stricker's command was never divulged.

After breakfast General Ross and his ADC were with the 85th Light Infantry at the front of the column. Admiral Cockburn was with the bulk of the column, which was still forming before following behind.

At 1 p.m. on September 12, Stricker moved forward a vanguard of 250 men of the 5th Mechanical Volunteers Regiment, commanded by Major Richard Heath. Both sides were advancing slowly. At a sudden turning in the road they came upon each other in a heavily wooded area. An ineffective volley was fired at the British advance party, numbering about fifty light infantrymen.

Ross ordered a return volley and then a charge to make the Americans think the entire British force was immediately behind him. A young private of Captain Edward Asquith's rifle company fired at the forty-eight-year-old Irish general, delivering a mortal wound. The ball passed through his right arm and into his breast, Ross slumped forward and nearly fell off his horse. The efforts of his ADC, Captain Duncan MacDougall, held him in place until many hands gently lifted the dying man and carried him to the shade of a nearby tree. Ross's horse ran back through the line of advancing redcoats. They could see the blood-spattered saddle and they knew who its master was.

Ross lived long enough to pass leadership of the army to Colonel Arthur Brooke of the 44th East Essex Regiment. The British 85th Foot advanced quickly towards the retreating American militia, eventually reaching General Stricker's main defence line of infantry and guns "behind a stout paling," immediately engaging them and being quickly supported by the other

British battalions. The 2nd Battalion Royal Marines was held in reserve while the Colonial Marines and the naval seamen and ships marines under Captain Robyns RM, took the extreme left of the British line.

Colonel Brooke ordered his field artillery and rocket batteries into place and began to fire on the American centre and left flank. As had happened before, Lieutenant John Lawrence RMA, commanding the Royal Marine Artillery firing Congreve rockets, greatly unnerved the American militia. Brooke ordered his infantry forward to flank the American line; this was countered by Stricker advancing the 39th and 51st Maryland Militia regiments into line on his left flank.

The 51st became confused in performing the wheeling into line movement. Colonel Brooke, seeing the American confusion, ordered a relentless volley of musketry, followed by a charge into the American left flank. Lieutenant Gleig of the 85th would later write of this episode,

> A hearty British cheer gave notice of our willingness to meet them, and firing and running we gradually closed upon them, with the design of bringing the bayonet into play. Volley upon volley having been given, we were now advanced within less than twenty yards of the American line; yet such was the denseness of the smoke, that it was only when a passing breeze swept away the cloud for a moment, that either force became visible to each other. The flashes of the enemy's muskets alone served as an object to aim at, as, without doubt, the flashes of our own muskets alone guided the enemy.[47]

The American 51st staggered under the weight of the assault and pulled back, taking part of the 39th with them. The American centre and right flank held steady with the Union Artillery and the 5th Mechanical Volunteers holding firm, "resting their arms on the palings, and taking deliberate aim," thereby inflicting heavy casualties on the British 44th and 21st Regiments. General Stricker, concerned that his exposed left flank would cause an American rout, ordered his troops to fall back on their reserve regiment, the 6th Maryland, waiting at Worthington Mill. As the Americans retreated the cohesion was lost, and as Lieutenant Scott RN, noted on turning the American left flank, "It was a second edition of the Bladensburg Races." The Royal Navy blue jackets captured one fieldpiece. In the words of Lieutenant Scott RN,

Actions in Maine, North Point, and Baltimore

It now became a regular chase and numerous Americans were taken prisoners. We popped upon one fellow, who impressed with the erroneous idea that he would receive no quarter, had determined to sell his life as dearly as possible. I observed him leveling his rifle, and called upon him to surrender. We were not half a dozen paces apart, but, instead of complying with my command, he fired, the ball grazed my left side cutting my flannel waistcoat, and unfortunately entered the breast of the young man close behind me, named Edmondson, who was attached to the *Albion*'s party.[48]

The American force was chased back past the 6th Maryland Militia at Cook's Tavern and a further seven miles to the main Baltimore defence line at Hampstead Hill. The British troops, much fatigued by the march and battle, stopped the advance at the sound of a bugle call to halt. Admiral Cockburn now returned to the field of battle, after escorting General Ross's body back to the fleet. He joined several soldiers filling their canteens and began to water his horse. Unexpectedly a volley was fired from the branches of nearby trees by American riflemen. This killed several men and grazed the horse's shoulder. The admiral had been the obvious target, but he remained unhurt.

At the close of day the British had 39 killed, 251 wounded, and 50 missing. The American losses were 24 killed, 139 wounded, and 50 prisoners. Two American field pieces were also captured.

The wounded men from both sides were carried to the Methodist meeting house. This being the only sizable building near to the scene, it was converted into a temporary hospital for both sides. The meeting house was placed under military guard. Amongst the severely wounded was Captain John Roybins RM. The dead for the most part were left where they fell as the British pursued the retreating Americans. These fallen soldiers were eventually buried in what was then a burial ground on the Weatherby farm. The site is now covered by the Norris Farm Landfill.

The next day at 1 a.m. in the pouring rain, the British army neared the Baltimore defensive lines at Hampstead Hill. Colonel Brooke was advised by his officers that an estimated force of 15,000 militia was strongly entrenched and supported by up to 100 naval guns, all sited in redoubts and laid in such a way as to give crossfire if attacked. Indeed, one observer noted that the naval entrenchments on Hampstead Hill had taken on the appearance of a fully armed frigate, with guns run out through the embrasures and with sailors armed with muskets, cutlasses, and boarding pikes. One hundred seventy US Marines were situated in the rear as a support for the batteries. Baltimore's City Council had formed a Committee of Public Safety in 1813, when the British began raids in the Chesapeake. The defences were constructed from that time forward and were renewed with intensity after the occupation of Washington, when Mayor Edward Johnston formed a replacement Committee of Vigilance and Safety to strengthen efforts to defend the city. Baltimoreans had raised half a million dollars towards the defence of the city. The command of Baltimore's land defences was given to Major General Smith, who achieved this post after much political controversy.

Colonel Brooke had serious reasons to reconsider his attack. He called for support from the Royal Navy vessels; when these ships fired at the American positions, the fall of shot was ineffective, as the ships' guns could not get enough elevation. He had also requested a diversionary naval attack in a separate location to make the Americans think a separate landing was taking place.

Brooke ultimately decided any further attempt by his army would only meet with devastatingly high casualties. In consequence he sent an officer to Admiral Cochrane, cancelling the naval diversion, then ordered a return of the army to the landing place. During this retirement the army deployed its artillery and rearguard infantry on more than one occasion, expecting to ward off an American attack. In each instance it was merely United States cavalry scouts that were encountered, and no further serious action was undertaken.

Heavy rains continued throughout the day. By completion of the re-embarkation it was reported that up to 200 prisoners had been taken by the British army.

The Bombardment of Baltimore

Before taking command of naval forces in North America, Admiral Cochrane had discussed at length with Lord Bathurst the overall strategy of the war and the economic implication of blockading the U.S. ports and providing Royal Navy protection to convoys of merchant vessels crossing the Atlantic to continue British maritime trade.

Actions in Maine, North Point, and Baltimore

Portrait of Rear Admiral George Cockburn RN
Lieutenant-Colonel of Royal Marines.

His predecessor, Admiral Sir John B. Warren, had been seen as not aggressive enough with his blockade and too complaining to the Admiralty when his vessels were needed for convoy duty. Admiral Cochrane would change all that. As soon as the British army in Europe did not need supplies from the New England states, the licences granted by Warren were cancelled, and New England was also subjected to blockade. The renewed effort in the Chesapeake meant as many as 200 vessels were lying idle in Baltimore, and hundreds more in other locations throughout the U.S. were unable to leave port. Those American privateers who did escape the blockade had to go as far as the coasts of Britain to find relatively unprotected prizes. In many instances only the prize vessels' cargo could be sold, and the ship itself would be destroyed at sea, the privateers unable to sail them back to America for fear of capture by the blockade.

Rockets, Bombs and Bayonets

The Royal Navy now had a stranglehold on the United States economy, and this was being ever tightened by Admiral Cochrane. This is why he wanted to preserve the army to hit larger, more valuable targets, such as Baltimore, New York, Rhode Island, Boston, and New Orleans. The destruction of these economic targets would destroy the United States war efforts from within, both monetarily and politically, not to mention the portion of prize money that would be Cochrane's share. The Admiral even employed a full time accountant on board ship, to keep his books up to date and to ensure his full payment from the prize agents.

After the Washington campaign, Cochrane, Cockburn, Malcolm, and Ross waited for the return of Captain Gordon in the *Seahorse;* he arrived on the 9th of September with his squadron fully intact and escorting an epic haul of twenty-one fully loaded prizes. HMS *Menelaus,* Captain Sir Peter Parker's ship, and his small squadron had also rejoined the fleet. Parker himself had been killed during a raid at the Battle of Caulk's Field. His body had been recovered and was sent to Bermuda for interment, eventually being sent on to England for final interment at his family vault in St. Margaret's, Westminster. The Royal Navy combined high command seemed to have some confusion on whether to attack Baltimore or New York. Cockburn provided a plan to attack Baltimore immediately; this was rejected by Cochrane. After deciding to take the bulk of the fleet northward, he recanted and decided to attack Baltimore, but using a plan other than Cockburn's.

By the evening of September 9, Vice Admiral Cochrane's combined fleet anchored off the Patuxent. Each moment of indecision and delay had only strengthened Baltimore's defences. The following morning saw fifty warships under a full spread of canvas heading for Baltimore.

September 10 and 11 saw much activity amongst the American defenders. Commodore John Rogers USN, and Major George Armistead USA, sent a communication to General Smith detailing the dispositions of officers and men of USS *Guerriere,* who had been distributed to various key locations on the approaches to the city, both on land and on the shore, the sailors manning batteries of varying size and numbers of guns.

On September 12 Admiral Cochrane transferred his flag from HMS *Tonnant* (80) to the shallow draught frigate HMS *Surprise* (38), commanded by his son Captain Thomas Cochrane RN. This frigate would allow Cochrane to sail closer to Baltimore and direct the naval attack on Fort McHenry.

Actions in Maine, North Point, and Baltimore

Captain of the Fleet Edward Codrington, newly appointed a rear admiral, wrote a letter to his wife in London:

> The work of destruction is now about to begin and there will probably be many broken heads tonight. The army with as many seamen and marines as possibly could be spared were all landed this morning and now are now on their march to the town of Baltimore. The bomb vessels, brigs & frigates, are all pushing up the river with an eagerness which must annoy the enemy, I presume as much as it delights me.[49]

Baltimore's manmade defences were considerable, but the natural obstacle of muddy water was best described by Midshipman Robert Barret RN, who served in HMS *Hebrus* (38):

> Departing from our gallant comrades, we proceeded, without delay, under sail, in company with frigates, sloops, and bombs, etc. To take up a position where we might be enabled to attack the sea defences of Baltimore. Leaving the line of battle ships, which on account of their size, could not proceed any farther than North Point, our frigates sailed through the mud for miles...As we proceeded up the river, doubtless the Americans were struck with panic and amazement, for although they built frigates at this port, yet they always sailed down the river, flying light, as far as Annapolis, where, I was informed, they completed for sea, by taking in their guns, provisions, and water.[50]

In the opposing navy, the progress of the British fleet was also under observation. Sailing Master George De La Roche USN, on board the sloop of war USS *Erie* (22), recorded in his diary,

> Having at daylight discovered that the British had succeeded in forcing three frigates inside the Man of War Shoals fifteen miles below, and were coming up with a fine breeze, contrary to our expectations. I sent word to Commo. J. Rogers then in command, and as our own broadside was too light to withstand frigates, was ordered to bring the ship near Baltre, again. Began to sink ships in the channel, and then was given by Commo. Rogers the command of the most

advanced battery between the Philadelphia & Sparrow's Point Road, three hundred yards in advance of all others, of three 12-pounders, thirty two officers & men, and military corps for small arms.[51]

USS *Erie* was positioned off Jackson's Wharf near Fells Point, where it ran out spring lines to enable it to swing around and use its armament of two long eighteen-pounders and twenty thirty-two-pounder carronades, in the event of British gunboats making it past the block ships and outer defences.

Another American naval officer concerned about the approach of the large enemy fleet was Commodore Oliver Hazard Perry USN. In a letter to a friend he wrote, "It is, at this moment, said the enemy are now standing up the river for this place with about forty sail. I shall stay by my ship and take no part in the militia fight. I expect to have to burn her." Perry had recently been placed in command of the new ship USS *Java*, under construction but not yet complete. Perry and his men were consigned to a battery of six-pounder guns with one eighteen-pounder. When the time came for action, his guns ran out of ammunition without damaging the British ships.

Three heavy metal chains had been suspended from blocks and stretched across from Lazarreto Point to Fort McHenry; in addition, a series of vessels had been sunk as block ships across the harbour. Lieutenant Solomon Rutter USN, sent a written report on September 11 detailing the distribution of naval manpower between barges (gunboats) and batteries. The report also stated three long eighteen-pounders at the Lazaretto, fit for service with 100 rounds of ammunition. Eight barges were up with long eight-pounders and four with long twelve-pounders and all with gunades (swivel guns of small calibre).[52]

Admiral Cochrane's bombardment squadron consisted of six frigates, five bomb ships, five schooners, one rocket ship, and one brig. The force also had a number of gunboats and smaller craft. As previously arranged the five bomb vessels took up a line abreast of Fort McHenry, approximately 2 3/4 miles from the fort and about 3 miles from Fort Covington. At 6:30 a.m. on September 13 the bomb ship HMS *Volcano* fired its thirteen-inch sea mortar, followed by another discharge from its ten-inch mortar. Both shells fell short of the bastions of Fort McHenry.

With the range checked a signal was raised, and *Volcano* moved closer to the fort, with its sister ships and the support vessels forming a half-circle two miles below Fort McHenry. The remainder of the bombardment squadron

Actions in Maine, North Point, and Baltimore

formed a second line behind the bomb ships and the rocket ship HMS *Erebus*. The guns at the fort began a brisk fire on their attackers, the shot and shell falling amongst the British squadron. Admiral Cochrane signalled a retirement of the force back to a safe distance of two miles from the fort. The American guns fell silent while the British rockets and mortar bombs continued falling on and beyond the fort.

From commencement till noon *Volcano* alone had expended seventy-three shells from each of its ten-inch and thirteen-inch mortars. *Aetna, Meteor, Terror,* and *Devastation* also kept up their fiery assault. Numerous shells fell behind the fort, one of which landed within a hundred yards of USS *Java* moored at Flanagan's and Parson's Wharf, nearly three miles distant.

The British had a clear view beyond the fort and into the North West Branch. Here could be seen numerous mastheads of merchant vessels, privateers, and the federal navy ships *Erie, Ontario,* and *Java,* all located in or near the dockyards at Fells Point. At the onset of the Royal Navy bombardment, Sailing Master Beverly Diggs USN, received orders to take several more vessels and sink them as block ships in the channel between Lazaretto Point and the fort.

US gun barge number 7, commanded by Diggs, towed the schooners *Packet* and *Enterprise,* the letter of marque vessels *Temperance* and *Father and Son,* plus some others and sunk these while under fire from the British fleet. A new large steamboat, the 130-foot *Chesapeake* of the Union line, was also used as a block ship, but it was allowed to stay afloat.

The bombardment continued during the day amidst heavy downpours of rain. The consumption of ammunition was excessive, and the bomb vessels and rocket ship transferred munitions from the large number of fleet tenders. The *Niles' Weekly Register* reported, "That at every discharge (a bomb ship) was forced two feet into the water by the force of it, thus straining every part from stem to stern." The heavy sea mortars had various types of ammunition; a thirteen-inch mortar could easily send a 190-pound cast iron exploding shell two miles. The bomb shell might be fused to explode over the target or explode on impact. Another type known as carcasses were incendiary bombs and meant to explode in flame and burn continuously to destroy wooden structures and ships. Only a handful of the latter were used at Baltimore.

Lieutenant Henry Newcomb USN, at Fort Covington made note in his report, "2 p.m., wind at the N.E. with heavy showers of rain." Within the same hour, a British mortar bomb flew at a high arc over the Patapasco River, landing squarely on a twenty-four-pounder mounted on the southwest bastion of Fort McHenry. None of the defenders had seen its flight, owing to the pouring rain. Third Lieutenant Levi Claggett of the Baltimore Artillery Company of Fencibles was killed instantly and four of his gun crew severely wounded.

When the wreckage was being cleared another shell came down and burst over the heads of the defenders. Private Isaac Monroe later described the event:

> Sergeant [John] Clemm, a young man of most amiable character, gentlemanly manners, and real courage, was killed by my side; a bomb bursting over our heads [when] a piece of the size of a dollar, two inches thick, passed through his body in a diagonal direction from his navel, and went into the ground upwards of two feet."[53]

The lookouts on the British ships reported seeing a large number of defenders running to and fro in confusion amongst the American battery. Admiral Cochrane took this to mean that the bombardment had succeeded and the American artillerymen were now deserting their posts. He ordered the signal to advance the squadron closer to the fort, where it would increase the destruction on the fort and force the abandonment of the shore batteries.

Fort McHenry was defended by 1,035 men, mainly United States Corps of Artillery and regulars from the 38th, 36th, and 14th United States Infantry. Other units of militia were also present, such as the US Sea Fencibles, the Baltimore Independent Artillery, and the Washington Artillery. A United States Navy contingent of sixty seamen from the Chesapeake Flotilla under Sailing Master Solomon Rodman also manned the fort's guns. The entire defence was under the command of Major George Armistead of the US Corps of Artillery.

Armistead later reported, "The bustle necessarily produced in removing the wounded and re-mounting the gun probably induced the enemy to suspect that we were in a state of confusion, as he brought three of his bomb ships to what I believe to be good striking distance."[54]

As the British ships neared the fort, Major Armistead mounted the parapet and studied the advance of the enemy, and when the distance was right he ordered a battery of twenty-four-pounders to open fire. Immediately after the initial American discharge, the thirty-six-pounder French-built naval guns

Actions in Maine, North Point, and Baltimore

under the direction of Sailing Master Rodman fired a single broadside in unison, just as if on shipboard. The sound of the heavy, repeated firing from Fort McHenry could be heard all over the city. The *Niles' Weekly Register* would later report that "the houses in the city were shaken to their foundations for never, perhaps from the time of invention of cannon to the present day, were the number of field pieces fired with so rapid succession."

By 3 p.m. the Americans had scored several hits on the nearest vessels. Bomb ships *Volcano* under Commander David Price RN, and *Devastation*, commanded by Captain Thomas Alexander RN, were hit several times, as was a nearby gunboat. The British rehoisted their sails and moved out of range. This time an even more severe bombardment followed. The fort's powder magazine was hit, but, fortunately for the defenders, the bomb failed to explode. The bombardment continued as the rain intensified

Later, as daylight began to fade to darkness, the city lights of Baltimore were ordered extinguished. As the rain continued, the bombardment did likewise. Admiral Cochrane put in motion the previously arranged diversionary attack on the far side of Baltimore harbour. This attack was to draw forces away from the landward defences at Hampstead Hill while Colonel Brooke launched the main attack at those defences.

Despite being pressed by Admiral Cockburn to attack, Brooke and his officers had decided the American position was too strong and sent a message to Admiral Cochrane to halt the diversionary attack. The messenger arrived too late.

Admiral Cochrane, unaware of Brooke's decision, proceeded with the attack on Ferry Branch. Several gunboats came alongside HMS *Surprise* to hear final instructions from the Admiral. At 10 p.m. twenty-eight-year-old Lieutenant Charles Napier RN, of HMS *Euryalus* (38), who had recently served as second in command to Captain Gordon in the successful offensive against Alexandria, was ordered to take command of the twenty gunboats and row close to the western shore, round the Point of Patapasco, and proceed up the river one and a half miles, then drop their grapnels and remain quiet until 1 a.m. At that time a signal would be given for the gunboats to engage the shore batteries on the Ferry Branch side of the river. At Fort Covington Lieutenant Newcomb noted in his report, "10 p.m., the enemies barges all in motion. Weather thick & hazy, with frequent showers of rain."

Lieutenant Napier's flotilla, armed with twelve, eighteen, and twenty-four-pounder cannon, silently slipped away from the larger British warships. Each oar was muffled and each command was whispered. The heavy rain and dark night caused some of the gunboats to unknowingly row towards the American defences at the Lazaretto. The main part of Napier's force continued past Fort McHenry and towards Fort Covington and Battery Babcock. Once abreast of Fort Covington the flotilla silently slipped their anchors into the water and positioned their craft with cannons facing the fort and began to wait for the signal at 1 a.m.

At Battery Babcock, six eighteen-pounder French naval guns, loaded with round shot and canister, stood ready and waiting. Sailing Master John Webster and his men were vigilant and began to notice the small glimmering lights in different places out in the darkness off shore near Fort Covington. Newcomb and his men also noticed the lights. Realizing these were lit matches used for detonating cannon, the American officers reacted.

Immediately both shore batteries opened up on the British boats lying two to three hundred yards out in the water. Fort Lookout also began firing out into the dark of the night, trying to find the British vessels. Napier's flotilla had been discovered. He had no alternative but to return the American fire.

The British boats off Lazaretto Point had also been spotted by the defenders. An urgent message was sent to Commodore Rogers by Lieutenant Solomon Frazer, indicating his belief that a landing at the Lazaretto was about to be attempted by the British. A detachment of Pennsylvania Riflemen led by Master's Mate Robert Stockholm was sent by Rogers to reinforce Frazer's battery. The wayward British gunboats quickly withdrew to the safety of the squadron, amidst a shower of grapeshot and cannon fire.

Lieutenant Napier kept his gunboats firing at the various shore batteries, which were now supported by the circular battery at Fort Lookout. The duel was maintained for about two hours. Napier decided to return his flotilla to the fleet. At least two of his gunboats had been severely damaged with a number of casualties; several British dead were floating in the river. The mandate of providing a diversion had been met as much as was possible under the circumstances. Napier decided to abort the attack at about 2 a.m.

On Wednesday, September 14, the British bomb ships fired the last of their rounds at Fort McHenry before hoisting the answer signal to the fleet order for cease fire. The time was 7 a.m. The British army was in full retirement back to

Actions in Maine, North Point, and Baltimore

the North Point anchorage. Commander Price of HMS *Volcano* entered in the ship's logbook that the vessel had expended 278 shells during the bombardment. By 9 a.m. the Americans could see clearly that the British fleet was sailing back to North Point inlet.

The night's casualties were light for the Americans, four defenders killed and twenty-four wounded. The British had lost an undetermined number of sailors and marines, killed or wounded, from Napier's gunboats but had no other deaths in the bombardment squadron. Baltimore had survived the heaviest bombardment of the war and thwarted the land attack, in both instances by anticipation, forethought, and preparation. As the British warships left, a single cannon was fired in defiance, and an oversized American flag was raised over Fort McHenry.

The pyrotechnic display was observed by lawyer Francis Scott Key, who was present and under Royal Marine guard on board a truce vessel, attempting to obtain the release of a Dr. William Beanes, who had been apprehended by the British for his attempts in arresting stragglers following the march on Washington. Key later wrote a poem that eventually became the United States' national anthem in 1931. This is perhaps the most well-known and enduring incident from the War of 1812.

The bombarding British fleet included five bomb vessels and one rocket ship. While overall command of each vessel was in the hands of a Royal Navy officer, the main armament was under the direction of the Royal Marines Artillery officer. HMS *Erebus*, a sloop fitted to fire Congreve rockets from the scuttles (apertures) in its sides, was commanded by Captain David E. Bartholomew RN, and the rocket detachment was under 1st Lieutenant Theophilus Samuel Beauchant RMA, who provided the "rockets' red glare" during the bombardment of Fort McHenry. The bomb vessels were HMS *Volcano*, Commander David Price RN, and 2nd Lieutenant J.P. Furzer RMA; HMS *Devastation*, Commander Thomas Alexander RN, and 1st Lieutenant James Adolphus Moore RMA; HMS *Terror*, Commander John Sheridan RN, and 1st Lieutenant J. Walker RMA; HMS *Aetna*, Captain Richard Kenah RN, and 2nd Lieutenant Robert Wright RMA; and HMS *Meteor*, Captain Samuel Roberts RN, and 1st Lieutenant H. A. Napier RMA. These vessels and their Royal Marine Artillery detachments fired the "bombs bursting in air."

In his dispatches Admiral Cochrane described the attack on Baltimore as a "demonstration" and indicated that the defeat of the American army at

North Point greatly contributed to the general alarm and despondency throughout the entire Baltimore area. Admiral Cockburn saw the land attack as a military failure, in which he saw Colonel Brooke as the weak link. Colonel Brooke's dispatch indicated that the withdrawal was in no way his fault. There was no retribution for any of these leading officers in this event, despite the disastrous consequences to the British position at the peace talks in Ghent.

Before dispersing his fleet back to Bermuda and Halifax on September 19, Cochrane learned that another British army of 7,000 veteran troops was in transit to Jamaica. He had already begun plans for an attack on New Orleans. He ordered Cockburn to have his ships refitted in Bermuda, then proceed to create a diversion by blockading the coasts of South Carolina and Georgia.

Admiral Malcolm, in his flagship HMS *Royal Oak* (74), and his squadron would maintain the blockade of the Chesapeake Bay. On October 4 he sent a force of ten ships and a number of barges up the Coan River with the intention of capturing three American schooners. The initial British boat assault was repulsed by the American militia. Then reinforcements arrived in the form of 3,000 British, consisting of the 21st North British Fusiliers, 44th East Essex Regiment, and Royal Marines and seamen. These were landed at Black Point on the Coan and on the Yeocomico River at Mundy Point and Ragged Point. A short battle ensued, and the Lancaster County militia retired to the Northumberland county courthouse. Further skirmishing took place against 100 militiamen under Lt. Col. Thomas Dowling and also Captain William Jett's riflemen. While a small number of British troops were killed and wounded, the most significant loss was that of Captain Richard Kenah RN, of HMS *Aetna*. He was killed by riflefire from Captain Jett's men. The British captured thirty to forty stands of arms with ammunition; they took livestock and burned several buildings and enabled refugee slaves to leave their masters. The British had a number of Colonial Marines guide their attacks, these men being former slaves from the area.

Actions in Maine, North Point, and Baltimore

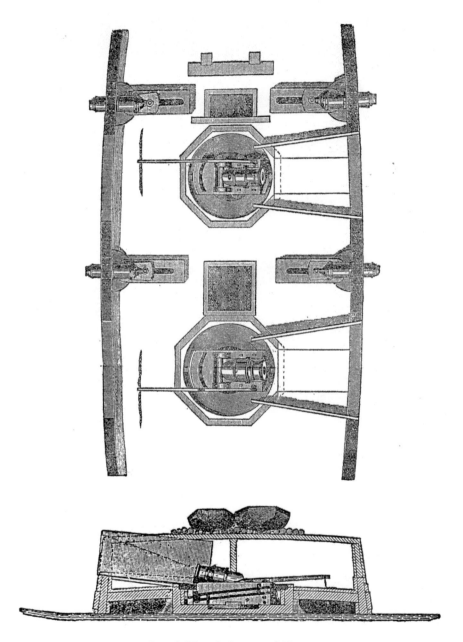

Bomb Vessel–Sectional View
From a drawing by Lieut.-General Sir W. Congreve

Captain
Royal Navy

Seaman
Royal Navy

8

A Dangerous Voyage

As the British fleets dispersed to Halifax and the Caribbean, the watch for American privateers was an ever-present task when convoying vessels to and from ports in Britain and the rest of Europe. One incident involved the bomb ship HMS *Volcano* escorting transports *Golden Fleece* and *Balahoo*, with 250 officers and men of the 85th Foot on board, including Lieutenant Gleig, in passage to Port Royal, Jamaica.

At 2 o'clock in the morning of October 31, a strange sail was reported astern of the British vessels. When in range the large American privateer fired three shots over the British vessels to make them heave-to. The American privateer was a clipper built schooner, painted black with a white streak along its side. It was later identified as *Saucy Jack* (7) out of Charlestown, South Carolina, commanded by Captain Jean Pierre Chazel, a naturalized American originally from Santo Domingo. All on board the bomb and transports went quickly to quarters and cleared for action. *Volcano* then closed with the *Golden Fleece* and indicated that it intended to make a fight of it. Both British vessels reduced sail, while the privateer closed astern, following in their wake. As daylight came on, the privateer set more sail and ran to the windward, keeping just out of gunshot. To bring it within gunshot, *Volcano* and *Golden Fleece* hoisted colours and fired a single gun each to signify defiance. *Volcano* then hoisted its fore and main sails in a lubberly manner. This was to make the predator believe they were ordinary merchant vessels. The American ship began to close into gunshot range while still not hoisting its own colours. From its build and rig it was recognized as a well-built large schooner with seven ports a side and apparently crowded with men. Only a few hands were kept on deck, both in the bomb and the transport, with the mortars and carronades on *Volcano* being hidden under tarpaulins and canvas to look like deck cargo. The bomb ship was described by Lieutenant Gleig as an "ugly, three-massed thing, with exactly the appearance of a merchantman."

Captain Chazel's schooner hoisted the American colours and fired a broadside at *Volcano*, and then one at *Golden Fleece*. The schooner, whose name was now close enough to read, then stood for *Volcano*, making a run at it to get alongside and board. As it approached, the transport *Golden Fleece*, which carried eight four-pounders, called the men to man the guns and fired broadside, which slammed into the American vessel. At the same time the *Volcano* got in two "well aimed broadsides" from its quickly stripped carronades. Lieutenant Furzer's Royal Marine Artillery detachment fired the two mortars that had been loaded prior to being hidden under tarpaulins, each with a keg of one hundred iron one-pound balls. The borders on *Saucy Jack*'s deck were hit hard, and many became casualties; but the schooner had too much speed and swept in, colliding with *Volcano*. The privateer sheared alongside, its seamen firing musketry. Lieutenant Furzer was shot dead "while in the act of flinging a hand-grenade amongst the close packed enemy." The Americans, despite being taken aback, tried to board the British vessel but before the grappling irons held, *Saucy Jack* sheared off and slid clear of the bomb vessel. Eight borders were left hanging on *Volcano*'s bowsprit and soon dropped into the sea.

Chazel quickly ordered his men to make all sail and made off as fast as he had come, with at least two round shots embedded in the hull. *Saucy Jack* also received a sharp fusillade from the soldiers of the 85th standing along the transport's bulwarks. Both British ships made sail to follow the enemy, *Volcano* "firing with great precision at the yards and rigging in the hope of disabling him." The American, however, managed to escape serious damage aloft. Lieutenant Gleig reported, "We had the mortification to see her, within a few minutes, beyond our reach." In addition to Lieutenant Furzer two seamen were killed; one gunner, RMA, and a seaman were wounded on

A Dangerous Voyage

board the bomb. The transport had no casualties. Furzer's body was buried next day in Jamaica, at Fort Rock, a short distance from Port Royal. Present were the officers of HMS *Volcano* plus several officers of the 85th.

On November 14 Captain Price wrote a letter to Lieutenant Colonel Furzer, Royal Marines Barracks, Stonehouse, Devon. The letter went by packet to Falmouth and then on to Stonehouse but was passed on to the elder Furzer's home at Budleigh Satterton near Exmouth, Devon. The letter contained the news of the death of his son. The letter's main content dealt mostly with the disposal of the young Furzer's personal effects and a codicil to his will that had been added just prior to his participation in the bombardment of Baltimore. The details of the exact disposition of his effects show the realization by this young officer of the dangers of his military calling. His father, also a Royal Marine officer, must have cherished this last link to his son. Six weeks after the bombardment of Baltimore, two of the British officers heavily involved in the action were now dead in very dissimilar circumstances.

Gunner
Royal Navy

Royal Marine
pouch ornament

Private
Royal Marines

9

Operations Against the Coast of Georgia and Alabama

Tangier Island, centrally located in Chesapeake Bay, is, in size, 1.2 square miles (3.2 square kilometres) off the mainland of Virginia and since the spring of 1814 had been the staging area of the Royal Navy's attacks in the Chesapeake area. After the attack on Baltimore, the British land forces regrouped at Fort Albion to await further orders on the next deployment.

While the local population were technically prisoners of war, they were allowed to continue their normal lives of crab fishing and farming. The British maintained good relations and purchased all food supplies from the locals and at Fort Albion dug wells and constructed officers' quarters, parade grounds, gardens, and numerous huts for new soldiers under instruction (Colonial Marines), and two redoubts had installed eight large cannons. Prior to embarking on the Baltimore campaign the local pastor, Reverend Joshua Thomas (known as Parson of the Islands), was asked to deliver a sermon to the troops. He complied, and in his sermon he warned the British against their impending defeat. Now after the withdrawal from Baltimore the British transports were back, and troops began preparations for further actions.

In this period the 3rd Battalion Royal Marines was reorganized with additional ships marines being added and a "combing" of the Colonial Marines, retaining the stronger best suited soldiers, while the remainder were placed as guards on ships and the naval base. Another change was the replacement of the commanding officer Major George Lewis RM, owing to health reasons, by Captain William Thomas Clements RM.

While the British were reorganizing and rearming for the coming offensive in New Orleans, Vice Admiral Cochrane had a special unit formed, much like the special forces of the modern era. The commanding officer of this unit was Major Edward Nicolls RM. He was given the local rank of Lieutenant Colonel. His second in command, Lieutenant Robert Henry RMA, was given the local rank of captain; 2nd Lieutenant William Allen RM, and 2nd Lieutenant J. McWilliam were both given the local rank of captain. Sergeant J. Chapman RM, was given the acting rank of lieutenant, and Adjt. Assistant Surgeon Gooder RN, promoted to surgeon. The rest of the party consisted of twelve RMA non-commissioned officers and gunners, plus sixty infantry marines, all picked men. With the unit were 180 Indians, including several chiefs of the Creek and Choctaw tribes. This unusual composite unit was embarked on four vessels under the command of Captain the Honourable Henry Percy RN. His ships were HMS *Hermes* (22) and HMS *Carron* (20), both corvettes. The two gun brigs were HMS *Childers* (18) and HMS *Sophie* (18). The *Sophie* under Captain Nicholas Lockyer RN, had just returned from Barataria, sixty miles southwest of New Orleans, in an unsuccessful attempt to gain the Baratarians as allies in the forthcoming attack on New Orleans.

The purpose of this special unit was to support the Creeks and Choctaws in their war against the Americans in West Florida and Alabama, thereby drawing away US forces from the New Orleans and Mississippi Valley areas. The special service party brought 1,000 muskets and ammunition, 300 red uniforms, and 3 light field guns.

On reaching Pensacola in August, Nicolls issued a proclamation stating his force was the advance guard of a British land force backed by a British and Spanish naval squadron coming to the aid of the native tribes. The Creek, Choctaw confederacy had already been defeated by the American forces. The mission to help the Indians was a failure. Colonel Nicolls and his party rejoined the four ships. Captain Percy suggested a second target and with Colonel Nicolls in agreement set off to attack Fort Bowyer on the entrance to Mobile Bay.

Admiral Cochrane had proposed to make Mobile Bay his base of operations against New Orleans. Fort Bowyer therefore had to be under British

Operations Agains the Coast of Georgia and Alabama

control. The approaches to the fort were difficult to navigate. It took from September 12 to 15 for the British ships to navigate shallow channels to within bombardment range. The Royal Marines were put ashore under acting captain Robert Henry RMA (Colonel Nicolls, ill with dysentery, returned to HMS *Hermes*). The marines landed two 5.5-inch howitzers and a mixed force of 120 Creek and Seminole Indians. Fort Bower was a recently built log fort; it had twenty-five guns, including three thirty-two-pounders, eight twenty-four-pounders and an eight-inch mortar. It was garrisoned by 300 regulars of the 2nd US Infantry and United States Artillery, commanded by Major William Lawrence USA. The British howitzers were set up just east of the semicircular fort, while sixty Indians under a Royal Marine lieutenant secured the landward approaches to the fort.

At 4 p.m. the American artillery opened up on the British ships and received a reply from the vessels, with the exchange of fire continuing till 7 p.m. In that time *Hermes* had its cable shot away. The vessel drifted in a strong current and grounded on a shoal 600 yards from the fort. The grounding was too hard to get off, and being within range of the forts heaviest guns it was pounded till it had to be abandoned and set on fire. Twenty-five seamen were killed on the ship and twenty-four wounded, including Colonel Nicolls, who was wounded in the head (eventually losing an eye) and in the legs. The survivors were picked up by *Sophie*, which had six killed and sixteen wounded; then the three remaining vessels hauled out of range. The landing force lost one marine killed and several wounded while being left stranded on shore. The unit now reformed out of range of the fort then marched along the coast towards Pensacola, where the party took over an old unused Spanish fort named San Carlos de Barrancas.

Three weeks later an American force of 3,000 men led by Major General Andrew Jackson USA, were sent to seize Pensacola, in retribution for allowing the British to use it as a base and to enforce Spain's neutrality in the region. The Americans attacked not only the Barrancas fort but also the Spanish-held fort of San Miguel, under the command of the governor, Mateo Gonzalez Manrique. The governor and his 500-man garrison surrendered after an American bayonet charge, leaving the British fort to face the Americans.

The overwhelming American attack forced Lieutenant Colonel Nicolls and his men to retreat from the fort and regain the ships in the harbour.

Sophie and *Childers,* under Captain J. B. Umfreyville RN, were now assisted by Captain Gordon in HMS *Seahorse,* who directed a bombardment at the Americans to give Nicolls and his men time to escape. During this retirement, the Barancas fort was blown up by the Royal Marines to prevent the forts guns being used against the fleet.

Back on Tangier Island in the Chesapeake, the 3rd Battalion Royal Marines, despite a large number of the soldiers suffering from dysentery, had been busy working to complete a fifty-bed hospital and barracks for 600 men, plus two large stores at Fort Albion. The battalion expected to spend the winter months on Tangier. On December 11 an order arrived for the battalion to embark on board the transport HMS *Regulus* (44) and sail to the coast of Georgia. On January 10, 1815, the battalion disembarked at Cumberland Island, having buried sixty-nine men at sea, including the surgeon.

At Cumberland Island, they met the fleet commanded by Admiral Cockburn: His Majesty's ships *Dragon* (74), *Brune* (56), *Severn* (40) *Hebrus* (36), *Rota* (38), and *Primrose* (18), the bomb vessels *Terror* and *Devastation,* both eight guns, and schooners *Canso* (10) and *Whiting* (12). Cockburn declared the island "occupied territory" and set up his headquarters in Dungeness Mansion. He also said that any enslaved Africans wishing to, could leave on the British ships. One group of sixty-six slaves paddled twenty-three miles in a wooden canoe to reach the island.

On landing, the 3rd Battalion was brigaded with the other two Royal Marine battalions and the West India Regiment. The entire brigade was placed under Lieutenant Colonel Sir Richard Williams RMA, the same officer who commanded at Ile aux Noix. The military force secured the island, crossed Cumberland Sound, and landed in a wooded area of the mainland at Kings Bay Plantation, with another force at Johnstone's Landing, next to a mill. Having met no resistance they proceeded along a narrow path leading to the fort at Point Pitre (Fort Peter), at the entrance to the St. Marys River.

The fort's garrison included the 1st US Rifle regiment and the 8th and 43rd US Infantry regiments under Captain Abraham A. Massias, who took up a position in the woods but was driven back; the fort with seven heavy guns was eventually captured by the British. Leaving three companies of marines at the fort, the main body crossed another branch of the river and entered the town of St. Marys at midnight of the 13th of January.

Operations Agains the Coast of Georgia and Alabama

An incident of note took place when the British passed through the woods. A sergeant of the 1st US Rifles had been severely wounded in the upper arm by a Royal Marine. He was then drawn up and placed against a tree and left to die. He was found by a private in the 3rd Battalion; this soldier marching in the rear of the column was the son of a surgeon in Devonshire. He carried a set of surgical instruments in his knapsack. On seeing the American bleeding severely he called for the help of a drummer and surgically removed the sergeant's arm at the socket. The wound healed, and the sergeant survived. As there was a great scarcity of medical assistants, Admiral Cockburn, on learning about the incident, ordered that the private was to receive the pay of an assistant surgeon.[55]

Captain Massias reported casualties of one killed, four wounded, and nine missing. He had also estimated the enemy force at 1,500, composed of "white and black men." The British reported three killed and five wounded. On January 15, the town of St. Marys was captured, along with two American gunboats and twelve merchant vessels, including the *Countess of Harcourt*, which an American privateer had taken on its passage to London from India. The British force ended its occupation after a week, then withdrew back to Cumberland Island, burning Fort Peter to the ground. On their return to Cumberland Island the 3rd Battalion Royal Marines were handed over to their new commanding officer, Major Andrew Kinsman RM.

The British presence was enough to draw away much of the United States Army that would have otherwise reinforced the American defence of New Orleans. Cockburn and his officers were planning a series of attacks on Savannah and South Carolina, amidst rumours of a peace treaty being signed. This news arrived officially on March 6 from the Prince Regent's dispatch, sent on board HMS *Pylades* (16). Admiral Cockburn was very disappointed that the United States had been allowed "status quo ante bellum" as part of the agreement. Reluctantly the British fleet obeyed orders and left, taking with it all the refugee slaves that had come to Cumberland Island.

By March 18 the British were on the way back to Bermuda. *Pylades* had brought the prize agent, who gave out the division of prize money from some of the ships and contraband taken earlier in the war. The dispatch also gave Cockburn the news that he was awarded the royal pleasure of the Prince Regent "to assume the style and dignity of a Knight Commander of the Military Order of the Bath."

Captain
Royal Marines

Lieutenant
Royal Navy

10

The New Orleans Campaign

New Orleans had been on the Royal Navy's list of priority targets since April of 1814. Admiral Cochrane had begun with a blockade of the American gulf coast in the early summer months. After the attack on Baltimore, Cochrane received the news of a further release of British regiments from Europe. He therefore attempted to encourage the Indian tribes involved in the Creek war against the Americans by sending Colonel Nicolls to reinforce the native tribes and draw away American forces from Louisiana and the Gulf coast, in particular from New Orleans and Mobile.

The British were working under the misunderstanding that the tribes were willing and able to comply, as based on the intelligence sent by Captain George Woodbine RM. Cochrane was unaware that the "Red Stick" Creeks had been beaten in the battle of Horseshoe Bend by forces under General Andrew Jackson. Nicolls' force and the Royal Navy ships were rebuffed at Fort Bower, thereby saving Mobile from attack. The British fell back to Pensacola in Spanish Florida, only to be pursued by Jackson, who forced the small British force to leave and then occupied the town to prevent further British usage. This was a serious act of provocation against Spain. The forcing of the Creek Indians to sign the treaty of Fort Jackson, which seized twenty-three million acres of native lands, forced friendly as well as hostile Creeks to move farther west.

Jackson's superiors were infuriated with his provocative acts of aggression; however, rather than censure him, they promoted him to the rank of major general in the army. In short, the US government had found an energetic, efficient and aggressive (some said ruthless) leader to defend some of the most vulnerable parts of the country.

Jackson's intense dislike for the British stemmed from his involvement in the Revolutionary War, when he and his brother were captured by the British (another brother was killed in action). As a prisoner Jackson was ordered to clean the boots of a Major Coffin. The thirteen-year-old refused and was slashed on the hands and head by the officer using his sword, leaving the wounded boy with an intense hatred of the British.

In 1814, New Orleans was upwards of 120 miles from the mouth of the Mississippi River. It had no elaborate defensive fort, such as Baltimore's Fort McHenry. The only serviceable forts were Fort St. Charles near the town, which could easily be overcome, and Fort St. Philip, situated at a bend in the Mississippi River. The main defence was the natural terrain of swamps, marches, and sluggish streams infested with predators such as snakes and alligators. Lake Borgne provided an inlet from the Gulf of Mexico midway between Mobile Bay and the Mississippi delta. To the north of New Orleans was Lake Ponchitrain. The local population were varied in nationality: French refugees from the slave revolt in Haiti, with Spanish, African, Anglo, and Creole peoples.

The British Admiralty had a report of the area by Captain James Stirling RN, written in 1813, which shaped their thinking that this mixture of "Foreign" residents might be inclined to form alliance against Washington. He even sent various plans on how the Americans could be defeated.

Stirling had misread the extent to which the white-dominated slave economy had been embraced by the Francophone Louisianans. The deciding factor was the activities of Colonel Nicolls' forces to enlist Creek Indians, slaves, and Spanish nationals. This exacerbated Louisianan fears that the British would take their lands and free their slaves. As long as Americans supported slavery and controlled the Indians, the white Louisianans would stand united against the British.

Admiral Cochrane had gone to Halifax to concentrate on plans for taking New Orleans and for acquiring boats suitable for Louisiana's bayous. The

The New Orleans Campaign

search for suitable watercraft was not up to his expectations, as Nova Scotia was in the middle of a shipbuilding boom. So the next option was to have boats built in Jamaica. He wanted shallow draft boats designed like Dutch *schuyts*. The Admiralty, however, hired and purchased local small craft, which had too great a draft and proved difficult in use. The Admiralty also disregarded Cochrane's request for warm clothing for the West Indian regiments, now mobilizing for the expedition to New Orleans, which was now common knowledge in Jamaica.

By November the military reinforcements were arriving from Spain and France. Major General John Keane would be in charge of the army until a more senior officer would arrive to replace the late Major General Ross.

Cochrane was understandably angry to find the knowledge of an attack on New Orleans was openly spoken of on the street. He discussed moving the attack to Long Island or New York but decided to keep the original plan. The British fleet with the army on board put to sea on November 26 and 27.

On December 8 Vice Admiral Cochrane, in his flagship HMS *Tonnant*, with several of the larger warships anchored off the Chandeleur Islands. Cochrane had sent orders for a flotilla consisting of the frigates, HMS *Seahorse*, HMS *Armide* (38), and the brig *Sophie* to leave Pensacola and proceed into Lake Borgne. When they were passing a small chain of islands, two large American gunboats fired on them and then retreated at speed from the area. Three other gunboats were spotted by lookouts on the British ships.

On December 10 to 12 the remainder of the British troopships arrived along with the remainder of the men of war. The larger seventy-fours anchored at the Chandeleur Islands; the frigates and smaller craft anchored close to Cat Island near the entrance to Lake Borgne. Cochrane and Keane decided to land at Bayou Catalan or Bienvenue, some sixty-two miles across Lake Borgne. The troops would have to travel in open boats; however, it would place the army only fifteen miles from New Orleans. It became imperative that the American gunboat fleet be eliminated. The battle for Lake Borgne was about to begin.

On the night of December 12, forty-two launches taken from fourteen major warships were assembled into three divisions under Captain Nicolas Lockyear of HMS *Sophie*, Captain Henry Montresor RN, of the brig HMS *Manley* (16) and Captain Samuel Roberts RN, of the bomb vessel HMS

Meteor. Each launch was armed with twenty-four, eighteen, and twelve-pounder carronades. The boats also carried 980 seamen and Royal Marines.

The Battle of Lake Borgne

The American force consisted of six Jeffersonian gunboats and other small craft:

> Gunboat 156, commanded by Lieutenant-Commandant Thomas Ap Catesby-Jones USN, had a long twenty-four-pounder, four twelve-pounder carronades, four swivel guns, and a crew of forty-one.
> Gunboat 23, under Lieutenant Isaac McKeene USN, carried a thirty-two-pounder, six long six-pounders, two five-inch howitzers, and four swivel guns, with a crew of thirty-nine men.
> Gunboat 162, commanded by Lieutenant Robert Spedden USN, was armed with a long twenty-four-pounder, four six-pounders, four swivel guns, and thirty-five men.
> Gunboats 5, and 163 were each armed with a long twenty-four-pounder and four six-pounders. Gunboat 5 was commanded by Sailing Master John D. Ferris USN, with thirty-six men, and Gunboat 163 was under Sailing Master George Ulick with thirty-one men.
> A schooner, USS *Seahorse*, with one six-pounder and fourteen men, was under Sailing Master William Johnson USN.
> A sloop, USS *Alligator*, with one four-pounder and eight men was under Sailing Master Richard S. Sheppard USN.

At 10 a.m. on December 13, Lieutenant Catsby-Jones saw the British boats rowing towards Passe Christian, where he believed they would disembark troops. He sent USS *Seahorse* to Bay St. Louis to destroy stores located in warehouses at that place. Captain Lockyear ordered some of his boats to pursue *Seahorse* and capture her. The schooner stationed itself under a commanding point of land, which had two six-pounder field guns. The combined firepower from *Seahorse* and the land guns were very destructive and drove off the British boats. Sailing Master Johnson realized his vessel would be captured when a larger British force arrived, so he set it on fire and destroyed the warehouses.

The New Orleans Campaign

At 1 a.m. on December 14, Lieutenant Catesby-Jones emulated the tactics of Macdonough at Plattsburgh; he moved his five largest gunboats in a close line abreast formation across the narrow Malheureux Island passage. Each boat had wound spring lines on their cables and had made every preparation possible to fight the British. At about 9:30 a.m. Captain Lockyer saw the sloop *Alligator* heading towards the five American gunboats. He signalled Captain Roberts to take a few boats and capture the sloop; this was done quickly and without much opposition.

The British rowed to within long gunshot distance of the American line. Lockyer had the British boats join together with grapnels and allowed the crews to have their breakfasts. The British had rowed for thirty-six hours, much of the way against a strong current. At 10 a.m., with breakfast over, the boats weighed anchor, and the men took to their oars and started pulling towards the American line, with the current strongly against them. The boats made at least three knots an hour and were fully exposed to a heavy and destructive fire of both round shot and grape.

By noon Captain Lockyer and Lieutenant George Pratt RN, in the same boat, closed on Gunboat 156, commanded by Catesby-Jones. The hand-to-hand fight resulted in heavy casualties on both sides. Catsby-Jones was severely wounded and Lieutenant Pratt mortally wounded; even Lockyer was wounded. Eventually Gunboat 156 was captured. Lockyer could see that the incoming British boats were still under heavy fire from the other American gunboats, so he ordered the guns of 156 along with his own boat to fire on the remaining American flotilla. Within five minutes the second and third divisions under Captains Montresor and Roberts secured all the American boats. The loss to the US Navy was six men killed, thirty-five wounded. The British loss was four Royal Naval officers, thirteen seamen, and one Royal Marine killed and eleven Royal Navy officers, one Royal Marine officer, fifty seamen, and eleven Royal Marines wounded. Captains Lockyer, Montresor, and Roberts were all promoted to post captain rank; many of the lieutenants and midshipmen were also advanced in rank. It is perhaps worth noting that one wounded British officer was the Battle of Trafalgar veteran Lieutenant John Franklin RN, later known as the renowned explorer Rear Admiral Sir John Franklin, KCH FRGS RN.

Rockets, Bombs and Bayonets

The Approach to New Orleans

On December 16 the Royal Navy began the disembarkation of the army. The first division of troops, including the 85th Regiment under Colonel William Thornton, landed at Isle-aux-Poix situated at the mouth of the Pearl River. This advanced guard was joined by the 4th (King's Own) Regiment, the 3/95th Rifle Regiment, a Royal Marine Artillery party armed with three three-pounder guns and three mobile mortars under Lieutenant John Lawrence RMA, and a small detachment of Royal Horse Artillery (on foot) armed with Congreve rockets. The senior army officer present was Major General John Keane.

The force of 1,688 men set off for Bayou Catalan (Bienvenue), some ten miles distant. The boats returned to the fleet for the next division of troops waiting at the anchorage off the Chandeleur Islands. It was estimated that Keane's force would be on its own for forty-eight hours before reinforcements could be expected. At the mouth of the bayou, an American outpost was captured while the garrison was asleep.

By the early morning of December 23, a reconnaissance was needed to define the closeness of the American positions. Two British officers dressed as local fishermen found out from the local inhabitants that no enemy troops were between them and the main road to New Orleans. The advance guard then pressed on through swamps and morasses overgrown with reeds and brushwood. Lieutenant Gleig of the 85th described the scene as "a tract inhabited only by alligators and wild duck."

Soon the British came to scrublands that led to fields of sugarcane and then a sugar factory building with slave huts nearby. Lastly, they saw the planter's house. Here they reached the main road. At this point a small American picket was surprised and captured; the troops were now about ten miles from the city. Keane and Thornton decided to march on.

A mile or so later the force turned off to the left and set up a defensive camp between the road and the Mississippi embankment. Major General Keane then decided to wait for the main body of the army at the Villere plantation.

As the British set up camp, it was observed that two vessels, a schooner and a ship, were at anchor some distance up the river towards the city, both apparently merchant vessels. Later in the afternoon several American scouting parties

The New Orleans Campaign

on horseback were observed by the outermost pickets. These horsemen were Mississippi Dragoons under Colonel Thomas Hinds. What was not observed were the two companies of American riflemen commanded by Captain Thomas Beale. Each sighting was met by a volley from the British pickets, resulting in the cavalry retiring as the main British force stood to arms. The "stand to" lasted only a short time, and then with no further enemy seen the soldiers returned to their camp work.

Lieutenant Gleig later wrote his impression of the events: "Our wonted confidence returned and again betook ourselves to our former occupation, remarking that, as the Americans had never yet dared to attack, there was no great possibility of their doing so on the present occasion, in this manner the day passed without any further alarm."

The Battle of the Villere Plantation

Major General Andrew Jackson USA, at 2 or 3 p.m. received intelligence on the arrival of British troops from Major Gabriel Villere, the son of the owner of the Villere plantation. Almost immediately another report came in from the Mississippi Dragoons. Jackson was furious and placed the city under martial law, informed Governor Clairborne, called out the militia, and sent for his highest ranking officers.

General Jackson's force was comprised of General John Coffee's brigade and Captain Thomas Beal's Orleans Rifle Company, totalling 648 men; the 7th US Infantry Regiment under Major Henry B. Piere USA, and the 44th Infantry Regiment under Major William Orlando Butler and Major Baker USA, with a total of 763 men in both units; Colonel John McKee USMC, with his 60 US Marines, and Lieutenant Samuel Spots USA, with twenty-two artillerymen; Plaunche's battalion (in French uniforms) and Darqin's Battalion of Free Men of Color, totalling 488 men; Colonel Thomas Hind's Mississippi Dragoons, totalling 186 cavalrymen—a total force of 2,167 troops. Major General William Carroll arrived with his force, boosting the American numbers to about 4,000.

Jackson had also called in the United States Navy in the form of Commodore Daniel Todd Paterson USN, and Captain John Dandridge Henley USN, the officer commanding the 230-ton schooner USS *Carolina* (14) moored in the Mississippi River.

Rockets, Bombs and Bayonets

The plan was for Captain Henley to drift *Carolina* downstream in the dark until it reached the British encampment. Once there and in position it would open fire at 7:30 p.m. on the British force, and that would signal the land attack to begin. Jackson placed General Coffee in charge of the troops making the attack, including the artillery and cavalry. The troops under Coffee's command were mostly the same militia that had defeated the Red Stick Creek and Chickasaw forces in a number of engagements, ending with the battle of Horseshoe Bend.

USS *Carolina* dropped quietly down the Mississippi River after dark on December 23. It towed two gunboats behind it and was followed a mile or so behind by the corvette USS *Louisiana* (16). *Carolina* approached the British position in complete silence; the picket guards repeatedly hailed but received no reply. Eventually the guards fired several musket shots in its direction. With still complete silence from the vessel, a few soldiers arose to see what was happening. All this time the British campfires kept burning brightly and were the only source of light and heat on an extremely dark night, two days after the new moon.

The ship anchored quietly on the far bank of the river opposite the British encampment. It then used its lines and gently hauled up its sails and swung at anchor, aligning itself broadside to the riverbank. At 7:30 p.m. a loud call was given out: "Give them this for the honor of America," instantly followed by the roar and flashes of its guns. A deadly shower of grapeshot tore into the tents and killed and wounded a number of soldiers, many still lying asleep around the campfires.

Snatching up their muskets, the majority of the soldiers ran for the cover of the riverside embankment, the three or four foot high dyke providing the only cover, and at once the redcoats returned fire at the flashes from the schooner's guns.

The 1st Royal Horse Artillery rocket troop under Captain Henry Lane RHA, managed to deploy their rockets and fired off a few in the direction of the gunfire, but these went wide or high and did not deter the enemy fire. Many of the British soldiers at the farthest away point from the river were still lying flat on the ground, escaping the worst of the grapeshot. They too were ordered to make for the shelter of the dyke. Gleig of the 85th described the scene:

The New Orleans Campaign

Laying ourselves along wherever we could find room we listened in painful suspense to the pattering of the shots and the shrieks and groans of those who lay wounded. Our fires, deserted by us and beat about by the enemy's shot, began to burn red and dull, and except where the flashes of the guns which played on us cast a momentary glare, not an object could be distinguished at the distance of a yard. In this state we lay for nearly an hour, unable to move from our ground or offer any opposition to those that kept us there.[56]

An hour after *Carolina* first fired, the land battle began. The British were surprised for a second time, even though General Coffee's men were late in attacking. Because of the inability to see clearly, his forces sent to flank the British got lost in the darkness. Gleig again described the action:

Desultory shots were heard on the right flank, succeeded by a blaze of musketry. It was quickly obvious that the British force was nearly surrounded, and by a greatly superior force. The 85th and 95th rushed from the dyke to support the pickets, the 4th stealing to the rear of the encampment from the riverbank, formed close column and remained as a reserve. A desperate close-quarter conflict at once ensued. Each officer, as he succeeded in collecting twenty or thirty men about him, plunged into the midst of the enemy's ranks, where it was fought hand to hand, bayonet to bayonet. Our men were mingled with the Americans repeatedly before they could tell whether they were among friends or foes, because, speaking the same language, there was no mark by which to distinguish anyone. None could tell what was going on in any quarter except where they chanced to be, and no part of the line could bring assistance to another.[57]

A later record of the attack came from Royal Navy Seaman G. Raymond, who wrote that the *Carolina* "did a great deal of mischief on that night. The troops had not been landed above two hours, and were just in the act of cooking some victuals, when this vessel opened a galling fire, and a large party of volunteers and regulars attacked in front."

The Americans made three fierce charges; each one in turn broke up the British formation, until on the fourth attempt, near midnight, the American force was beaten back in great confusion. The darkness made pursuit out of the question; the exhausted and tired British doubled the guards and waited for another attack. None came, as the lead elements of the British main force in the form of the Grenadier Company of the 93rd Sutherland Highlanders were beginning to reach the field.

The greatest loss was to the 3rd Battalion of the 95th Rifles; the commanding officer, Major Samuel Mitchell, and 41 of his men were missing, while 23 were killed and another 58 wounded, a total of 123 casualties, or more than one-fifth of the entire unit.

As daylight began on a frosty December 24, the schooner *Carolina* reopened fire, sending the British back to the riverside embankment. The soldiers were cold, tired, and hungry, but whenever they tried to light a fire or prepare food they were immediately shelled. USS *Louisiana* moved closer to *Carolina,* and both ships kept up the bombardment.

At this point it was realized that Major General Keane's choice of encampment was not a good one. With his troops trapped, he had to withdraw without causing a rout. It was decided to move the troops, company by company as darkness arrived, to a village of huts a short way across and beyond the road. The high road was left to the protection of a picket.

The afternoon of the 24th saw the arrival of the main body of the British army. The sound of firing had been heard during the night when crossing Lake Borgne. The sailors rowed their hardest, and on landing the troops disembarked rapidly.

December 24 was the day a peace treaty between the two warring nations was signed. This was also the day that casualties were recorded. The Americans lost 24 killed, 115 wounded, and 74 missing. The British casualties were 46 killed, 167 wounded, and 64 missing.

On Christmas Day, as high winds and sleet continued, Lieutenant General Sir Edward Packenham, the new commander in chief, arrived on site, along with Major General Sir Samuel Gibbs and Colonel Alexander Dickson RA (Wellington's Peninsula artillery commander). After a staff discussion it was decided that the first order of business was the removal of the American ships. This would enable a clear passage for the army to proceed without interference. The British force now numbered about 4,700 men, all of whom were in a much happier state of morale.

Packenham and Dickson ordered the construction of a battery on the embankment opposite the schooner. It was mounted with two 5 1/2"

The New Orleans Campaign

howitzers and six field guns manned by the newly arrived Royal Artillery brigade and a 5 1/2" mortar manned by Lieutenant Lawrence's Royal Marine Artillery gunners. A furnace for heating "hot shot" was constructed out of broken gun barrels damaged in the bombardment.

On daybreak of December 26 the battery began to bombard *Carolina* with shells and red-hot shot. "It was not long before we could perceive her crew hastening into their boats, while the smoke, which began to rise from her decks, proved that the balls had taken effect. She was on fire, and being abandoned without resistance in little more than an hour, she blew up,"[58] as later written by Lieutenant Gleig. An attempt to deal similarly with the *Louisiana* failed. As the Royal Artillery turned the guns to the corvette, it was seen that it had hoisted down its boats, and they began to row, towing the vessel away from the action. One shell did land on the deck and caused "considerable execution," but other than that it escaped further damage.

The danger of enemy ships on the river having been removed, the rest of the day was spent in bringing forward ammunition and stores just arrived from the fleet. This enabled the army to have a general advance the next day. The Royal Navy also sent four eighteen-pounder ships guns to replace those used against the American ships in the river. These were accompanied by a naval brigade of ship's marines and seamen numbering more than five hundred. Additional Royal Marine gunners from the various ships' detachments followed to service the river battery.

In the evening, parties of American riflemen became more active in sniping at the pickets; some heavy firing caused the alarm to be given, and the troops stood to arms in expectation of an attack in force.

The army moved forward the next morning in two brigades. The 3/95th Rifles went first in skirmish order ahead of the main force. The light companies of several regiments formed a separate unit under Lt. Colonel Robert Rennie of the 21st. These soldiers were employed in clearing any snipers from the cypress swampland that flanked the advance. The 1st Brigade was under General Keane and had Lawrence's RMA mortar unit attached. The 2nd Brigade was under Major General Gibbs. The British force now consisted of the 4th King's Own, 21st Royal North British Fusiliers, 44th East Essex, 85th Bucks Light Infantry, 93rd Sutherland Highlanders, two battalions of the West India Regiment, the 1st and 5th, the 14th The Duchess of York's Own regiment of Light Dragoons, Royal Artillery and Royal Horse

Artillery batteries, rocket batteries, Royal Engineers, and the Royal Marine Artillery with mortars and light guns.

The army marched about five miles and had no opposition. On reaching the enemy breastworks along the Rodriguez Canal, they could see a ditch, about forty yards in front and extending into a morass on their left, with the high road on the right. The ditch and breastworks were still unfinished but quite formidable, particularly with the water obstacle in between. On the road and at intervals in the breastworks were mounted powerful batteries. The ship *Louisiana* and a number of gunboats flanked the American position from the river. It soon became apparent that this was to be the field of battle before entering the city. The name of this place was the Chalmette Plantation.

When the British force came in range General Jackson immediately ordered his cannon to open fire with round shot and grape. The British guns were quickly deployed and returned fire. The leading infantry column deployed and advanced towards the canal in front of the American positions. The field commander halted his troops and ordered them to shelter in a narrow gully. Now hidden from American view, the soldiers crouched down while a scout checked the depth of the canal in front of the American position.

The British field artillery was now deployed and in full counter battery fire. The Royal Marine Artillery had its mortars set up, and as the gunfire raged, it soon became obvious that the British were outgunned. The superior numbers of American guns and heavier weight of metal thrown, together with the crossfire from the American boats, were gaining the upper hand.

Within an hour the unprotected British guns were practically silenced; two field guns and a mortar had been dismounted and disabled. These weapons were saved by a party of seamen who "running forward to where they lay on the ground lifted them up and, in spite of the enemy's fire, bore them off." USS *Louisiana* alone had fired 700 rounds at the British force.

The infantry were recalled and fell back for two miles, to be beyond the reach of the American guns. Here the army bivouacked. Colonel Dickson noted,

> It is difficult to express how much the black troops suffered from the excessive cold, which they are so little accustomed to, and also so improvided with warm clothing to protect them from it. Several have died from mere cold and the whole appear quite torpid and

The New Orleans Campaign

unequal to any exertion; I am convinced that little or no benefit will be derived from these troops while exposed to such cold.[59]

Admiral Cochrane met with the general and his staff to discuss the formidable nature of the American defensive works and how best to defeat them. It was decided to issue orders to the fleet to send for a number of ships' twenty-four-pounder and eighteen-pounder guns, with as much ammunition as could be transported, a number of ships' boats, to be used in a flanking attempt across the Mississippi River, and a force of 3,000 seamen and Royal Marines to support the army. Admiral Cochrane was very much interested in seizing prize ships and cargos located in the port of New Orleans. He knew the war would not last forever, and this was his chance to become an even wealthier man while continuing the mission of damaging the American economy.

In the meantime attempts were made by the army to find a way around or across the swamp to the American left flank. None were found; in the meantime Jackson's forces could be observed working on the defences, making them practically impregnable.

Jackson also had some of *Louisiana's* sailors with their heaviest guns land on the right bank of the river and construct a battery there. He could now cover the river and his right flank and also be able to enfilade any frontal attack from this position. Brigadier General David Morgan was sent up to 1,200 troops to defend this position.

On December 31 General Packenham received the shipment of heavy naval guns, both eighteen-pounder long guns and twenty-four-pounder carronades. These weapons were dragged across the swampy countryside on reed mats by teams of sailors. Along with the guns came Admiral Plutney Malcolm RN, with a force of sailors in ships' boats of various sizes, many loaded with supplies and ammunition for the army. The waterways were often difficult to navigate, and the British force had to be vigilant against attack. Six days before, a boat containing thirty-seven men and two officers of the 14th Light Dragoons was surprised and captured while the oarsmen were taking a rest.

Once on site the weapons were placed in a line along with the field artillery, about 800 yards from the enemy. Two eighteen-pounders were placed on the road next to the river. The RMA Company with their three mortars and two carronades were posted in the rear right of the line along with the RHA rocket troop. Next to them was a battery of Royal Artillery guns, nine- and six-pounders and howitzers. Further to the right was a battery of eighteen-pounders and twenty-four-pounder carronades plus a second rocket battery.

The work in setting up the batteries was carried out in a torrential downpour and virtual darkness. The ground was little better than a quagmire. Colonel Dickson and Lieutenant Colonel John Fox Burgoyne of the Royal Engineers had sugar barrels (hogsheads) taken from the surrounding warehouses and rolled to the front, placed upright on the parapet. and used as improvised firing platforms. These were makeshift at best and did not help with accuracy when the firing began. There was much discussion amongst the officers as to the value of many thousands of pounds sterling of sugar wasted in such a manner. Another more urgent concern was the sparse supply of ammunition; the guns could not keep up a bombardment for long.

Packenham had two columns of his infantry at the ready to advance on New Year's Day 1815. The morning was cold and misty when the British artillery opened up. The American troops were on parade in full dress and were momentarily caught off guard. After the first British shells hit the breastworks, the American counterfire became more accurate than the British. Even the heavy flanking fire from across the river enfiladed the British gunline.

Three hours after the first shots Packenham cancelled the infantry assault. By noon, five of the British guns were dismounted or disabled and put out of action, while the Americans had lost three guns. The British were also nearly out of ammunition. They had been able to discharge up to 276 pounds per salvo, while the American batteries were able to fire up to 225 pounds per salvo. After dark the disabled guns were brought back through the mud.

The British loss for the day was twenty-three killed and forty-one wounded, mostly Royal Artillery gunners, compared with eleven Americans killed and twenty-three wounded. The British officers killed were Lieutenant Alexander Ramsay RA, Lieutenant Peter Wright Royal Engineers, and Lieutenant John Blakney 44th Foot. The American riflemen kept up their nightly sniping to ensure the British had as little rest as possible.

The following morning, Packenham's reinforcements arrived at the main anchorage at the Chandeleur Islands. The Royal Engineers with the sappers and

The New Orleans Campaign

miners had improved the road from the bayou to the Villere canal and lengthened and widened the canal, making it easier for the boats to reach the river. This also improved the flow of supplies and ammunition to the troops.

Major General John Lambert's troops arrived on the 6th of January. These were two of the best Peninsular battalions (with each soldier carrying an artillery round in his knapsack), the 7th Royal Fusiliers and the 43rd Monmouth Light Infantry Regiments. Packenham was so pleased to have these fresh troops that he held a review, which happened to be within range of the American guns. The review in brilliant sunshine, complete with the assembled bands playing music, provided the Americans with a chance to work on improving their defences without hindrance, not to mention the intelligence blunder.

The British Attack on the West Bank

The next day, Cochrane's boats were drawn up close to the twelve-foot-high embankment or levee next to the Mississippi River. The night of the 7th was the time fixed for the flanking troops crossing the river to attack the large guns on the American right. To protect the crossing of the Mississippi, a battery was mounted consisting of two mortars manned by the Royal Marine Artillery and two eighteen-pounder naval guns manned by seamen. Colonel Thornton had under his command his 85th Regiment; a battalion of ships marines, commanded by Brevet Major Thomas Adair RM, and Captain John Robyns RM (this battalion was 400 strong, including twenty-two Royal Marine officers); Captain Lane's 1st Rocket Brigade RHA, and Lieutenant Lawrence's Royal Marine Artillery party. The Royal Navy also fielded a smaller battalion of about 200 officers and seamen, "all trained to small arms" and led by Captain Rowland Money RN. The 5th Battalion West India Regiment was also part of the intended assault force, numbering some 1,900 men.

The navy had assembled more than forty boats and crews under Captain Samuel Roberts RN, of HMS *Meteor*, to row them across the river. It was estimated that at least two trips would be required to land the entire force. Thornton and his officers watched as the Royal Engineers and the Royal Sappers and Miners broke through the levy to fill the canal up to river height. Without any warning a large portion of the embankment gave way, unleashing a deluge of water into the canal, swamping all but a few boats and damaging a number. This would severely reduce the attacking force.

The near disaster held up the departure of Thornton's force and caused it to be reduced to only the 85th, the Royal Marines, and the Royal Navy. The West India Regiment stood down and returned to the reserve of the main force under Packenham. The boats were refloated as quickly as possible, but by the time this was done and the flotilla was crossing against the strong cross current, the attack was hours behind schedule. The force assembled on the opposite bank as daybreak arrived and the sound of sporadic gunfire was heard from across the river. Leaving a company of marines behind to guard the boats, the rest of the troops immediately marched on the battery. Just then the signal rocket was fired, signalling that Packenham's frontal assault was beginning, despite the enfilading battery on the right bank still being in American hands.

Brigadier General David Morgan, in charge of the American right bank, was informed by Commodore Patterson USN, that the British had landed and were at Andry's plantation, and four gunboats were supporting the British flank from the river. Morgan sent a detachment of 150 Louisiana Militia under Major Paul Arnaud to oppose the British. After firing a volley, the militia retired. Another force of 170 Grey's Kentucky militia, under Lieutenant Colonel John Davis, was moved forward to Mayhew's Canal, where they combined with Arnaud's force.

Thornton's troops reached the American line and were greeted with another militia volley. In reply a heavy volley from the British front line along with gun and rocket fire from the flanking gunboats sent the Louisiana militia out of the area, leaving the Kentuckians exchanging fire with the British regulars. Thornton could now hear the heavy firing across the river, making his attack ever more urgent.

The Kentucky riflemen were inflicting more casualties than they received. Then an order from General Morgan had them fall back to another line of defence closer to the battery. This line was 300 yards long, placing them in a single line spread-out formation, with several yards between each man. Colonel Davis directed his men fire into the solid line of soldiers and sailors bearing down on them. A shower of rockets, followed by carronade fire from the British boats, now close alongside the river bank, outflanking the Kentucky force, caused them to break and retire.

Thornton ordered an immediate and determined charge. At this moment 2nd Lieutenant Henry Elliot of the Royal Marines observed that

The New Orleans Campaign

the enemy's right flank was accessible. He ordered his men to oblique to the left, passing a ditch and unfinished breastwork, and they were quickly in the rear of the Americans. Lieutenant Acheson Crozier RM, with his company of marines and the skirmishers of the 85th in close support, turned the enemy flank and captured a field piece. This carried the 85th and the remainder of the navy and marine brigades into the battery, forcing out the American naval gunners and infantry, and capturing the colours of the New Orleans Regiment of Militia.

The retreating Americans were pursued for about two miles, after which the battery was consolidated and made serviceable, while the infantry prepared for a possible counterattack. It was later reported that the American artillery was spiked; however, the Royal Marine Artillery detachment found no problem on reloading and directing fire on the American guns at Line Jackson.

Lieutenant Gleig recorded the event in this manner: "Our People had no time to waste in distant fighting and hurried on to storm the works, upon which a panic seized the Americans. They lost their order and fled, leaving us in possession of their tents and of eighteen pieces of Cannon."[60]

The short, brisk fight had left a number of British severely wounded. These included Colonel Thornton, wounded for a second time, first at Bladensburg and now at New Orleans. Captain Money RN, was severely wounded, with both bones of his right leg broken by a musket shot. Also Midshipman George Woolcombe Esq. RN, of HMS *Tonnant* was severely wounded. He was mentioned in dispatches for having "Particularly distinguished himself" while leading his seamen into the battery.

A number of other officers and men had less severe wounds. First Lieutenant Gilbert Elliot RM, was hit in the torso; the ball struck a toothpick case in his waistcoat pocket, which was shattered to atoms. Another marine officer, 2nd Lieutenant Henry Elliott, was hit in the breastplate, the ball taking away the tail of the lion and passing through the cross belt. A third Royal Marine, Lieutenant Charles Morgan, was also slightly wounded in the same attack.

On retirement the British artillerists made certain all eighteen captured guns were made unusable and all military stores destroyed. Notably, one ten-inch brass howitzer amongst the captured weapons was inscribed "Taken at the surrender of York Town 1781." The British force, with thirty prisoners, was able to retire without any molestation from the American forces. The

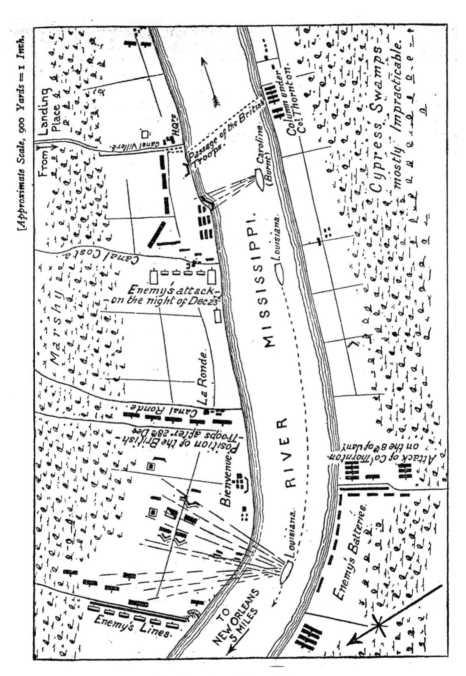

The Attack on New Orleans
December 1814-January 1815

The New Orleans Campaign

trip back was made much easier by the current of the Mississippi flowing in the right direction.

The Battle of Chalmette Plantation

From the earliest reports of a British force nearing New Orleans, Major General Jackson had endeavoured to build defences to defeat whatever the British could throw at him. He had three defensive lines: Line Jackson at Chalmette Plantation, behind that Line Dupree, and closer to Fort St. Charles and New Orleans, Line Montreuil. These defensive lines were constructed using 900 slaves gathered from local plantations. These slaves were given great motivation to work and fight. Jackson said, "If you will go, and the battle is fought and the victory gained on Israel's side, you shall be free."

At each stage he fortified his defenseworks with the heaviest guns available, even removing armament from the American naval vessels. He sent for thousands of veteran Indian fighters from Kentucky and even cut a deal with the Baratarian pirates, the Lafitte brothers and their followers, whom he had previously referred to as "Hellish Banditti" and who even provided the defence with a large quantity of gunpowder.

After the earlier battle with the British, Jackson's spies had informed him of General Packenham's intention to mount a full scale attack on the morning of January 8. On that day Packenham set up his army with the 1st brigade under General Lambert, consisting of the 14th Light Dragoons, the 7th Royal Fusiliers, the 43rd Monmouth Light Infantry, and lastly the 5th West India Regiment, returned from Thornton's amphibious attack. These troops were all held as a reserve in the rear of the attacking columns.

The right wing of the army was the 2nd Brigade under Major General Samuel Gibbs; this was the 4th King's Own, the 44th East Essex, 21st Royal North British Fusiliers. The 3/95th Rifle regiment, about 400 strong, under the command of Captain James Travers formed extended files and proceeded ahead of the main force.

On the left was Major General Keane's 3rd Brigade. The lead unit was Colonel Rennie's light brigade consisting of the light companies. The rest of Keane's brigade was the 93rd Sutherland Highlanders, and 1st West India Regiment.

The Royal Artillery had twenty-six guns of various types, with the heaviest being naval guns, while the batteries had the capacity to fire salvos of up to 360 pounds. The persistent problem of undersupply of ammunition was still a great concern to the British high command.

Packenham's plan was to advance with the two columns towards Jackson's line, with the main thrust on the right against the Tennessee and Kentucky militia with Gibbs' force some 2,200 men. Captain Brevet Lieutenant Colonel the Honourable Thomas Mullins, commanding the 44th Regiment, was very dissatisfied with the plan of attack, which saw his regiment leading while carrying ladders and fascines (bundles of wooden poles lashed together, which can be dropped into a sunken obstacle to allow men to cross). He felt that "his regiment was sent as a forlorn hope, and was doomed" to be sacrificed for the glory of the others.

The left column under Keane was to form up with 1,200 soldiers of the 93rd Highlanders supported by two companies of the 95th Rifles and two companies of the 43rd Light Infantry. A further 1,200 men were in reserve, but ready to advance at any given time.

At daybreak the heavy mist blocked the view of each army of the other. The order was given to open fire from the artillery batteries. This was replied to by the American gunners. The American drummers began to play "Yankee Doodle" while Jackson's men peered into the smoke and fog for any sign of movement. The British signal rocket was fired, and the order "Forward!" was given. Rennie's light companies surged ahead, using the skirmishing tactics for which they were specially trained. The bulk of the army was marching in compact, close company formation. The two columns strode into the deadly fog of battle, drummers tapped out the marching beat, and the war pipes of the 93rd droned into life, sending out an eerie message to the American defenders. The Scots were uniformed in government tartan trews (trousers) and wearing an unbecoming form of Kilmarnock bonnet. They marched into the roar of cannon fire and musketry. Cannonballs, grapeshot, rifle balls, and buckshot whistled through the air from an enemy almost unseen behind parapets.

Within a few minutes Morgan's guns on the west side of the river opened up. Immediately Packenham and his staff realized that Thornton's attack had not been completed. General Gibbs's column was marching directly towards the mouths of a battery of eighteen-pounders. Jackson's infantry could now see the redcoats and began sporadic firing. The mist that had protected the British was now dissipating, and their ranks were now in full view of the enemy.

The New Orleans Campaign

The cypress woods were filled with American riflemen. These shot into the British lines without being seen. General Gibbs was hit and mortally wounded. The two columns reached the ditch; however, the 44th had failed to pick up the fascines and ladders, which had been placed in a redoubt in the British front line. The regiment had to go back 500 yards to collect the equipment, then return to the battle, which was now in dire straits for the British. Lieutenant Colonel Mullins had led his regiment past the needed equipment and was totally responsible for the disastrous mistake. When his regiment rejoined the battle he was conspicuously absent.

The left column light companies and a spiking party from the Royal Artillery under 1st Lieutenant Charles Ford RA, all led by Lieutenant Colonel Rennie, were able to force themselves into the forward levee redoubt containing four guns, manned by the 7th US infantry, Beal's Rifle Company, and a detachment of United States Marines. Rennie was struck twice in the head with rifle balls and fell dead while leading his men. The hand-to-hand struggle continued till the light companies were on the parapet and the embrasures, driving the Americans out, but they could not penetrate further.

The light companies (or what was left of them) now dug into the exterior of the ditch and held the redoubt, hoping for supports to arrive. The fighting was so close and intense that one light company officer is reported to have engaged the enemy by throwing stones. When it was obvious the attack had failed, some of the men placed their caps on the end of their bayonets and waved them to encourage a volley from the Americans. This happened, and the light companies jumped out and ran for their own lines as fast as they could. They reached them, just out of musket range when the smoke cleared. Only three of the officers of this detachment escaped, Lieutenant Joseph Hutchison, with three bullets through his cap, and Lieutenant Charles Lorentz, slightly wounded, both from the 7th, and Lieutenant Alexander Steele of the 43rd, unscathed.

Sergeant John Spencer Cooper of the 7th Royal Fusiliers, waiting with his battalion in reserve, later recalled the retirement of the light companies from the levee redoubt:

> At last, the companies bolted from the ditch and ran off stoopingly in different directions. One of them, named Henry Axhorn, a smart

young fellow, received a ball above his hip, which ran up his body, and stuck near his eye. It was extracted in a hospital at New Orleans. He joined us again after the peace, much altered in shape, and not fit for further service. Our Light Company went into this action sixty-four strong, and returned sixteen having lost forty-eight.[61]

The 93rd Highlanders charged forward in a diagonal direction across the front of the American positions, the pipers playing "Moneymusk," the traditional pipe tune for the charge of the Sutherland Highlanders. Lieutenant Charles Henry Gordon described the advance of the 93rd:

A most destructive and murderous fire was opened on our column of round, grape, musquetry, rifle and buckshot along the whole course and length of their line in front, as well as on our left flank. Not daunted, however, we continued our advance which in one minute would have carried us into their ditch, when we received a peremptory order to halt—this was indeed the moment of trial. The officers and men being as it were mowed down by ranks.[62]

The regiment was finally ordered to retire, which they did in parade-ground precision, leaving three-quarters of their total strength killed or wounded on the field. They had lost their three most senior officers plus another ten wounded and four more missing.

The right column under Major General Gibbs stopped under the weight of enemy fire. The 44th East Essex Regiment retrieved the fascines and ladders needed for the assault, but it was too late. Major General Packenham rode forward to the head of Gibbs's column, calling out, "Lost from the want of courage" in an attempt to spur the troops on. This worked for a few yards, and then he and his horse under him were hit by grapeshot.

Packenham's ADC, Major Duncan MacDougall of the 85th, got the general to his feet and was mounting MacDougall's horse when another shot hit the general. He fell back into MacDougall's arms, uttering a few words; then he expired. His body was then removed from the field. Major General Keane had also been severely wounded; this meant the three most senior major generals in the British army were now all *hors de combat*.

Both columns fell back about 250 yards, as Major General Lambert (now in charge) brought forward his reserve battalions and consolidated a

The New Orleans Campaign

line. All the troops were ordered to lie down; however, the heavy guns from Jackson's line were still causing casualties. Captain John Cooke of the 43rd recalled, "For five hours the enemy plied us with grape and round shot, some of the wounded lying in the mud or even on the wet grass, managed to crawl away; but every now and then some unfortunate man was lifted off the ground by round shot, and lay killed or mangled."[63]

The advanced files of riflemen from the 95th were the last to return. They had surprisingly light casualties, owing to their extended formation. They lost 11 killed and 101 wounded. They had been close enough to the American works to begin to cut steps into the embankment in order to breach the line when the main force arrived.

The British lay in place all day until finally ordered to retire. Major Joseph Hutchison of the 7th Royal Fusiliers wrote in his memoir that "on assembling the troops when out of fire, only 15 men were found serviceable out of 85 of which the company was composed one hour before. I received seven shots through my clothes and cape."[64]

Lambert had sent Colonel Dickinson of the artillery to check the status of Colonel Thornton's capture of the American battery on the west side of the Mississippi. Dickson's report stated that an infantry and artillery force of no less than 2,000 men would be needed to hold the west-side battery. General Lambert knew the situation was unsustainable and subsequently ordered the retirement and evacuation of the west bank troops.

Sergeant Cooper of the 7th Royal Fusiliers related his recollections on the order given to advance the reserve battalions:

> Just before the order was given to lie down, my right hand man received a bullet in his forehead, and fell dead across my feet. This man was drunk the night before, and cursing the seven year's men for wishing to be discharged. Poor Fitzpatrick had been considered an honest man; but his knapsack, when opened, showed him to have been a sly thief. Another man, about ten or twelve files on my right, was smashed to pieces by a cannon ball. I felt something strike my cap; I took it off, and found sticking to it a portion of his brains, about the size of a marble. A young man on my left got a wound on the top of his head, and ran to the surgeon behind us; he was dressed and sent into his place again. Close to him, another man had his

arm so badly fractured near the shoulder that it was taken out of the cup. A few yards behind sat a black man, with the lower part of his face shot away; his eyes were gone, and the bones of his brow all jagged, and dripping blood. Near him in a ditch, lay one of the 43rd trying to hold in his bowels. The enemy kept pounding away at us all day; during which a shower of grape came whizzing like a flock of partridges, and struck Major King dead.[65]

The British sent forward a white flag of truce to negotiate a two-day ceasefire in order to bury the dead and assist the wounded. General Jackson agreed. In his memoirs Sergeant Cooper recalled,

> An American officer strutted about, sword in hand, on his side of the ditch, to our great amusement. An American soldier, looking at the long rows of the slain, exclaimed "I never saw the like of that!" One of our party sneeringly said. "That's nowt, man; if you'd been wi' us in Spain, you would ha' seen far worse!" While removing the bodies, I stripped two poor fellows of their shirts; they were bloody enough, but I wanted them sadly. The funeral being over, and the truce having expired, we returned to our huts in haste, and then the game of cannonading began again.[66]

The British officers were buried in the garden of the plantation, while the rank and file were buried in mass graves on the southern edge of the plantation. It is believed a Mississippi River flood disinterred the bodies, which were swept away throughout the delta. The bodies of Generals Packenham and Gibbs were preserved in barrels of spirits and returned to Britain to be interned there. A twin statue to them is in St. Paul's Cathedral, London. The loss to the British force was 291 killed, 1,267 wounded, and 484 missing, presumed captured. America's loss was 13 killed, 39 wounded, and 19 missing.

The Corduroy Road—The British Army Retires

The British encampment was still within range of some of Jackson's artillery. Sergeant Cooper went on,

> Exposed as we were to the enemy's fire, brushing and parading were continued. Getting myself ready for parade one morning, I saw a man

The New Orleans Campaign

who was doing the same, struck by a round shot. Another, lying in his hut, had both legs shot off. One day I had occasion to fetch water from a ditch in front of our lines; seeing smoke rise from the enemy's batteries, I perceived a ball coming straight at me. To avoid it, I fell flat. However, it struck boggy ground just before me, and sank. A shot fell one night within three feet of the hut in which four of us slept; it burst, made a large hole, but did no harm. I never heard the explosion. Another of these ugly customers passed over us, dropped upon a man's knapsack, and drove it several feet down in the soft earth.[67]

During this time several attempts were made to entice piquet guards to desert. Sometimes this worked; other times it did not. A piquet of the 95th Rifles had an incident that was described by Lieutenant Gleig of the 85th:

A Rifleman on sentry was exposed to the solicitations of another of these gentry. (An American Officer) He heard all his generous offers of money, land and promotion; but pretending he did not, he begged him to come a little nearer and "tell him all about it." The Yankee elated at his success walked up to the post, and when he was well within range the rifleman leveled and shot him in the arm. Then walking forward, he led him prisoner to the guardroom; on the way informing him of what a real soldier thought of such sneaking attempts on his fidelity.[68]

From January 11 to 17 the British army was slowly withdrawn along a seventy-mile route where a "rough corduroy road," made of crushed reeds and other vegetation, was laid down by Royal Sappers and Miners along with the Pioneer companies of the various regiments. The road or causeway stretched along the side of Bayou Bienvenue, with the intention that it would provide a safe footing for thousands of soldiers, sailors, and marines. The wounded and sick were conveyed in boats back to Lake Borgne and then to the fleet at the Chandeleur Islands.

The next consideration was to save the artillery and whatever equipment could be salvaged from the expedition, through alligator-infested swamps, with only a few of the foot soldiers having the privilege of a boat ride.

The smaller field artillery was all retrieved using boats; the heavier naval cannons were spiked and disabled beyond use. By January 18 the bulk of the infantry had secretly left. Sergeant Cooper picks up the story:

On the evening of the 18th, the order to retreat came, and we began to move after darkness set in, leaving the piquets at their respective posts. The road we took had never before been trodden by man, and it was both difficult and dangerous. To construct it, small parties had been employed in treading down the tall reeds or canes that grew on the edge of a deep creek. These being twelve or fourteen feet in length overlapped each other when trodden down, and so formed a kind of basket road. This strange path, being under laid by a stratum of rotten bog, was deceitful; and the night being dark, no one could see where to step. One officer slipped through this bending, swinging path, and sank up to his armpits. A canteen strap under those parts served to hoist him out of his dilemma. A Bugler of the 95th Rifles sank overhead and was lost. I had a taste of the same, but only with one leg; the other stood on firmer stuff.

We marched in this way till near daybreak, when we were completely stopped by a wide, deep bog, like a cesspool. Till the foremost got over, we lay down till daylight among the wet grass. In this horrible swamp three or four poor fellows were sticking up to their middles. They were still sinking, and would have perished, when a boat having Admirals Malcolm and Cochrane on board, came down the creek. The boat stopped, and some sailors with shovels cut the prisoners out.

I made a short circuit, and got safely over, by stepping on the roots of some large plants that grew there. Just beyond the bog lay a splendid dead alligator, twelve to fourteen feet long. At length we reached the sea side, and encamped. Not a shot had been fired at our rearguard during the retreat.[69]

The 7th Fusiliers were the last unit to re-embark on January 27. In his memoirs Major Joseph Hutchison wrote, "The road was in such a deplorable state & in many places impassable. Three or four men in search of better footing, leaving the rushes, sank to rise no more."[70]

The American forces, for the most part, did not interfere with the British withdrawal. General Jackson was still reinforcing his position, being under the belief that the British would regroup and return to New Orleans with a force of 25,000 men. Colonel Hind's Mississippi Dragoons did manage to capture

The New Orleans Campaign

four British stragglers, and when the army was embarking cannon fire killed one and wounded two of Colonel Hind's Dragoons who came too close.

Andrew Jackson would later commend his troops on their heroism; however, he reneged on his promise of freedom to the slave soldiers. James Roberts, a sixty-year-old slave who had been promised his freedom, confronted the general, saying, "I did fight manfully and gained the victory, now where is my freedom?"

Jackson, taken aback, replied, "I think you are very presumptuous."

The slave and all 900 of his fellows were returned to their owners. James Roberts was furious at having been "duped by the white man."[71]

The Attack on Fort St. Philip

In December of 1814, American costal craft had observed the Royal Navy fleet under Admiral Cochrane approaching the Chandeleur Islands. This intelligence was relayed on December 17 to Major Walter Hampden Overton of the 3rd US Rifle Corps, the commanding officer of Fort St. Philip.

Fort St. Phillip was located at Plaquemines Bend in Plaquemines Parish about forty miles from the mouth of the Mississippi River and about seventy miles from New Orleans. It had twenty-nine twenty-four-pounder cannons, two thirty-two-pounder cannons, two howitzers, an eight-inch and a 5 1/2 inch, one thirteen-inch mortar and an additional six-pounder cannon—in all, thirty-five pieces of artillery manned by 117 US artillerymen, 163 infantrymen, and 84 militia.

On news of the British fleet, Overton began to strengthen his position with the hasty construction of a battery on the opposite side of the river and the installation of a signal station three miles downriver as an early warning post. He also constructed an earthen fortification at the rear of the fort as a defence position from a landward assault. He also improved the overhead protection for his gunners, to reduce casualties from shrapnel.

He further improved the fort with the demolition of the old powder magazine and the construction of several separate magazines, heavily protected with wooden supports and thick sod above. Several gun carriages were repaired, and the distribution of the artillery was improved to help give interlocking fire across the river.

On December 30, the Royal Navy sent a strike force consisting of the sloop HMS *Herald* (20), the brig of war HMS *Pigmy* (18), the schooner

HMS *Thistle* (10), and the two bomb ships, HMS *Aetna* and *Volcano,* along with a number of launches, gigs, and several gunboats, with a number of Royal Marine infantry. All intended to capture the fort and force a passage to support the main assault on New Orleans.

The small fleet found the Mississippi difficult to navigate. The South Pass entrance to the delta had shifting sandbanks and a torturous channel, followed by a strong river current requiring a great deal of warping to and fro and towing, all needed to close on the American fort. On January 8, the American Gunboat 65 arrived at Fort St. Philip and was set up to cover the battery on the opposite side of the river and to support the rear of the fort. Lieutenant Thomas S. Cunningham USN, had some forty sailors in the gunboat; some of these would help reinforce the artillery units in the fort.

On January 9 the first British vessels were sighted by the signal station guard. These men abandoned their post about 1 p.m. when it was observed several boats were landing Royal Marines. In their hurry to escape the advance of the marines, the guard omitted to fire the buildings and the lime kiln, which Major Overton ordered destroyed. By 2 p.m. the position was taken without incident and occupied; it would serve as a base camp for the British force.

At 3 p.m. the British advanced several boats to within a mile and a half of the fort. The guns on the left side of the fort opened fire. The two heavy thirty-two-pounder guns, located in what was known as the "Water Battery," also opened fire, these two guns being serviced by Lieutenant Cunningham and his sailors.

The British retreated, after noting the American fall of shot. The two bomb vessels advanced and took up position broadside to the fort at 3,960 yards and hoisted their battle ensigns. The Royal Marine Artillery detachments, under Lieutenant Robert Henry in *Volcano* (replacing Lieutenant Furzer, killed at sea) and Lieutenant Robert Wright of *Aetna,* prepared for a long bombardment. The ship's log of HMS *Volcano* gives the details of the prolonged bombardment:

> January 9th 1815: *Aetna* in company. At noon came-to in six fathoms near the south shore of the Mississippi. Anchored. Warped ship inshore with hawsers: made fast to a tree. 1:40 p.m. sprung the ship stern to shore. Let go stream anchor and veered cable: secured ship.

The New Orleans Campaign

> Began firing, about 3,700 yards from Fort Placmain. 2:30 p.m., fired thirty 13-inch and twenty 10-inch. Warped to S.W.S.
> January 10th: 10 a.m., commenced firing. Fired all day: forty 13-inch, forty 10-inch. Fired at by the fort heavily but no shot reached within 300 yards.
> January 11th: Fired forty-six 13-inch and forty-six 10-inch.
> January 12th: Fired thirty-five 13-inch, morning; twenty-one, afternoon. One 13-inch shell burst in leaving the mortar, damaged main yard and rigging, deck (main) started in several places, shrouds cut, broke down bulkhead. None hurt.

The damages to *Volcano* were made good, and the ship was ready for action the next morning.

The log lists no shell expenditure for January 13, 15, or 16. However the American official report states that the firing continued from the 9th to the 17th "without intermission."

> January 14th: Fired thirteen 13-inch; seventeen 10-inch, and three carcasses (one 13-inch, two 10-inch).
> January 17th: Ship opened fire 10 a.m. Enemy shells burst near.

The same day the British received intelligence regarding the defeat of the army at New Orleans on January 8. The following day all preparations were made to move off. On January 19 the vessels all weighed anchor, and with the wind behind them they made sail and proceeded down the Mississippi to return to the main fleet.

On the receiving end of the bombardment, the American defence was later recorded by Major A. Lacarriere Latour US Army Engineers.

> The first shot from the enemy fell short, but the next burst over the interior of the fort. All that day and night the firing continued, with only short intervals, generally a shell every two minutes. No injury was done to the men or works, as the shells, from the nature of the soil, sunk in the ground, without bursting, or burst under the ground, at so great a depth as to produce no other effect than a tremendous motion.
> In the night several boats approached near the Fort, and came so close as to allow us almost distinctly to hear their crews conversing.

Rockets, Bombs and Bayonets

They fired several rounds of grape and round-shot over and into the fort. The wind blowing fair up the river and in gusts during the night, this approach of the enemy was only considered as an effort to divert our attention from their vessels, which might attempt to pass under our smoke. Their attack was therefore received in silence, and our attention directed to the vessels alone. Finding we were not to be moved by this stratagem, they retired, and during the rest of the night fired a few shells from their boats stationed on both sides of the river.

On the 10th the bombardment was continued with the same vivacity as on the former day, except that a cessation occurred of about two hours at noon and sundown, which respite was daily granted us during the remainder of the siege. Occasionally on these two days a fire was opened from the batteries of the Fort, but the shot fell short. The third day of the bombardment several pieces of shells struck the flag-staff and in one instance nailed the halyards to the mast, in another severed them in the midst of the fire; the topmast was lowered down, and it took nearly an hour to have the flag replaced on the mast. This was done by a sailor who had the courage to stand on the cross-trees, exposed as a mark, and though the fire from the enemy was very brisk and well directed, and several shells burst over his head, he escaped unhurt.

The evening of this day the enemy directed their fire with great exactness at the contractor's store, supposing it to be the main magazine. Several whole shells passed through the building, and two burst in it, killing one man and wounding another; but as their spies had only described the magazine in the state in which it was a few days before the attack commenced, they were deceived; and by making every effort to lodge shells in the before-mentioned building, which had the appearance of the powder magazine in its former state, the magazine itself escaped, having only been struck two or three times by fragments of shells.

At four this evening the garrison opened an animated fire for a quarter of an hour on the bomb vessels from all the guns that bear on them, but apparently without any other effect than deranging their fire; it served however, to animate our men, showed the quickness

The New Orleans Campaign

and precision with which our guns were pointed and served, and gave a foretaste of what might be expected should the enemy attempt to pass.

On the 12th, 13th, and 14th the firing continued with the usual intervals, doing comparatively little injury; the enemy probably were aware of the inefficiency of their shells when discharged so as to alight whole in the interior of the works, now arranged their fuses, so that the shells burst in the air over the works, and scattered fragments in every direction. The evening of the 14th a man was killed on the right battery, another slightly wounded, a man on the centre battery lost his leg, and several of the gun-carriages were materially injured; on the right and centre batteries, the thirty-two-pounder in the covert-way, in the angle of the Spanish bastion, was struck five times, and for upwards of an hour was rendered unserviceable. Several shells entered the blacksmith's shop; one burst near the main magazine, and another passed into the ditch through the magazine in the covert way.[72]

Major Latour's report went on to describe the building of wooden structures to help protect the men servicing the guns and also to protect them from the near constant rainfall, which lasted throughout the siege. The Fort's interior was "nearly a pond of water," and the tents were all "torn by shells," making them unusable. In the evening of January 15, several boats arrived, loaded with ammunition from New Orleans; the supplies included fuses for the fort's thirteen-inch mortar, which the artillerymen could not manufacture. They also brought the news of the British defeat on January 8.

January 16 was a day spent in replenishing the magazines. As the weather was warmer, the American defenders returned to their guns in high spirits with the news of the British defeat and at being able to "annoy the enemy" with a rejuvenated supply of munitions.

January 17 saw a reduction in fire from the bomb vessels until later in the evening, when, the American report stated, "they threw shells more frequently than before." They also state, "one of our shells struck one of their bomb vessels; we distinctly heard the shock, and for near five minutes the fire from one of the vessels was discontinued." The British continued firing throughout the night, with several hits on the parapet, one bursting through the ditch and into the centre bastion.

On January 18 the British force received the news of the army withdrawal and the move back to the main fleet. Firing continued while the ships prepared for their own leaving.

At daylight on January 19 the British weighed anchor and sailed down the Mississippi without hindrance of any kind. The Americans counted 100 shells that had buried themselves inside the fort. All buildings were in ruins, and the ground for half a mile around was torn up in every direction. They also estimated that more than 1,000 shells were expended, using more than 20,000 pounds of powder. Major Overton later wrote of the action, "The enemy left scarcely ten feet of this garrison untouched."

The American loss was two killed and one wounded from Captain Murray's artillery, three wounded from Captain Woolstonecraft's artillery, two wounded from Captain Wade's 7th Infantry, and one wounded from Captain Brountin's 7th Infantry. The British loss in men has never been disclosed; the assumption is that none were killed or seriously wounded.[73]

11

The Second Attack on Fort Bower, the Last Land Action in the South

When the British army reached the coast of Lake Bourne, the various regiments boarded the waiting transport vessels. Sergeant Cooper tells of his regiment boarding the transport *Fox;* at the same time he tells of a distressing event: "Several boats came alongside, full of women belonging to the 93rd Regiment, seeking after their husbands; but as that corps had lost five or six hundred men on the 8th, many of these poor creatures would seek in vain."[74] Cooper's estimate was somewhat off. The return of the 93rd shows 128 other ranks killed, along with three senior officers. Many more were wounded, and a number remained in the care of the American forces, while a number of officers and men were captured. The ship's logs of the fleet transports showed 53 women and 104 children embarked with the 93rd to New Orleans; 5 children were born on the way to America and 4 died on the return.

Bad weather held back the British fleet from leaving the anchorage at the Chandeleur Islands. During this delay, Admirals Cochrane and Malcolm together with Major General Lambert decided to try another attempt at attacking New Orleans. This was a resurrection of Cochrane's original plan of attack, using the town of Mobile as a base from which an army could advance. Dauphin Island was chosen as a staging and rest area and was held under occupation during the attack on Fort Bower.

On January 10 a battery on the far bank of the island was captured and found to be constructed of barrels of brown sugar. During the occupation, soldiers from both West Indian regiments began to eat a quantity of the fortification, which they seemed very fond of, and in consequence soldiers from other British regiments began to acquire the same brown sugar for the purpose of sweetening their cocoa.

On February 5 the Royal Navy sailed towards Mobile Point, eventually settling into semicircle position with twenty-five major war vessels, about five miles from Fort Bower at the mouth of Mobile Bay. Behind the first line were another thirteen ships awaiting the return of the vessels of the Mississippi Squadron. Lambert's army of 5,000 soldiers was landed, a brigade containing the 4th, 44th, and 21st Infantry regiments and several Royal Artillery batteries, armed with four eighteen-pounder cannon, two 8-inch howitzers, three 5 1/2 inch howitzers, and a number of 4.4-inch field mortars. Lieutenant John Lawrence, RMA, and his twenty-five-man Royal Marine Artillery unit landed from HMS *Tonnant*, this time armed with Congreve rockets. HMS *Volcano* and *Aetna* with the rest of the small Mississippi squadron arrived to rejoin the main fleet on February 10. They added their firepower to the bombardment.

The defenders of Fort Bower had kept up a constant fire on the British since they had first landed and set up their siege artillery. General Lambert sent forward a flag of truce and persuaded Major William Lawrence that further resistance would only result in the needless slaughter of the defenders. On February 12 Major Lawrence and his officers and men of the 2nd US Infantry surrendered the fort and marched into captivity as prisoners of war. British casualties were 13 dead and 18 wounded, while the Americans had 1 killed, 10 wounded, and a total of 374 captured. The colours of the 2nd US Infantry were taken as a prize of war and still reside at the Royal Hospital Chelsea in London.

The British advance on Mobile was halted when the sloop HMS *Brazen* (18) arrived with news of the peace treaty. Cochrane and Lambert then began preparations to return to Halifax and Bermuda and eventually on to Britain. Lambert and some of the army would even take part in the Battle of Waterloo.

On Dauphin Island the officers of the 7th Fusiliers, 43rd Infantry, and the 14th Light Dragoons launched a lighthearted but spirited campaign of

The Second Attack on Fort Bower...

throwing fir cones at the officers of the 85th Light Infantry, 93rd Highlanders, and the 95th Rifles. Other pastimes were organized, such as a theatrical play. These lighthearted episodes helped to keep the troops occupied during the wait for troopships to take on provisions for the long voyage from America to Britain.

The other concerns were the local reptile population becoming more active. Snakes were very numerous and even found in the soldiers' beds. Alligators were seen to wander throughout camp, in one instance entering a tent with a mother and child inside. No harm came to either, but the episode made vigilance on everyone's part a constant necessity. It was not long before the officers switched their fishing and hunting activities to the demise of snakes and alligators rather than ducks and fish.

The Royal Navy fleet in the Chesapeake was also informed of the peace treaty. Their last engagement in war was the Battle of the Ice Mound on February 7, 1815. A tender from HMS *Dauntless* (20) was sent ashore near Choptank River to obtain supplies. It returned with two escaped slaves and was attacked by a company of troops from the 48th Regiment of Maryland Militia. The boat was stuck fast on an ice flow. After a two-hour fight three Royal Marines and thirteen sailors under Lieutenant Matthew Phibbs RN, and the two slaves were captured. Also taken were a twelve-pound carronade, a swivel gun, and small arms.

The Royal Navy at Halifax kept a strong presence in North American waters, including the bomb vessels HMS *Meteor, Aetna,* and *Vesuvius,* which finally returned to the United Kingdom in August 1815. A return to normal relations with the United States took place gradually. The British army returned a number of regiments to the United Kingdom as well as keeping a strong presence in her various Canadian colonies.

Appendix I

The Treaty of Ghent

At various times during the war both sides attempted negotiations with each other. However, each attempt failed. In late 1814 the American government realized that the country was nearly bankrupt, the British naval and military forces would continue to strangle the US economy, and, despite British setbacks at Baltimore and Plattsburgh, the enemy would continue to build up their strength to ultimately gain a complete military victory, to match the economic victory they were clearly obtaining.

The British were also under extreme pressure to conclude this war and return to a peacetime economy for the first time in about twenty years. However, the European political situation was such that Field Marshal Arthur Wellesley, the Duke of Wellington, declared that the European situation demanded a large presence of British troops to maintain stability, and in his opinion to completely win the war against America the Royal Navy would have to completely dominate the Great Lakes.

In article 10 of the treaty, both nations agreed to use their best efforts to promote the entire abolition of slavery. Unfortunately, the United States found that this would became a principle cause of the most costly war in her history, the American Civil War.

Appendix II

Who Won the War of 1812?

The British, Americans, and Canadians all claim to have won the war. The Americans call this the "Second War of Independence." In Britain and Canada it is seen as a war for Canada's very existence.

The United States' economy slowed, staggered, and came near to complete destruction owing to the Royal Navy's blockade and suppression of trade. The British economy actually grew during this same period, despite fighting two wars simultaneously.

The Royal Navy lost approximately 1 percent of its strength. The United States Navy (not counting privateers) lost 20 percent of its strength.

US casualties were higher than British and Canadian casualties.

US prisoners of war were far more numerous (mostly sailors) than British prisoners.

None of the stated goals of the United States were obtained; neither side lost territory.

America believes it won the war on the strength of the victories at Plattsburgh, Baltimore, and New Orleans. These victories were followed closely by the ratification of the Treaty of Ghent. This certainly can give the impression that the U.S. won the war.

Rockets, Bombs and Bayonets

Britain recognizes its military winning a war by the awarding of battle honours. The British Honours for the War of 1812 are: Detroit 16 Aug 1812, Queenstown 13 Oct 1812, Miami 23 April 1813, Niagara 25 July 1814, and Bladensburg 24 Aug 1814.

Canada had a few units that survived disbandment after the war. They were rewarded with the Niagara 25th July 1814 battle honour.

In September 2012 the Canadian government recognized the wider contribution of Canada's forces and awarded the following honours to the modern units that perpetuate those from the War of 1812: Detroit, Queenstown, Maumee, Niagara, Chateauguay, Chrysler's Farm, and a general Defence of Canada 1812–1815 honour.

A unique battle honour was awarded by King George III to the De Meuron Regiment. This came in the form of a specially engraved spearhead for their colours. It is inscribed *"7 au 14 Septembre 1814 a PLATZBOURG couvrant la retraite de L'ARMEE ANGLAISE."* This unique award was obtained for them by Sir John C. Sherbrooke, who had served alongside this same regiment in 1799 in India. The spearhead is preserved in the Musee d'Histoire, Neuchatel, Switzerland.

The demobilization of British forces, including the mercenary regiments, saw many officers placed on half-pay lists, with the majority never returning to active service. The massive army was eventually dissolved back into British daily life, but only after the final defeat of Napoleon at Waterloo.

The mercenary regiments saw their officers retained on half-pay lists while their men were given the option of remaining in Britain or returning to Europe. Many of the De Meuron Regiment elected to remain in the Canadas. One hundred soldiers became part of Lord Selkirk's expedition to the Red River in 1816.

Appendix III

Timeline of Reconciliation and Co-operation

The last angry shots of the War of 1812 were fired between USS *Peacock* and East Indiaman *Nautilus* on June 30, 1815, in the Indian Ocean, long after the Treaty of Ghent ended the last war between the English-speaking peoples. A new era of political diplomacy began, with many difficult situations between America, Britain, and the newly emerging nation The Dominion of Canada.

Renewed warfare was always an underlying fear for at least the next one hundred years. The Rush-Bagot Treaty of 1817 saw the demilitarization of the Great Lakes; however, the guns were only feet away under the deck, being used as ballast!

The First Seminole War of 1818 saw a highly controversial incident in which two British subjects were executed under the orders of Major General Andrew Jackson—Robert Chrysler Armbrister, a former Royal Navy midshipman who had served as an auxiliary 2nd lieutenant in the British Corps of Colonial Marines under Major Edward Nicolls RM, and Alexander George Arbuthnot, a Scottish merchant and translator—along with two Creek-Seminole leaders. Arbuthnot had been granted clemency by the court, but Jackson insisted on his and Armbrister's execution (along with a number of Seminoles). This was perceived as an act of barbarity in Britain and elsewhere.

The House of Representatives of the United States disapproved of the proceedings in the trial and the execution of the men. Jackson escaped Congressional censure for his actions by a vote of 107 to 63.

In 1826 the British government decided to move the capital of Upper and Lower Canada from the vulnerable border region. Lieutenant Colonel John By of the Royal Engineers was assigned to build a navigable waterway between Kingston and the Ottawa River. A new town was established in 1826 and named Bytown; in 1855 it was renamed Ottawa. The waterway was constructed as a defensible military canal, protected by strong stone-built forts and blockhouses, to deter any future military action by the United States.

Half-pay British officers and enlisted veterans were encouraged to settle in the Canadian provinces and join the militia to help form a second hidden boundary line of defence running through Rice Lake and across Upper Canada, again to deter any U.S. invasion.

The Oregon Crisis of 1818 to 1846 and the Maine-New Brunswick (Aroostook) War resulted in the Webster-Ashburn treaty of 1842, a political sore spot between Britain and the United States. The Patriot Rebellions in 1837 to 1838 saw British troops quelling internal dissent. All of these events kept a feeling of unease in the Canadas and in the mother country.

The Battle of the Windmill (near Prescott) in 1838 saw the Royal Navy, Royal Marines, Royal Artillery, and the 83rd Regiment, with several units of Canadian militia, involved in a bloody encounter with the Onondaga Hunters, from Oswego and Sackets Harbor, NY. The Royal Marines, led by Lieutenant Charles Arthur Parker RM, endured 50 percent of their number wounded, including Lieutenant Parker, and one killed. Private Robert Kershaw RM, was the last Royal Marine killed in defending the soil of Upper Canada.

The Pig War boundary dispute, on San Juan Island in 1859, was another near-war situation. Again the Royal Navy and the Royal Marines were in the forefront of British–Canadian defence. The 9th US Infantry was present, looking after American interests on the island. Two interesting personalities were present during the confrontation, Captain George E. Pickett of the 9th U.S. Infantry, later known as the leader of General Pickett's charge at Gettysburg, and Colour Sergeant John Prettyjohns RM, one of the first Victoria Cross winners in the Crimean War.

The Trent affair in 1861, along with the St. Albans Raid in 1864, kept war tensions high during the US Civil War. The Royal Navy continually

Appendix III

patrolled the Atlantic, Pacific, and Gulf of Mexico waters and was ready to blockade the north at any time. British shipbuilders, including William Simons of HMS *Confiance* and *Linnet* fame, were building blockade runners for the Confederate cause.

The Fenian Raids of 1866 and 1870 saw many Irish American veterans of the US Civil War attack Canada. The Canadian militia took the brunt of the fighting; the Royal Navy and the Royal Marines were still present in the Great Lakes and took part in repulsing these attacks.

The American policy of pursuing a "manifest destiny" in expanding her territory became an increasing concern for both Britain and Canada, especially when the United States became more industrialized and acquired more and more territory by war and by purchase.

The new Dominion of Canada assumed the defence of her own territory in 1867 with a small "permanent force" of trained regular soldiers and kept up a strong militia. The Royal Navy would remain the dominion's maritime protector until 1910, when the Canadian navy took over.

The Treaty of Washington in 1871 saw the first inclusion of the Canadian Commissioner in talks to settle various disputes. The Commissioner was Sir John A. Macdonald, Canada's first Prime Minister.

The first British and American co-operation took place at Alexandria, Egypt, in 1885. When Christians and hundreds of others were being massacred, the USMC and Blue Jackets from the U.S. European Squadron, under Captain Henry Clay Cochrane, USMC, joined with the Royal Marines; both provided security for fleeing civilians of all nations.

In 1893 the Royal Marines Artillery plus a sub unit of Royal Marines Submarine Miners were sent to Esquimalt to upgrade military installations (Fort Rod Hill) and mine the approaches to Esquimalt and Vancouver Harbour. The force remained onsite till 1899, while the Canadian government never actually purchased the required mines. The detachment did upgrade the defences at Esquimalt and Victoria. They also trained two battalions of the 5th Regiment of Canadian Artillery.

The next significant event of U.S. and British forces' co-operation was in China in 1900. Marines from both countries combined into one unified unit during the defence of the legations in Peking. Captain Lewis Stratford Tollemache Halliday, RMLI, and Captain John T. Meyers, USMC, agreed to use seniority of officers and non-commissioned officers of both units to pass down the chain of command as the more senior marines became casualties. Captain Halliday was wounded and awarded the Victoria Cross for bravery in this action. The relief force coming to the aid of the legations also contained naval and marine forces of both nations, as well as many others.

World War I saw Britain, Canada, and the United States at war with a common enemy. Both marine corps saw action at sea and in the fields of Flanders, where the USMC gained the nickname "Devil Dogs."

After WWI both Canada and the United States developed theoretical plans to invade each other. Canada's "Defence Plan No. 1" was developed by Colonel J. Sutherland "Buster" Brown. This plan envisaged using Canada's 4,000 regulars and 38,000 militia to occupy a number of U.S. cities in the west and other attacks in the east.

The U.S. plan was "War Plan Red." This plan was designed to eliminate the British Empire, including Canada. It was one of a number of colour-coded plans, such as War Plan Yellow against Japan. Oddly enough, there was no War Plan Black against Germany.

World War II again saw the USMC and Royal Marines combining forces, in the Pacific theatre against the Empire of Japan. Canada, Britain, and the United States lost many troops to the initial Japanese attacks. The war in the Pacific was conducted with mainly U.S. and U.K. forces, while Canadians fought mainly in Europe.

The Cold war against the Communist world saw the United States, Great Britain, and Canada as allies.

In the Korean War, 41 Independent Commando Royal Marines was attached to the United States 1st Marine Division, serving in raids on Wonsan Harbour and Sorye Dong, and during the Chosin Reservoir campaign. They were awarded the Presidential Unit Citation. Other Royal Marines served on Royal Navy vessels throughout the war. Canadian, U.S., and British army units all served under the U.N. banner.

Since Korea, the British, Canadian, and U.S. forces have fought in Iraq and Afghanistan. Today, in the twenty-first century, the nations of the free world have never been more united in peace and war.

Endnotes

[1] Privy Council: *Regulations and Instructions Relating to His Majesty's Service at Sea.* 1808, p. 422.
[2] Field, Cyril. *Britain's Sea Soldiers,* "Memoirs of Lord St. Vincent," p. 204
[3] Gordon, L.L. *British Battles and Medals.* p. 57
[4] Blumberg, H.E. *Royal Marines Records 1793-1836.* Special Publication #4 RM HQ, 1983. p. 22.
[5] Downs, P & J. *Sea Soldier: Journal of Maj. T.M. Wybourn RM.* pp. 191-192.
[6] Palmer. *History of Lake Champlain 1609-1814.* pp. 175-176.
[7] Ibid.
[8] Craig, A. *The Sheet Anchor Vol. XXV* No. 2.
[9] Palmer. *History of Lake Champlain.* p. 182.
[10] Craig, A. *The Sheet Anchor Vol. XXV* No.1 & No. 2.
[11] Latimer, S. *1812 War With America.* p. 279; Morgan, J.C. *Emigrants Notebook and Guide.* p. 333.
[12] Laughton, Frazer & Carr. *The Royal Marine Artillery 1804-1923.* p. 249.
[13] Sturdevant. "Recollections of the Battle of Sandy Creek," *Waterdown Daily Times,* 1893, July 17, p. 3.
[14] Chester, G. *Battle of Big Sandy.* p. 135.
[15] Ibid. p. 134.
[16] Ibid. p. 204-205
[17] *Letterbook of Isaac Chauncey.* New York Historical Society.
[18] Field, Cyril. *Britain's Sea Soldiers.*
[19] Smith. *The Autobiography of Lieutenant-General Sir Harry Smith.* p. 197.
[20] Marine. *The British Invasion of Maryland.* p. 114.

21 Adams. *The War of 1812.* p. 229.

22 Cole. *Memoirs of British Generals Distinguised During the Peninsula Wars Vol.2.* p. 315.

23 "Britons, Strike Home!" Popular song of the period after "Rule Britannia" and "Hearts of Oak." From the opera *Bonduca* by Henry Purcell, 1695.

24 Mahan. *Seapower and the War of 1812.* p. 249.

25 Everest. *War in the Champlain Valley.* p. 150-152; Izard to Armstrong 31 July 1814; Latimer. *1812 War with America.* p. 263.

26 Richards. *Memoir of Alexander Macomb the Major General.* p. 82.

27 Latimer. *1812 War with America.* p. 352; Preston. *The Journals of Sir. F.P. Robinson G.C.B.* ch. 37.

28 Wood. *Plattsburgh 1814: Extracts from Diary Captain Afterwards Colonel J.H. Wood RA.*

29 *The Publications of the Champlain Society. Vol. III, Part I, p. 397.*

30 Craig, A. "The Diary of Captain James Ballingall RM." *The Sheet Anchor,* XVII, No. 2, RMHS. 1993.

31 *Some Account of the Public Life of Sir George Prevost Bart.* Appendix XXX, p. 78 & 79.

32 Ibid. p. 80.

33 Ibid. p. 82

34 *The Publications of the Champlain Society. Vol. III, Part I, p. 382; Some Account of the Public Life of Sir George Prevost Bart.* Appendix XXX, p. 83.

35 *Bryden Testimony at Courts Martial of British Officers & Men 1815.*

36 *Lt. Bell's Testimony the Court Martial of Capt. Daniel Pring and Officers & Men on Lake Champlain 1815.*

37 *The Centenary of the Battle of Plattsburgh.* University of the State of New York, 1914. p. 34.

38 Fitz-Enz. *The Final Invasion.* p. 234; *Niles Weekly Register, Vol. 8, 1815.* p. 173.

39 *Plattsburgh Republican,* Sept. 22, 1877.

40 Hitsman. *The Incredible War of 1812.* p. 254; Latimer. *1812 War with America.* p. 354.

41 Herkalo. *The Battles at Plattsburgh September 11, 1814.* p. 102.

42 Hayden. *The Historical Record of the 76th "Hindoostan" Regiment.* p. 104.

43 Ibid. p. 105.

44 Wood. *Plattsburgh 1814.* p. 13.

Endnotes

45 *Reminiscences of Gen. Sir Thomas M. Brisbane (Bart).* p. 29.
46 Ibid.
47 Gleig. *A Subaltern in America.* p. 133.
48 Scott. *Recollections of a Naval Life Vol. III.* p. 336.
49 Sheads. *The Rockets Red Glare.* p. 91.
50 Barrett. *Naval Recollections.* p. 462.
51 Roche. "A Seaman's Notebook" *Maryland Historical Magazine 42.*
52 Sheads. *The Rockets Red Glare.* p. 80.
53 Ibid. p. 95.
54 Ibid.
55 Field. *Britain's Sea Soldiers.* p. 301; Nicolas. *The Historical Records of the Royal Marine Forces Vol. II.* p. 287.
56 Carr-Laughton, Fraser. *The Royal Marine Artillery Vol. I.* p. 284.
57 Ibid.
58 Ibid. p. 286.
59 Latimer. *1812 War with America.* p. 379.
60 Carr-Laughton, Fraser. *The Royal Marine Artillery Vol. I.* p. 293.
61 Cooper. *Rough Notes on Seven Campaigns.* p. 140.
62 Latimer. *1812 War with America.* p. 385.
63 Cooke. *A Narrative of Events in the South of France and the Attack on New Orleans of John Henry Cooke, 1835.* T&W Boone, New Bond St., London. p. 240.
64 National Army Museum Memoir by John Hutchison.
65 Latimer. *1812 War with America.* p. 387; Cooper. *Rough Notes on Seven Campaigns.* p. 141.
66 Ibid; Ibid p. 142.
67 Cooper. *Rough Notes on Seven Campaigns.* p. 143.
68 Cope. *The History of the Rifle Brigade.* p. 190.
69 Cooper. *Rough Notes on Seven Campaigns.* p. 144-145.
70 National Army Museum Memoir by John Hutchison.
71 Horton. *Slavery and the Making of America.* p. 82.
72 Latour. *Historical Memoir of the War in West Florida and Louisiana in 1814-1815.* p.191-194.
73 Ibid. p. 195-197.
74 Cooper. *Rough Notes on Seven Campaigns.* p. 146.

Select Bibliography

Adams, Henry. *The War of 1812.* Cooper Square Press, 1999.

Barrett, Richard E. *Naval Recollections.* United Service Journal, April, 1841.

Brisbane, T.M. *Reminicences of Gen. Sir Thomas M. Brisbane (Bart).* Edinburgh: Thomas Constable, 1850.

Burgoyne, Roderick H. *Historical Records of the 93rd Sutherland Highlanders.* London: R Bentley & Son, 1883.

Charbonneau, Andre. *The Fortifications of Ile-aux-Noix.* Ottawa: Publishing, Supply and Services, 1994.

Chester, Gregory. *Battle of Big Sandy.* Gregory Chester, 2007.

Clarke, James. *Historical Record and Regimental Memoir of The Royal Scots Fusiliers.* Edinburgh: Banks & Co., 1885.

Clowes, Sir William L. *The Royal Navy: A History from the Earliest Times to 1900.* London: S. Low, 1897.

Cole, John William. *Memoirs of British Generals Distinguished During the Peninsula Wars Vol II.* London: Richard Bentley, 1856.

Cooper, John S. *Rough Notes of Seven Campaigns in Portugal, Spain, France and America During the Years 1809–1815.* Spellmount, 1996.

Duncan, Francis Major RA. *History of the Royal Regiment of Artillery, vol. II.* London: John Murray, 1879.

Everest, Allen S. *The War of 1812 in the Champlain Valley.* Syracuse: Syracuse University Press, 1981.

Select Bibliography

Field, Cyril, Colonel R.M.L.I. *Britain's Sea—Soldiers.* Liverpool: Lyceum Press, 1924.

Fitz-Enz, David G., Colonel. *The Final Invasion.* New York: Cooper Square Press, 2001.

Filion, Mario. *Le Blockhaus de la riviere Lacolle.* Municipalite de Saint-Paul-de-Ile-aux-Noix: 1998.

Fraser, E. & L. G. Carr-Laughton. *The Royal Marine Artillery 1804—1923.* Whitehall: The Royal United Service Institution, 1930.

Gleig, George R. *The Campaigns of the British Army at Washington and New Orleans.* London: John Murray, 1827.

Gordon, Major L.L. *British Battles & Medals 4th Edition.* London: Spink & Son, 1971.

Hayden, F.A. *The Historical Record of the 76th "Hindoostan" Regiment.* The Johnson's Head, 1909.

Herkalo, Kieth A. *September Eleventh 1814: The Battles at Plattsburgh.* Lulu Press, 2007.

Heidler, David S., and Jeanne T. Heidler. *Encyclopedia of the War of 1812.* Santa Barbara: Naval Institute Press, 1997.

Hitsman. J. Mackay. *The Incredible War of 1812.* Toronto: University of Toronto Press, 1965.

Horton, James O. *Slavery and the Making of America.* Oxford University Press, 2005.

Irving, Homfray. *Officers of the British Forces in Canada During the War of 1812–15.* Welland: Welland Tribune, 1908.

Keyes, Roger, Admiral of the Fleet. *Amphibious Warfare and Combined Operations.* London: Cambridge University Press, 1943.

Lambert, Andrew. *The Challenge.* London: Faber & Faber, 2012.

Latimer, Jon. *1812 War with America.* Cambridge, Mass: Harvard University Press, 2009.

Latour. *Historical Memoir of the War in West Florida and Louisiana in 1814-1815.* University Press of Florida, 1999.

Mahan, Alfred T. *Sea Power in its Relations to the War of 1812.* London: Sampson Low, Marston & Co. Ltd., 1903.

Marine, William B. *The British Invasion of Maryland 1812–1815.* Maryland: Society of the War of 1812 in Maryland, 1913.

Munday, John. *Naval Cannon.* Buckinghamshire: Shire Publications Ltd., 1998.

New York Historical Society Letterbook of Commodore Isaac Chauncey. New York City.

Nicholas, Paul Harris, Lieutenant RM. *The Historical Records of the Royal Marine Forces.* London: T. & W. Boone, 1845.

Pack, James, Captain, RN. *The Man Who Burned the White House.* Elmsworth: Kenneth Mason, 1987.

Palmer, Peter S. *History of Lake Champlain 1609–1814.* Fleischmanns, N.Y.: Purple Mountain Press, 1992.

Preston, Richard A. *The Journals of Sir F.P. Robinson G.C.B.* Toronto: University of Toronto Press, 1956.

Prevost, George, Sir. *Some Account of the Public Life of the late Lieut-General Sir George Prevost, Bart.* Printed for T. Cadell, Strand and T. Egerton, Whitehall, 1823.

Privy Council. *Regulations and Instructions to His Majesty's Service at Sea.* London: 1808.

Pullen, H.E. *The Shannon and the Chesapeake.* Toronto: McLelland & Stewart, 1970.

Richards, George H. *Memoir of Alexander Macomb the Major General.* New York: McElrath, Bangs & Co., 1833.

Scott, James, Captain, RN. *Recollections of a Naval Life.* Vol. 3. Oxford: Oxford University Press, 1834.

Sheads, Scott S. *The Rockets' Red Glare.* Centerville: Tidewater Publishers, 1986.

Skaggs, David C. *Thomas Macdonough Master of Command in the Early US Navy.* Naval Institute Press, 2003.

Smith, G.C. *The Autobiography of Lt. General Sir Harry Smith.* London: John Murray, Albemarle St., William Clowes & Sons Ltd., 1903.

Smith, Joshua M. *Battle for the Bay: Naval War of 1812.* Gregg Centre, 2011.

Select Bibliography

Smyth. B, Lieutenant, Lancashire Fusiliers. *History of the XX Regiment.* London: Simpkin, Marshall, & Co. 1889.

War Office. *A List of Officers of the Army and Royal Marines on Full or Half Pay.* January 1, 1821.

Wood. J.H., Col. *Plattsburgh 1814: Extracts from the Diary of Captain afterwards Colonel J.H. Wood RA.*

Wybourn, T. Marmaduke. *Sea Soldier. An Officer of Marines with Duncan, Nelson, Collingwood and Cockburn: The Letters and Journal of Major T Marmaduke Wybourn, RM, 1797–1813.* Edited by Anne Petrides and Jonathan Downs. Tunbridge Wells: Parapress, 2000.

Manuscripts

Hooper Thomas. *The Naval Station at Ile-aux-Noix, 1812–1834.* Unpublished.

Hutchison, Joseph, Major. *A Memoir by Major Joseph Hutchison, 1815.* London: National Army Museum Archives, Chelsea.

Lee David. *#47 Theme Papers, Ile-aux-Noix.* National Historic Sites Service, Dept. Indian Affairs, 1967.

Anonymous. *The Court Martial of Capt. Daniel Pring & the Officers & Men on Lake Champlain.* 1815.

Periodicals

Blumberg, H. E. *Royal Marines Records 1793–1836: Special Publication,* no. 4. RMHS, 1983.

Craig. A. "The Diary of Captain James Ballingall, RM—Service on the Great Lakes of Canada, 1841." *The Sheet Anchor* Vol. XVIII, no. 2. RMHS, 1993.

Craig. A. "Lower Canada Preserved—1st Bn RM in Canada—1812." *The Sheet Anchor* Vol. XXV, no. 2. RMHS, 2000.

Roche. "A Seaman's Notebook." *Maryland Historical Magazine* 42. Baltimore: 1947.

Sturdevant, J.M, Doctor. "Recollections of the Battle of Sandy Creek." *Waterdown Daily Times,* 1873.

Index

Abbot, Joel Midshipman USN, 67
Abernathie, T. Major RM, 14
Ackley, Gad Captain NY Militia, 46, 48
Ackley, Joseph, 26
Adair, Thomas Brvt. Major RM, 159
Alexander, Thomas Captain RN, 129, 131
Alexandria, Virginia, 55, 56, 129, 185
Allen, William Lt. Act/Captain RM, 140
Allen, William Midshipman RN, 96
Anaconda, Privateer, 22
Anderson, Alexander Captain RM, 14, 21, 24, 65-67, 82, 83, 90, 100. 101
Appling, Daniel Major US Rifles, 44-48, 73, 75, 76
Armistead, George Major USA, 124, 128
Armistead, Lewis Lieutenant US Rifles, 47
Armstrong, John, Secretary of State, 60, 70
Arnaud, Paul Major, 160
Ashmore, John Lieutenant RM, 42, 65, 66, 88
Asquith, Edward Captain, 119
Atlas, US Privateer, 22

Auna-Maria, Dispatch Boat, 55
Axhorn, Henry Private, 165

Baker, Major US Infantry, 151
Baker, William Sergeant, 28
Balchild, George E. Lieutenant RMA, 13, 18, 20, 24, 33, 42, 70, 78, 111, 113
Ballingall, David J. Captain RM, 83, 188, 193
Baltimore, Maryland, 22, 56, 58, 64, 118, 119, 121, 122
Barclay, Robert H. Captain RN, 23
Barney, Joshua Commodore USN, 55, 58, 59, 60, 61, 62
Barret, Robert Midshipman RN, 125
Bartholomew, David E. Captain RN, 131
Barton, Samuel Lieutenant RM, 30, 32, 34, 35
Bathurst, Earl, 69, 70, 106, 122
Baynes, Edward Adjutant General, 69, 73, 109, 112
Bayou, Bienvenue (Catalan), 147, 150,

Index

169
Beachaunt, Theophilus S. Lieutenant RMA, 131
Beal, Thomas Captain, 151, 165
Beanes, Dr. William, 131
Beckwith, Sir Thomas S. Quartermaster General, 19, 75, 76
Bell, Christopher J. Midshipman RN, 88, 95, 96, 188
Benedict, Maryland, 58, 59, 64
Big Sandy Creek, NY, 44, 45, 46, 50, 65, 73
Bissell, Daniel General USA, 28, 34
Bladensburg, Maryland, 59, 60-64, 118, 120, 161, 182
Blainey, Daniel Lieutenant USA, 39
Blakney, John Lieutenant, 158
Bodell, John Midshipman RN, 92
Bond, Ensign, 86
Brisbane, Thomas Maj. General, 70-76, 106-114, 189, 190.
Brooke, Arthur Colonel, 119-122, 129, 132
Brooks, Alexander Captain US Artillery, 110
Brountin, Captain US Infantry, 176
Brown, J Corporal RM, 32
Brum, Mr Sailing Master USN, 99
Bryden, Robert A. Sailing Master, 88, 90, 99, 188
Budd, Charles A. Midshipman USN, 97
Burgoyne, John F. Colonel RE, 158
Butler, William O. Major US Infantry, 151

Caldwell, Glassen Lieutenant RM, 65, 66, 98
Caldwell, William R. Lieutenant RM, 30, 35, 66, 88, 98
Carroll, William Major General, 151
Cartwright, Edward Captain, 31, 33
Cassin, Stephen Lieutenant USN, 27, 43, 94, 96, 99
Castine Fund, 117
Catesby-Jones, Thomas Lt. USN, 148, 149
Caulk's Field, Maryland, 124
Chalmette Plantation, 156, 163
Chandeleur Islands, 147, 150, 158, 169, 171, 177
Chapman, J. Sgt. Act/Lieutenant RM, 140
Chapman, John Ensign, 74
Chauncey, Isaac Commodore USN, 37, 50, 70, 113, 187, 192
Chazel, Jean P., 135, 136
Chazy N.Y., 71-73, 82, 85-89, 101, 111, 112
Chesapeake Bay, 20, 51, 55, 56, 63, 66, 123, 132, 139, 179
Chesapeake, Steamboat, 127
Childs, Joseph Lieutenant RM, 65, 66, 90
Chittenden, Martin Gov. Vermont, 79
Chrisjohn, Jim Oneida Warrior, 48
Claggett, Levi Lieutenant, 128
Clairborne, William C.C. Governor, 151
Clements, William T. Captain RM, 140
Clemm, John Sergeant, 128
Cochrane, Sir Alexander F. I. Vice Admiral RN, 51, 54-56, 59, 64, 118, 122-124, 126-129, 131, 140, 145-147, 157, 170, 171, 177, 178

Cochrane, Thomas Captain RN, 124
Cochrane, William Brevet Major ADC, 108
Cockburn, Sir George Rear Admiral RN, 13, 18-20, 51, 52, 54, 55, 58, 59, 61-63, 118, 119, 121, 123, 124, 129, 132, 142, 143, 193
Codrington, Edward Rear Admiral RN, 64, 125
Coffee, John Brigadier General, 151-153
Congreve Rocket, 19, 63, 80, 120, 131, 150, 178
Conover, Thomas Midshipman USN, 96
Cooke, John Captain, 167, 189
Cooper, John S. Sergeant, 165, 167-169, 177, 189, 190
Coore, Foster L. Major ADC, 87, 89
Coulter, John Lieutenant RM, 42
Cox, Henry Ships Carpenter RN, 89, 98
Cox, Thomas S. Lieutenant RM, 46-50
Crab Island, NY, 73, 77, 97, 102-104, 115
Craney Island, Virginia, 19-20
Creswick, Charles Lieutenant RN, 35, 99
Crozier, Acheson Lieutenant RM, 161
Culver Hill, NY, 74
Cunningham, Thomas S. Lieutenant USN, 172

Dauphin Island, Alabama, 177-178
Davis, John Lt. Colonel, 160
DeBersey, Rudolph Captain, 39
De Graffenreid, Frederic Subaltern, 77
De La Roche, George Sailing Master USN, 125
De Meuron-Bayard, Francois Lt. Colonel, 76

De Rottenburg, Baron George F. Maj. General, 69, 70, 75, 110, 113
De Salaberry, Charles-Michel Lt. Colonel, 69
Diadem, Transport, 23
Dickman, William H. Midshipman RN, 98
Dickson, Alexander Colonel RA, 154, 156, 158, 167
Diggs, Beverly Sailing Master, 127
Diomede, Transport, 23
Doty, Simeon Private, 104
Dowling, Thomas Lt. Colonel, 132
Downie, George Post Captain RN, 72, 73, 81-93, 99-101, 103, 105, 113
Drew, William Lieutenant RN, 99
Drummond, Sir George Lieutenant General, 37, 39, 40
Duell, Thomas Lieutenant RN, 88
Duncan, Silas Lieutenant USN, 75

Edmondson, Arthur Captain's Clerk RN, 121
Eli, Dr. Samuel, 49
Ellard, Henry Captain, 31, 35
Elliot, Gilbert Lieutenant RM, 161
Elliott, Henry Lieutenant RM, 160, 161
Emmerson, Edward Captain USA, 19
Everard, Thomas Captain RN, 26

Fennell, John Lieutenant RM, 25, 66
Ferris, John D. Sailing Master USN, 148
Fisher, Peter Post Captain RN, 44, 67, 68
Fischer, Victor Lt. Colonel, 38
Fitzpatrick, Lieutenant, 86
Flying Squadron, 9, 14, 15

Index

Ford, Charles Lieutenant RA, 165
Forlorn Hope, 32, 164
Forsyth, Benjamin Major 1st US Rifles, 28-31, 73
Fort Albion, 139, 142
Fort Barrancas, 141, 142
Fort Bower, 140, 141, 145, 177, 178
Fort Brown, 73, 78
Fort Erie, 25, 41, 78
Fort McHenry, 124, 126, 128-131, 146
Fort Moreau, 73, 76, 105
Fort Ontario (Oswego), 37-39, 81
Fort Peter, 142, 143
Fort Scott, 73
Fort St. Charles, 146, 163
Fort St. Philip, 146, 171, 172
Fort Warburton (Fort Washington), 55
Fort Wellington, 24
Fox, Transport, 23, 177
Franklin, John Lieutenant RN, 149
Frazer, Solomon Lieutenant USN, 130
Fulford, Henry Private, 161
Furzer, J. P. Lieutenant RMA, 131, 136, 137, 172

Gaines, Edmond P. General USA, 45, 49
Gamble, Peter Lieutenant USN, 92
Gell, Thomas Captain, 117
Gibbs, Sir Samuel Maj. General, 154, 155, 163-166, 168
Gleig, George R. Lieutenant, 59, 120, 135, 136, 150-153, 155, 161, 169, 189, 191
Golden Fleece, Transport, 135, 136
Gooder, Mr. Assistant Surgeon, 140
Gordon, Charles H. Lieutenant, 166

Gordon, Frederic Captain RA, 79
Gordon, James A. Captain RN, 55, 56, 124, 129, 142
Gore, Charles Lieutenant ADC, 113
Gosselin, Gerard Maj. General, 117
Gracie, James Lieutenant, 60
Grahame, Fortesque Lieutenant RM, 42
Gratton, William Lieutenant, 69
Greene, William Brevet Major, 108, 110
Grifith, Edward Rear Admiral RN, 68, 117
Grifith, Valentine Lieutenant RM, 25
Gunn, William Midshipman RN, 101

Halifax, Nova Scotia, 22, 23, 40, 44, 65, 68, 118, 132, 135, 146, 178, 179
Hamilton N.Y. (Waddington), 27
Hammond, William Ensign RM, 52
Hampton, Virginia, 18, 20, 21, 24
Hanchett, John M. Captain RN, 19
Handcock, Richard B. Major, 30-32
Harrison, James H. Captain RM, 61
Hatch, George Lieutenant, 109
Heath, Richard Major, 119
Heathrington, Edward Lieutenant, 109
Henley, John D. Captain USN, 151, 152
Henley, Robert Master Commandant USN, 90
Henry, Robert Lt. Act/ Captain RMA, 140, 141, 172
Hewett, John Lieutenant RM, 2, 39-41
Hicks, William Act. Lieutenant RN, 35, 97, 98, 100, 102
Hill, Josiah Lieutenant US Rifles, 46, 47
Hinds, Thomas Colonel, 151, 170, 171
Hoare, Charles Masters Mate RN, 46-49

Holgate, Bennet Captain, 31
Holtoway, William Captain RM, 39, 40
Holy Stones, 88
Hornby, William RN, 99
Hot Shot, 38, 77, 93, 94, 155
Houghton, Charles E. D. P. Midshipman RN, 95
Hubbel, Julius C. Judge, 103
Hutchison, Joseph Lieutenant, 165
Hutchison, Joseph Major, 167, 170, 193

Icicle, Tender, 88, 89, 95, 101
Ile aux Noix, 24-32, 42-44, 65-68, 72, 81-85, 101, 112, 142, 190, 191,193
Izard, George Maj. General USA, 35, 43, 70, 79, 106, 113, 188

Jackson, Andrew Maj. General, 141, 145, 146, 151, 152, 156 157, 163, 164, 167, 168, 170, 171, 183, 184
Jackson, Francis Boatswain RN, 101
Jebb, Joshua Lieutenant RE, 71
Jett, William Captain, 132
Johnson, Edward Mayor, 122
Johnson, Simon Private US Rifles, 47, 48
Johnson, William Sailing Master USN, 148
Jones, John E. Lieutenant RM, 25, 66

Keane, John Maj. General, 147, 150, 154, 155, 163, 164, 166
Kemp, Sir James Maj. General, 70, 113
Kenah, Richard Captain RN, 131, 132
Kennedy, John M. Ensign, 107, 108
Kent Island, Maryland, 22
Key, Francis S., 131

King George III, 11, 13, 19. 182
Kingsbury, Robert Lieutenant, 75
Kinsman, Andrew Major RM, 143

La Colle Mill, 28, 29, 42, 67, 107
Lake Borgne, 146-148, 154, 169
Lake Champlain, 26, 27, 33, 42-44, 65, 68, 81, 82, 88, 96, 113, 187, 188, 192, 193
Lake Ontario, 45, 65, 81, 101, 113
Lambert, Sir John Maj. General, 159, 163, 166, 167, 177, 178
Lane, Henry Captain RHA, 152, 159
Lang, John Lieutenant, 75
Larabee, Adam Lieutenant US Artillery, 34
Latour, A. Laccarriere Major USA Engineers, 173, 175, 189
Lawrence, John Lieutenant RMA, 120, 150, 155, 159, 178
Lawrence, William Major USA, 141, 178
Lawrie, James Lieutenant, 40
Lee, Richard Lieutenant RN, 104
Leonard, Luther Captain US Artillery, 73, 74, 75
Lewis, G. Major RM, 51-54, 140
Lindesay, Patrick Lt. Colonel, 108
Lockyer, Nicholas Captain RN, 140, 148 149
Lorentz, Charles Lieutenant, 165
Louder, Edward N. Captain RM, 21
Lundy's Lane, 41
Lynch, Robert B. Major RM, 30, 32, 42
Lynnhaven Bay, 22

Macomb, Alexander General USA, 28, 30, 70, 72, 73, 75, 77, 78, 79, 85,

Index

106, 107, 112-114, 188, 192

Macdonough, Thomas Commodor USN, 27, 33, 35, 42, 43, 67, 70, 75, 76, 78, 80, 90-93, 97, 99, 101-103, 105, 111, 149, 192

MacDougall, Duncan Major ADC, 119, 166

Madison, James President of the USA, 56, 60, 62-64, 78

Malcolm, James Major RM, 14, 24, 25, 39, 40, 51, 52, 54, 118

Malcolm, Sir Plutney Rear Admiral RN, 54, 64, 118, 124, 132, 157, 170, 177

Mann, James Doctor, 73, 97, 102

Manrique, Mateo G., 141

Marsh, John Lieutenant RMA, 25, 41

Massias, Abraham A. Captain US Rifles, 142, 143

Matthey, Frederic Captain, 111

McGhie, James Lieutenant RN, 91, 92, 102

McGlassin, George Captain US Infantry, 78

McIntosh, Major US Dragoons, 45

McKee, John Colonel USMC, 151

McKeene, Isaac Lieutenant USN, 148

McKenzie, Daniel T. Boy RN, 11

McMillan, Alexander Captain, 38

McPherson, Robert H. Captain USA, 31, 34

McVeagh, Patrick Lieutenant RM, 46-49

McWilliam, J Lieutenant Act. Captain, 140

Melvin, George W. US Artillery, 45

Melwood, Maryland, 59

Middleton, Samuel Captain RM, 66

Mitchell, George E. Lt. Colonel USA, 38, 39

Mitchell, Samuel Major, 154

Mitton, John Lieutenant RM, 25

Money, Rowland Captain RN, 159, 161

"Moneymusk," Pipe tune, 166

Monroe, Isaac Private, 128

Monroe, James Secretary of State, 17, 60

Montgomery, Captain Union Artillery, 118

Montressor, Henry Captain RN, 149

Mooers, Benjamin General NY Militia, 70, 109

Moore, James A. Lieutenant RMA, 131

Morgan, John C. Lieutenant RM, 39

Morgan, Charles Lieutenant RM, 161

Morgan, David Brig. General USA, 157, 160, 164

Mould, Thomas Captain RM, 25

Mulcaster, William Captain RN, 39, 40

Mullins, Thomas Captain Bvt. Lt. Colonel, 164, 165

Murray, John Lt. Colonel, 26

Murray, Sir George Lieutenant General, 115

Murray, Captain US Artillery, 176

Napier, Charles Lieutenant RN, 129, 130

Napier, Charles Lt. Colonel, 20

Napier, H. A. Lieutenant RMA, 131

Nautilus, East Indiaman, 183

Nelson, Horatio Admiral RN, 10, 13, 82, 88, 104, 193

Nemesis, Transport, 23

New Orleans, Louisiana, 124, 132, 140, 143, 145-147, 150, 157, 161-163, 166, 170-173, 175, 177, 181, 189, 191

Newcomb, Henry Lieutenant USN, 127, 129, 130

Nicolls, Edward Major Bvt. Colonel RM, 140, 142, 145, 146, 183

Nichols, Caleb, 104

Norfolk Navy Yard, 19, 20

North Point, Maryland, 117-119, 125, 131, 132

Nourse, Joseph Captain RN, 55

Odelltown L.C., 29, 72, 112

Ogalvie, George Lieutenant, 109

Oliver, Lieutenant Canadian Militia, 87, 95

Oswego, New York, 2, 37-39, 41, 44, 45, 81, 184

Otter Creek, Vermont, 27, 42, 43

Overton, Walter H. Major, 171, 172, 176

Packenham, Sir Edward Lieutenant General, 154, 157-160, 163, 164, 166, 168

Parke, Thomas A. Captain RMA, 13, 14, 20, 22, 24, 27, 33, 34, 70, 78, 110

Parker, Sir Peter Captain RN, 56, 124

Patterson, Daniel T. Commodore USN, 160

Pauling, Hiram Midshipman USN, 96

Paul, William Lieutenant RN, 151

Pearce, George Lieutenant USN, 39, 45

Pechell, Samuel J.B. Captain RN, 19

Penobscott, Maine, 117, 118

Pensacola, Spanish Florida, 140, 141, 145, 147

Percy, The Honourable Henry Captain RN, 140

Perry, Oliver H. Commodore USN, 126

Phelps, Benajah, 102

Phibbs, Matthew Lieutenant RN, 179

Phillips, John A. Lieutenant RM, 42

Piere, Henry B. Major US Infantry, 151

Plattsburgh NY, 6, 7, 26-28, 65, 66, 70, 72-77, 79, 84, 86, 88, 97, 102, 105, 107, 108, 110-114, 149, 180, 181, 188, 191, 193

Plattsburgh Republican (Newspaper), 28, 188

Popham, Sir Home Commodore RN, 15

Popham, Stephen Captain RN, 45-50

Power, Sir Manley Maj. General, 71, 73, 75, 77, 107-109, 112

Pratt, George Lieutenant RN, 149

Prevost, Sir George Lieutenant General, 13, 23-27, 37, 41, 42, 64, 68-73, 75-79, 84-87, 92, 105-108, 110-115, 117, 188, 192

Price, David Commander RN, 129, 131, 137

Prince Regent, 63, 86, 113, 143

Pring, Daniel Commander RN, 26, 27, 33-35, 42-44, 67, 72, 82, 84, 87, 91, 93, 99-103, 105, 188

Purchas, John Captain, 109

Pym, Mr Midshipman RN, 96, 98

Quebec City, LC, 24, 68, 84

Ramsay, Alexander Lieutenant RA, 158

Index

Raumzie, Captain Canadian Militia, 87, 95
Raymond G. Seaman RN, 153
Raynham, Mark Lieutenant RN, 88, 94, 105
Rennie, Robert Captain Bvt. Lt. Colonel, 155, 163-165
Roberts, James (Slave), 171
Roberts, Samuel Captain RN, 131, 147, 149, 159
Robertson, James Lieutenant RN, 72, 81, 82, 84, 93, 99, 100, 102
Robertson, James Midshipman RN, 96
Robinson, Sir Frederick P. Maj. General, 71, 73, 75, 76, 106-109, 112, 188, 192
Robyns John Captain RM, 59, 120, 121, 159
Rodman, Solomon Sailing Master USN, 128, 129
Rogers, John Commodore USN, 124, 125, 130
Ross, Robert Major General, 54, 55, 58-64, 118, 119, 121, 124, 147
Rowe, James Lieutenant RN, 48
Runk, George W. Lieutenant US Infantry, 77
Rutter, Solomon Lieutenant USN, 126

Sackets Harbour NY, 37, 39, 44, 45, 49, 50, 69, 70, 82, 83, 113, 184
Sailly, Peter, 42
Saucy Jack, Privateer, 135, 136
Sawyer, Sir Herbert Vice Admiral RN, 17
Scott, James Lieutenant RN, 59, 120
Scott, Judge, 120

Sheldon, Walter Lieutenant US Artillery, 34
Sheppard, Richard S. Sailing Master USN, 148
Sherbrooke, Sir John C. Governor General, 23, 115, 117, 182
Sheridan, John Commander RN, 131
Short, James Captain RM, 44
Simmonds, Mr Masters Mate RN, 99
Simons, William Shipbuilder, 26, 42, 68, 82, 83, 89, 185
Simpson, Pilot, 97
Sinclair, John S. Major & ADC RA, 78, 79, 110
Skenadore, Adam Oneida Chief, 46, 47
Slavery, 146, 180, 189, 191
Smith, Henry G.W. Captain, 58
Smith, Richard Captain USMC, 45
Smith, Samuel Major General, 122, 124
Spedden, Robert Lieutenant USN, 148
Sperry, Gilead Captain NY Cavalry, 74
Spilsbury, Francis B. Captain RN, 45-47, 49
Spots, Samuel Lieutenant US Artillery, 151
Sproul, John Captain US Infantry, 73, 75
Stafford, Hiram Lieutenant NY Cavalry, 74
Stafford, Job NY Militia, 43
Standish, Matthew M. Coronet NY Cavalry, 74
Steele, Alexander Lieutenant, 165
Steele, Richard C. Lieutenant RMA, 25
Stevens, John H. Lieutenant RMA, 18, 27, 38, 40, 113
Stirling, James Captain RN, 146
Stockholm, Robert Masters Mate, 130

Stricker, John Brigadier General USA, 118-120
Strong, Samuel General Vermont Militia, 109
Stuart, Charles, 14
Sturdevant, J.M. Private, 47
Success, Transport, 23
Sumpter, William Lieutenant US Light Artillery, 110
Swift, John Brigadier General NYV, 44
Swiftsure (Steam Vessel), 24

Tangier Island, Virginia, 51, 52, 139, 142
Thomas, Rev. Joshua, 139
Thorn, Nathaniel Major, 107
Thornton, Arthur W. Captain US Artillery, 43
Thornton William B. Lt. Colonel, 59, 60, 150, 159-161, 163, 164, 167
Tingey, Thomas Captain USN, 63
Totten, Joseph G. Lt. Colonel US Engineers, 28, 34, 73, 107
Travers, James Captain, 163
Treaty of Ghent, 54, 115, 180, 181, 183
Triphook, Thomas Lieutenant, 66
Turner, Ezra Captain NY Militia, 28

Ulick, George Sailing Master USN, 148
Umfreyville, J.B. Captain RN, 142
Upton, Clotworthy Captain RN, 84

Vallette, Elie A. F. Sailing Master USN, 93
Vaughan, Daniel Captain NY Militia, 77
Vergennes, Vermont, 43, 67, 83, 102
Vignau, Edouard Lieutenant, 111
Villere Plantation, 150, 151

Villere, Gabrielle Major, 151
Wade, Captain US Infantry, 176
Wainwright, John Captain RN, 64
Walker, J. Lieutenant RMA, 131
Warren, Sir John Borlese Vice Admiral RN, 17-19, 21-13, 26, 51, 123
Washington D.C., 54, 58-60, 62-64, 70, 72, 122, 124, 131, 146, 191
Watson, William Captain ADC, 86
Webster, John Sailing Master, 130
Weller, Lt. Colonel, 25
Wellington, Duke of, 14, 15, 54, 69, 114, 154, 180
Welshman, George T. Lieutenant, 117
Wemyss, Robert Sailing Master RN, 98
West, John Lieutenant, 74
Westropp, John L. Captain, 74
Wilkinson, James Major General USA, 24, 28, 29, 30, 33-35
Williams, Eleazer, 107
Williams, Richard Lt. Colonel RMA, 13, 14, 20, 24-27, 30-33, 65, 142
Willington, James Captain (Brevet Lt. Colonel), 74
Windler, William H. General USA, 60, 62
Wood, James H. Lieutenant RA, 77, 111
Woodbine, George Captain RM, 145
Wool, John E. Major US Infantry, 73, 74
Woolcombe, George Midshipman RN, 161
Woolsey, Melancthon T. Captain USN, 39, 44-46
Woolstonecraft, Captain US Artillery, 176
Wright, Daniel General NY Militia, 43, 109

Index

Wright, Peter Lieutenant RE, 158
Wright, Robert Lieutenant RMA, 131, 172
Wybourn, Marmaduke Captain RM, 19, 187, 193

Yeo, Sir James L. Commodore RN, 26, 37, 39, 40, 41, 44, 45, 49, 50, 65, 68, 69, 82, 103, 113
Youngs, White Captain US Infantry, 105

United States of America Regiments:
1st US Light Artillery, 31, 34
1st US Rifle Regiment, 28-30, 44, 46, 73, 142
1st Baltimore Hussars, 119
2nd US Light Artillery, 45
2nd US Infantry, 141, 178
3rd US Artillery, 38
3rd US Rifle Regiment, 171
5th Mechanical Volunteers, 119, 120
6th US Infantry, 77
6th Maryland Militia, 118, 120, 121
7th US Infantry, 151, 165, 176
8th US Infantry, 142
9th US Infantry, 184
13th US Infantry, 73
14th US Infantry, 128
15th US Infantry, 78, 105
20th US Infantry, 19
27th Maryland Militia, 118
36th US Infantry, 128
36th NY Militia, 28
38th US Infantry, 128
39th Maryland Militia, 118, 120
43rd US Infantry, 142
44th US Infantry, 151
48th Maryland Militia, 179
51st Maryland Militia, 118, 120
55th NY Militia, 45
68th James City Light Infantry, 21
85th US Infantry, 21
Baltimore Artillery Company of Fencibles, 128
Beal's Rifle Company, 151, 165
Darquin's Battalion of Militia, 151
Grey's Kentucky Militia, 160, 164
Lancaster County Militia, 132
Mississippi Dragoons, 151, 170, 171
New York Cavalry, 74
Plaunche's Battalion of Militia, 151
Union Artillery, 118
United States Corps of Artillery, 128, 141
US Engineers, 73, 107, 173
US Marine Corps, 17, 19, 45, 60, 62, 122, 151, 165, 185, 186
Washington Artillery, 128

British Regiments
1/27th Inniskilling Regiment, 71, 108
2/8th Kings Regiment, 71
1st West India Regiment, 155, 163
3rd Buffs, 71, 74, 75, 107
4th Kings Own Regiment, 54, 150, 153, 155, 163, 178
5th Northumberland, 71
5th West India Regiment, 155, 159, 160, 163
7th Royal Fusiliers, 159, 163, 165, 167, 170, 178
9th East Norfolk, 70

10th Royal Veteran Battalion, 25
13th Somersetshire, 25, 30-32, 35, 65, 66, 71
14th The Duchess of York's Own Light Dragoons, 155, 157, 163, 178
19th Light Dragoons, 71, 75, 108
21st Royal North British Fusiliers, 54, 60, 62, 120, 132, 155, 163, 178
29th Worcestershire Regiment, 117
37th North Hampshire Regiment, 70
39th Dorsetshire, 71, 73, 86, 91, 96, 105, 107, 108
41st Regiment, 31
43rd Monmouthshire Light Infantry, 159, 163-165, 167, 168, 178
44th East Essex Regiment, 54, 119, 120, 132, 155, 158, 163-166, 178
49th Herefordshire, 65, 71
57th West Middlesex Regiment, 70
58th Rutlandshire Regiment, 71, 74
60th Rifles (Royal American Regiment), 117
62nd Wiltshire Regiment, 117
76th Hindoostan Regiment, 71, 107-109, 188, 191
81st Regiment, 70
85th Bucks Volunteers Light Infantry, 54, 59, 60, 119, 120, 135-137, 150, 152, 153, 155, 159-161, 166, 169, 179
88th Connaught Rangers, 69, 71
93rd Sutherland Highlanders, 154, 155, 163, 164, 166, 177, 179, 190
95th Rifles, 150, 153-155, 163, 164, 167, 169, 170, 179
98th Regiment, 117

102nd New South Wales Regiment, 19, 20, 22
103rd Regiment, 28, 108
Canadian Chasseurs (Chasseurs Britanniques), 19-21
De Meuron Regiment, 71, 76, 77, 105, 107, 110-112, 182
De Watteville Regiment, 37-39

Canadian Regiments:
Canadian Chasseurs, 70, 107, 111
Canadian Fencibles, 31, 32
Canadian Voltigeurs, 31, 32, 70
Frontier Light Infantry, 29, 30, 35, 70
Glengarry Light Infantry, 37, 38

Royal Marines Forces
1st Battalion Royal Marines, 15, 21, 23, 24, 65-67, 193
2nd Battalion Royal Marines, 14, 15, 23-25, 27, 37, 39, 40, 52, 62, 118, 120
3rd Battalion Royal Marines, 52, 54, 59, 139, 142, 143
Battalion of Ships Marines, 52, 120, 139, 148, 149, 155, 157, 159-161
Colonial Marines, 52, 56, 118, 120, 132, 139, 183
Royal Marine Artillery Companies, 13, 14, 18, 20, 25, 28, 30, 34, 38, 40-42, 61, 66, 69, 72, 78, 87, 95, 110, 131, 136, 140, 150, 155, 156, 157, 159, 161, 172, 178, 187, 189, 191
Royal Marine Artillery Rocket Companies, 18-20, 23, 24, 33, 38, 40, 42, 52, 61, 75, 113, 120, 131, 150, 178

Index

Royal Engineers, 25, 156, 158, 159, 184
Royal Horse Artillery, 150, 152, 156, 158, 159
Royal Regiment of Artillery, 25, 70, 71, 75, 77, 78, 79, 87, 107, 108, 110, 111, 117, 155, 158, 163, 165, 178, 184,190
Royal Sappers and Miners, 71, 72, 158, 159, 169

Royal Navy Vessels
Blucher, Gunboat, 95, 98
Colonel Murray, Gunboat, 88, 95, 96
General Brock, Gunboat, 98
General Drummond, Gunboat, 88
General Simcoe, Gunboat, 95
HMS *Aetna*, 55, 127, 131, 132, 172, 178, 179
HMS *Ajax*, 84
HMS *Albion*, 52, 121
HMS *Armide*, 147
HMS *Brazen*, 178
HMS *Brune*, 142
HMS *Canso*, 142
HMS *Carron*, 140
HMS *Ceylon*, 84, 88
HMS *Childers*, 140, 142
HMS *Chubb*, 33, 42, 89, 90-92
HMS *Confiance*, 44, 67, 68, 81-93, 98-101, 103, 106, 185
HMS *Dauntless*, 179
HMS *Devastation*, 55, 127, 129, 131, 142
HMS *Discovery*, 78
HMS *Dragon*, 142
HMS *Erebus*, 55, 56, 127, 131
HMS *Euryalus*, 55, 56, 129
HMS *Fairy*, 56
HMS *Finch*, 89, 101
HMS *Hebrus*, 125, 142
HMS *Herald*, 171
HMS *Hermes*, 140, 141
HMS *Iphigenia*, 56
HMS *Junon*, 84
HMS *Leopard*, 84
HMS *Linnet*, 42, 67, 82, 89, 90, 91, 93, 98-101, 185
HMS *Manly*, 55
HMS *Marlborough*, 19
HMS *Menelaus*, 56, 124
HMS *Meteor*, 55, 56, 78, 127, 131, 148, 159, 179
HMS *Montreal*, 45, 81
HMS *Nereide*, 50
HMS *Niagara*, 42, 45
HMS *Pigmy*, 171
HMS *Pompee*, 66
HMS *Primrose*, 142
HMS *Prince Regent*, 37
HMS *Princess Charlotte*, 37, 40
HMS *Pylades*, 143
HMS *Rota*, 142
HMS *Royal Oak*, 132
HMS *Regulus*, 142
HMS *San Domingo*, 19, 21, 26
HMS *Seahorse*, 55, 56, 124, 142, 147
HMS *Severn*, 55, 142
HMS *Sophie*, 140-142, 147
HMS *St. Lawrence*, 50, 113
HMS *Surprise*, 124, 129
HMS *Tendos*, 117
HMS *Terror*, 127, 131, 142
HMS *Thistle*, 172

HMS *Tonnant*, 54, 64, 124, 147, 161, 178
HMS *Tremendous*, 11
HMS *Vesuvius*, 179
HMS *Volcano*, 126, 127, 129, 131, 135-137, 172, 173, 178
HMS *Warspite*, 84
HMS *Wasp*, 26
HMS *Whiting*, 142
HMS *Wolfe*, 26, 101
Lord Wellington, Gunboat, 95, 96, 98
Marshal Beresford, Gunboat, 95, 96
Sir George Prevost, Gunboat, 88
Sir Hope Popham, Gunboat, 95-97
Sir Sydney Beckwith, Gunboat, 88, 98
Sir James L. Yeo, Gunboat, 94, 95

United States Vessels:
Borer, Gunboat, 96
Gunboat 156, p. 148, 149
Gunboat 162, p. 148
Gunboat 163, p. 148
Gunboat 23, p. 148
Gunboat 5, p.148
Gunboat 65, p. 172
Gunboat 7 (Gun Barge), 127
US Sea Fencibles, 128
USS *Adams*, 22, 117
USS *Alligator*, 148, 149
USS *Carolina*, 151-155
USS *Constellation*, 19
USS *Eagle*, 79, 89-91, 93, 98-100
USS *Erie*, 125-127
USS *Growler*, 39, 79
USS *Guerriere*, 124
USS *Java*, 126, 127

USS *Louisiana*, 152, 154-157
USS *Mohawk*, 50
USS *Ontario*, 127
USS *Peacock*, 183
USS *Penelope*, 39
USS *Preble*, 89, 94, 97
USS *Saratoga*, 42, 75, 89-93, 98-103
USS *Seahorse*, 148
USS *Superior*, 50
USS *Ticonderoga*, 43, 89, 94-100

Lightning Source UK Ltd.
Milton Keynes UK
UKHW020734281119
354348UK00009B/1956/P